Israeli And Palestinian Terrorism: The 'Unintentional' Agents

Geoffrey Whitfield

Emeth Press

Israeli And Palestinian Terrorism:
The 'Unintentional' Agents

Copyright © 2009 Geoffrey Whitfield
Printed in the United States of America on acid-free paper

All rights reserved. No part of this book may be reproduced, or stored in a retrieval system or transmitted in any form or by any means, electronic, mechanical, photocopying, recording, scanning or otherwise, except as permitted by the 1976 United States Copyright Act, or with the prior written permission of Emeth Press. Requests for permission should be addressed to: Emeth Press, P. O. Box 23961, Lexington, KY 40523-3961.
http://www.emethpress.com.

Library of Congress Cataloging-in-Publication Data

Whitfield, Geoffrey Victor.
  Israeli and Palestinian terrorism : the 'unintentional' agents / Geoffrey Whitfield.
       p. cm.
  Includes bibliographical references and index.
  ISBN 978-0-9819582-3-1 (alk. paper)
  1. Terrorism--Israel--History. 2. Terrorism--Palestine--History. 3. Terrorism--Religious aspects. 4. Arab-Israeli conflict. 5. Arab-Israeli relations. I. Title.
  HV6433.I75W477 2009
  363.325095694--dc22   2009020776

Dedication

to the conflict-prevention and peace workers
throughout the world:
who, where there's despair, bring hope,
who, where there's hatred, bring love,
who, where there's darkness, bring light....
who give without counting the cost,
who labour and ask for no reward....
To the channels of peace...and those who endure.

(Adapted from St Richard of Chichester and St Francis of Assisi)

Contents

Abbreviations and Glossary	7
Preface	11
Acknowledgements	19
Introduction	21
Chapter 1 The Usual, Predictable, Suspects: The Over-Zealous	27
Chapter 2 The Unintentional Jewish Agents in Terrorism in the 20th Century: A Dialectic of Gush Emunim and The Settler Movement	41
Chapter 3 The Early, Unintentional, Christian Agents, 1800-1845: The London Society for Promoting Christianity Among the Jews	83
Chapter 4 Israel Past and Present: The Land of Too Many Covenants	121
Chapter 5 The 21st Century: The Bridge Is Not Safe	135
Afterword and Postscript	161
Bibliography	169
Index	195
About the Author	205

Abbreviations and Glossary

AHLC	Ad Hoc Liaison Committee – the co-ordination mechanism for development assistance in the oPt
aka	also known as
Ashkenazi	Jews who originated in Europe
BMS	Baptist Missionary Society
B'tselem	The Israeli Centre for Human Rights in the Occupied Territories
cherem	A Rabbinical prohibition for Jews
CMJ	Churches Ministry Among Jewish People
CUP	Cambridge University Press
Debellatio	The political process of debilitating a people so that they can not govern themselves and have to be governed by another more powerful neighbour
Din Moser and Din Rodef	Rabbinic rulings that forbid soldiers to evacuate settlements.
Firman	A government licence to construct buildings in the Ottoman Empire
Ha'aretz	A daily newspaper in Israel
Hafrada	Used to describe separation by race, and a form of apartheid practised by Israel against Palestinians
Halakhah	Halacha or Halaka, codes of Jewish Law, derived from the Torah by the rabbis and frequently spelt differently by separate writers
Haluka	Financial aid from Diaspora Jews to Jews in Palestine in the nineteenth century
Haredim	A theologically ultra-conservative group of Orthodox Jews
Histradut	An Israeli Trade Union
Hitnachalut	Gush Emunim strategy to set up what began as outposts of squatters, which could be temporary, but developed into a settlement
HRH	His Royal Highness
ICAHD	Israeli Committee Against House Demolitions
ICG	International Crisis Group
ICJ	International Court of Justice
ICRC	International Committee of the Red Cross

8 Abbreviations and Glossary

IDF	Israel Defence Force
Kach	A militant Jewish group, created by Rabbi Kahane in the 1970s, committed to the expulsion of Arabs from Israel and banned in 1994
LJS	London Jews Society
LMS	London Missionary Society
LSPCAJ	London Society for the Promotion of Christianity Amongst the Jews and London Society for Promoting Christianity Among the Jews
Millennium	The thousand year reign of Jesus Christ on earth
Millet	This legal word was used to describe a community that was free to organise itself, but its leader was accountable to the Turkish authorities for their behaviour
Mizrah	A religious group of Jews, closely connected to the Sephardi, sometimes called the Oriental, largely originating in the Middle East and North Africa, especially the Arab world
Nakbah	The Palestinian word for the catastrophe of 14 May, 1948, which marks the establishment of the State of Israel and the destruction of Palestinian society which existed until the war of 1948
Nahal	The "Pioneering Fighting Youth" organisation
Nishool	Word used to describe dispossession and a form of apartheid against Palestinians by Israel
OCHA	United Nations Office for the Coordination of Humanitarian Affairs
oPt	Occupied Palestinian Territories
OUP	Oxford University Press
PA	Palestinian Authority
PLC	The Palestinian Legislative Council
PLO	Palestine Liberation Organisation
PNC	Palestine National Council
Politicide	Described by Baruch Kimmerling as the process used to destroy the political and national viability of a people and thus deny it the possibility of genuine self determination
RHR	Rabbis for Human Rights
SCM	Student Christian Movement
Sephardi	Jews who originated largely in Spain, Portugal and North Africa, frequently associated by others to the Mizrahi
SOAS	School of Oriental and African Studies, University of London
SUNY	State University of New York
Talmud	The collection of rabbinic writings, containing the Mishnah and the Gemara codes, and only second in importance to the Torah for Jews
Torah	The Jewish Law – the first five books of the Bible, Genesis,

	Exodus, Leviticus, Numbers and Deuteronomy
UN	United Nations
Yedioth Ahronot	A daily newspaper in Israel
Yeshiva	A theological school within the Jewish educational system in Israel which primarily focuses on the Jewish religion

Preface

This book is about my Jewish and Arab friends. There are many people throughout the world who have a deep affection for Jews and Arabs in Israel and Palestine, but also serious frustration and anger. We look with horror at what they do to each other and are torn by the conflict and we want to shout, "Stop! – Stop what you are doing to each other, stop threatening each other, terrorising each other and stop what you are doing to yourselves!"

So this book is torn between anger on behalf of friends – and anger at them as well. Many of my personal friends and colleagues join me in little short of fury and impatience, particularly with the corrosive views and actions of extreme religious, ideological groups who have a strange view of devotion. Those groups find it acceptable to bully another people by taking their land, building homes on it, confiscating their resources and cutting off normal community life by a Matrix of Control. Others, who are different, but equally devout, will nonetheless witness suicide bombings, hear the threats to Jewish existence, but not stand up to cry, "Never – Not in our name"!

And what do we do about those who come from other countries, such as the USA and the United Kingdom, and who are perceived to support unspeakable inhumanity? Are we not also ashamed of what our forebears did, no doubt with good intentions, but who obsessively started and supported a movement to return the Jews to land at the expense of the indigenous Arabs? To challenge, continually, any fundamental assumption, based on a few limited, ancient texts, that God selected one people to have exclusive rights to a particular piece of territory, is a crucial task. Are we not appalled that people focus on so-called sacred scripture and only see one interpretation that suits their ideology instead of being expansive and inclusive? And are we not furious that a proper, just structure has still not been created, helped by the international community, to bring a viable quality of life for both peoples?

Some will find me critical of Israelis in this book and they will be right, because I am. Some will find me critical of Palestinians and they will also be right, because I am. One can always be critical of friends – it is called, "holding them to the highest"! If some find me more critical of Israel than Palestine, as I am, it is because I always reckon that the emphasis for change is largely in the hands of the stronger party.

Until, "To forgive and to be forgiven" becomes part of their dialogue, this is what this book is about – my friends.

Sources

The requirement of providing evidence, which involves human behaviour and religious faith, is different from that of science where different kinds of proof are possible. In the following chapters, strong, objective evidence has been gained from personal experience of working with Israelis and Palestinians on projects in Israel and Palestine since 1993. What began as a project to supply books for an Arab village library in Israel, developed into supporting a mixed youth club, including a summer camp, with volunteer English students as part of the staff. This was to lead to a number of mixed projects, from working with a range of organisations to the training of staff in health centres in Israel and the West Bank. Before the Second Intifada, links had been successfully forged with separate Jewish and Palestinian professional organisations, and decisions had been made to conduct joint training workshops. Despite the maturity and professionalism of the Israelis, such was the fear in the land that both Israeli groups, separately, withdrew from their commitments. With hindsight, it could have been more creative if they had been able to contain their fear and to provide a model for joint activities for any organisations, but those decisions are extremely difficult and costly.

One project that has been sustained, commenced in 2000 and expanded into an annual Conflict-Prevention sports project and is entitled Football for Peace. (F4P). Originally entitled World Sports Peace Project, it grew to involve hundreds of youngsters from numerous towns in Israel.[1] They were supported by scores of staff and students from British and European universities, notably the University of Brighton, as well as English Premier League football clubs and runners in the Flora London Marathon. The different projects expanded to include the British Council and Israeli and Palestinian organisations.

The work led to research, involving interviews with people in Israel, Palestine and the UK, exchanges with colleagues and through extensive reading of relevant literature. I include material from the archives of CMJ in St Albans, the LSPCAJ archives in the Bodleian Library, Oxford, the University of London Special Collections, Senate House Library, British Library, SOAS Special Collections and SOAS Library with its LMS and LSPCAJ Archives, Durham University Library, Sussex University Library and the Library of the Institute of Development Studies at the University of Sussex. The primary sources have included politicians, diplomats, scholars, activists, journalists and peace agency workers. Significant work by scholars, academics and other writers from different disciplines are also included. Each reference is listed in the footnotes.

The Book

It has been suggested that coverage of the overall Israeli-Palestinian conflict requires a series of volumes, and not just one. The series would need to include a wide range of subjects, including British duplicity, their complicity with Arabs, anti-semitism in Britain and Europe, American duplicity with AIPAC and Christian fundamentalists, Arab duplicity, the Arab threat to the very existence of Israel, the Holocaust and Israeli chicanery. There could be others. This particular book would be one of those volumes. It is less to be construed as an empirical treatise with a solution, so much as a pointer to the gradual corruption of apparently, well-intended religious systems. It focuses on two unintentional agents of terrorism in the last two hundred years, which are still active and which are motivated by their limited interpretations of the Abrahamic Covenant. They are the settler movement of Gush Emunim and the earlier Christian organisation, now called, The Church's Ministry Among Jewish People. This book points to parts of the disease within the conflict but, despite what some might demand, it does not pretend to be part of the cure.

All sides in destructive disputes have their narratives. In Israel and Palestine, there are serious, crippling internal divisions and no policies that draw them close, to unite them. Palestinians have Fatah, Hamas, Islamic Jihad and other smaller groups, while Israel has Kadima, Likud, Yisrael Beiteinu, Labour and smaller groups too. The ideological divisions between them have contributed to the political disasters over the years and such is still the case.

The intention of this particular volume is to bring to the fore what the research has revealed to be a fundamental issue, i.e. the commitment to the Abrahamic Covenant, as held by certain religious groups, without which there would be a different attitude to the land and the people. Two particular organisations have, as "Unintentional Agents," caused havoc in the situation, despite their avowed intentions for good. The bodies involved may resent any suggestion that their work has any direct connection to terrorism, and would be angry at such an idea. Let me be clear, therefore, that no such argument is made that they have been directly involved in such activities. Indeed, it is not intended to apportion blame for the Middle East situation on either Israelis or Palestinians, although it may give that appearance, but to point out that the responsibility is mutual. Nonetheless, it is held that, for many, the logical consequence of their religious ideologies has led to extremist positions of violence in both Israeli and Palestinian communities in their attempts to possess the land, at the expense of the other. Such violence can be perceived as state and non-state terrorism.

There are endless arguments about who began the violence, Arabs or Jews, and one questions the relevance of the "chicken and egg" dilemma: which came first? With hindsight, it can be perceived that the return of Jews to Palestine would eventually cause conflict. Such was the case, well before the establishment of the state of Israel in 1947. By that time there had been enough experiences of violence and terror in and by both communities. The primary issue concerned the acquisition and control of the land. After the Six Day War of 1967, the Palestinians increasingly came to experience the loss of their land to the settler movement, led by Gush Emunim, and the means used to expel them from their homes. This gave rise to Arab resistance and both peoples resorted to increasing measures of violence to achieve their aims. This was to lead to acts of perceived terrorism, with each side blaming the other for the atrocities, and portraying themselves as the victims and defenders. The historical background to this can be seen in the return of Jews to Israel in the 19th century, through the British missionary organisation, the London Society for Promoting Christianity Among the Jews (LSPCAJ). The seeds that were sown by that organisation flourished, producing a harvest of perceived terrorism and counter terrorism in the 20th century and thereafter. But is it possible to be clear about which came first, the takeover of the West Bank and Gaza by Israel and their state terrorism of the Palestinians, or the Palestinian actions against the Jews? And is the question of importance any longer?

Both organisations assert that their aspirations have been based on their understanding of the promise made to Abraham by God that the land should be exclusively possessed by the Jews. This book holds that the different Old Testament Covenants are, and always have been, of immense significance because they represent the foundations of sufficiently powerful constituencies that have influence and, therefore, cannot be put to one side. That, nonetheless, is also a large part of the problem. A thorough exploration of the root of religion in this context has still not been sufficiently undertaken, and is seriously overdue. Quite naturally, not everyone will agree with what I write but my intention is to bring about an ongoing, intellectual engagement with the subject. It deserves a shared quest for a richer and more positive outcome for truth, avoiding partisan positions and clamorous interventions.

This book, therefore, explores, sympathetically but objectively, the roots and outcome of the Abrahamic Covenant through two prime movers in the conflict, i.e. the London Society for Promoting Christianity Among the Jews (LSPCAJ) and the settler movement of Gush Emunim. These are seen as the "Unintentional Agents" in the Israeli-Palestinian catastrophe for, apart from some possible extremists, they could not have envisaged or intended the destructive outcome of their endeavours. In working through the masses of source material, it was inevitable that those sources would interweave with each other, rather than present a simple, clear, step by step story.

The first four chapters are seen retrospectively. In Chapter 1, I have set the scene with the circumstances which have aggravated the situation in the region throughout the 20th century and thereafter. The next two chapters take up the bulk of the material so that readers can have a clearer understanding of two of the catalytic "Unintentional Agents" to the impasse. Chapter 2 describes the work of Gush Emunim and the settler movement as it expanded from its preliminary programmes to become a fully operational movement following the Yom Kippur War of 1973. In this chapter, I have incorporated the insights of a significant number of Israeli writers. Despite its wide range, it makes no claim to be exhaustive, although it is likely to prove to be controversial. That movement became the focus of the militant religious Zionist movement to expel the Palestinians and to occupy and control the Promised Land, in preparation for the coming of Messiah.

What they have done has been described as akin to acts of terrorism against a Palestinian civilian population. In response, there have been Palestinian terrorist attacks against Jewish communities. Although Gush Emunim has no formal connection with the LSPCAJ, currently named Church's Ministry Among Jewish People (CMJ), both organisations have common drives and goals which, as such, have not been exposed until now. Chapter 3, therefore, switches further back in time and looks at the Christian involvement in the return of the Jews to Palestine in the early 19th century, beginning with the work of the LSPCAJ as a missionary organisation, focused on the conversion of the Jews. There is little doubt that the British public was strongly influenced, and somewhat prepared to have sympathy for the Jews through the work of LSPCAJ during the previous hundred years. Its expansion into an evangelical-political-ideological organisation, with strategic connections in British society, facilitated the Balfour Declaration of 1917 and the founding of the State of Israel in 1948. The roots of the two organisations, Jewish and Christian, are not only theological but ideological as well. Both draw on their interpretations of the Abrahamic Covenant and their traditions to facilitate the coming of Messiah on the one hand, and the return of Jesus Christ on the other. This involves a particular exclusive view of the land and the people. It is argued that these religious quests have become disastrous for both Israelis and Palestinians for they do not lead anywhere, beyond the impasse to peace.

It is correct that both LSPCAJ and Gush Emunim have their focus on the end of the world and judgement, through the culmination of their respective belief systems, one in the return of Jesus Christ and the other in the coming of God's Messiah. What will follow will be the reward of the believer and the punishment of the non-believer in dramatic, apocalyptic terms.[2] The triumphalist, destructive notion of such a deity is sincerely held by many Christians and Jews. A certain type of faith and action will be rewarded, while others will be punished. This presupposes a certain type of God, with an accompanying belief system of loyalty and obedience, bringing redemption for a proportion, but destruction for the majority. The outcome for billions of non-believers is predicted to be violent, but just! Such theological literalism appears to be accepted without examination, or any questioning of the ethics and morality of such a divinity.

The literal interpretation of the Bible has been a problematical issue for centuries, as Professor Norman Vance of Sussex University has noted. In a personal communication,[3] he writes that as far back as the 2nd century, the Greek physician, Galen, complained that Moses, traditionally credited with authorship of the Torah, had not produced a philosophical or scientific story of creation. What Moses had written was one that was theological.[4] Vance also notes that Adamantius Origen. AD 185-AD 254 and other Post-Apostolic church fathers were impatient with the obsessive literalism and conclusions of Rabbinic exegesis.[5] Within Judaism, there was controversy between the Sadducees and the Pharisees, the former rejecting the Oral Law, as brought together in the Mishnah and Talmud. In the account of his meeting with the Sadducees, the words of Jesus implied that technical understanding of the writings depended on understanding the spirit behind the letter.[6] The issue of literalism and interpretation has been discussed and argued by many through the years.[7] They will surface regularly throughout these pages and when the texts of the Bible are mentioned, they can be read as part of the biblical narrative, without involving any value judgement.

Chapter 4 goes even further back, into history and pre-history, and discusses the evolution of the Abrahamic Covenant that became distorted into an ideology of land possession through the separate Covenants of Moses, Joshua and David. They led to the conquest, occupation and control of both the land and people of Canaan by the twelve ancient tribes of Israel, culminating in King David settling Jerusalem as his capital in 1011 BC. There are similarities with events from 1948 in which Israel extended its boundaries through war, occupation and control. It has maintained new boundaries by structured state terrorism against the indigenous people, despite UN Resolutions 194, 242, and 338, and the Advisory Opinion of the International Court of Justice on 9 July, 2004. Thus the religion of the Covenants has supported the creation, development and extension of the State of Israel. At its extreme, religious Zionists seek not for a democratic state, open to all its citizens, but one that is only for Jews. Their exclusive ideology, with its oppressive outworking, was to lead to non-state, Palestinian terrorism, especially after 1994, when a cycle of reciprocal terrorism ensued, beginning on 25 February, 1994, with the massacre of Palestinian worshippers in the Al-Aqsa mosque by a Jewish settler, Dr Baruch Goldstein. The violent, cause and effect, syndrome remains an unresolved political tension between Israel and its Arab neighbours in the region.

"The 21st Century, The Bridge is Not Safe" in Chapter 5, highlights some of the faulty, dangerous structures in Israel and Palestine, which result in obstacles and perils for the wider global community. The subjects of racism and Apartheid, when introduced, cannot avoid controversy and disputation. Some of the fierce, ongoing disputes which rage about the Gaza strip, and the mutual accusations of Palestinian terrorism and Israeli state terrorism, are also brought forward in this chapter. The future decades look increasingly insecure, until viable alternatives can be found to current intransigent, ideological positions. This is the challenge and opportunity for future generations of Arabs and Jews. The obstacles and openings for the future are raised in the final, "Afterword and Postscript."

Two factors will be left aside in this book, not because they are unimportant but because they would be a distraction from its primary process. One is the disputed issue of Dispensationalism, which is a particular, literal interpretation about the end of the world and the judgement of God. Although the Dispensation movement has had its followers since the 19th century, it is a road down which I have little interest in travelling, especially as there are those who have previously applied themselves to the task.[8] To give time and space to such views of God may be important for some, but there are other matters which, to me, are of far greater importance. Any judgement of the human race by God, I prefer to leave aside. The second factor is that of Islam, which is far more significant and worthy of respect, and deserves a fuller exposition by those able to perform the task with honour and distinction.

Notes

[1] Whitfield G.V., *Amity in the Middle East* (Brighton: The Alpha Press, 2006).
[2] The Book of Revelation 20. 1-15.
[3] Note sent to the author on 1 September, 2008.
[4] Walzer R., *Galen on Jews and Christians* (London: OUP, 1949).
[5] Hansen R.P.C. *Allegory and Event: A Study in the Sources and Significance of Origen's Interpretation of Scripture* (London: SCM, 1959), 12.
[6] Matthew 22. 29.
[7] Horan M., *Jesus and the Trojan War* (Exeter: Imprint Academic, 2007).
[8] Sizer S., *Christian Zionism* (Leicester: IVP, 2004).

Acknowledgements

From Autumn, 2004, my first two years of work at the Research Institute for Human Rights and Social Justice at the London Metropolitan University were very creative. The book might have moved on to become a product of the School of Oriental and African Studies (SOAS) but the demand, unfortunately too late in the day, for a working knowledge of Hebrew, meant a parting of the ways from that otherwise, highly regarded institution and my fine group of fellow research students. Aided and abetted by gifted and supportive family and friends, it was completed privately in Lewes, East Sussex, in 2008 and 2009.

I worry about those whose names I have failed to include but, first, my appreciation beyond words to my always supportive and patient wife, Jean. Further afield, my eldest son Robert and his wife and family in Hawai'i who allowed me so much time to use their resources, one month in 2008. Nearer home my two families in Lewes, East Sussex, Sarah Pearson and Colin Whitfield, along with their supportive tribes. for the space and backup they gave me; not to leave out Emma Jane and Sean Kelly in Bisley, Surrey, immense encouragers, one and all. The expertise and patience of my friends and colleagues at Christ Church, Lewes, East Sussex, have been a constant, invaluable support and resource ever since our arrival in the town in 2004.

The reinforcement of many friends, colleagues, partners-in-writing, fellow-researchers, interviewees, collaborators from near and far, readers of chapters, scholars, encouragers, creative critics, and many more; Gideon Aran, Canon Gavin Ashenden, James Atherton, Uri Avnery, Professor Paul Ballard, Helen Baron, Stephen Bates, Professor Eyal Benvenisti, Professor Anat Biletzki, Andrew Buxton, Peter Cane, Sister Catherine, Eric Chandler, Geoffrey Cleave, Professor Ronald Clements, Peter Colvin, Rt. Rev. Bishop Kenneth Cragg, Professor Michael Feige, Neil Fisher, Rabbi David Goldberg, Sohil Haj, David Hallam, Professor Jeff Halper, Adam Lausch-Holubowicz, Michael Horan, Jad Isaac, Alex Jacob, Pam Jenkins, Professor Gabriel Josipovici, Ghada Karmi, Don Lewis, Tim Llewellyn, Rabbi Jonathan Magonet, Professor Moshe Ma'oz, Sister Maria, Brother Thomas Moore Mann OFM, Colin Morris, William Morris, Canon Paul Oestreicher, Professor Stephen Orchard, Ari Rath, Avi Ravitzki, Susan Rees, Professor Tanya Reinhart, Rt. Rev. Bishop Riah al Assal, Danny Rubinstein, Walid Salem, Peter Salinger, J. Clayton Schroeder, Canon Peter Sills, Professor Ken Smith, Robert Smith, Norman Stockton, Jeanne Thomas, Rabbi Pete Tobias, Professor Norman Vance, Richard Vogler, Sir Harold Walker, Professor Haddon Willmer and, especially, my publisher, Professor Larry Wood of Emeth Press, Lexington, Kentucky.

In addition to the above, the writings of so many; some friends, others strangers, of whom these are but a few: Hanan Ashrawi, Canon Naim Ateek, President Jimmy Carter, Kathleen Cavanaugh, Ron David, Professor W. D. Davies, Professor John Dugard, Robert Fisk, Shlomo Gazit, Gershom Gorenberg, Shir Hever, Michael Keating, Professor Baruch Kimmerling, Keith Clements, Professor David Kretzmer, Professor Ian Lustick, Oliver McTernan, John Mearsheimer and Stephen Walt, Professor Jürgen Moltmann, Rabbi Jeffrey Newman, Ephraim Nimni, Greg Philo and Mike Berry, Gabriel Piterberg, Professor Edward Sa'id, Avi Shlaim, Professor David Shulman, Professor Laurence Silberstein, Stephen Sizer, Ehud Sprinzak, Timothy Stunt, Milton Viorst, Idith Zertal and Akiva Eldar.

The resourceful, painstaking, courteous, backroom staff of the archives and libraries of the Bodleian Library, Oxford, the British Library, Church's Ministry Among Jewish People, St Albans (now in Nottingham, England), Durham University Library, Lewes Library, Special Collections Senate House Library, SOAS Library, University of London Research Library, University of Sussex Library and the Library of the Institute of Development Studies at the University of Sussex.

Introduction

In the context of terrorism between the two primary adversary peoples, there is a paradox – even a contradiction – between those who, in their religion, focus on love, justice and mercy but then deal in violence on an alarming scale. The issue in Israel and Palestine is about more than religion; it is far more to do with the land, which both peoples claim to be theirs by divine right. Once the Jews set up the World Zionist Council in Basel in 1897 and made plans to create a state within the Muslim Ottoman Empire, the die was cast for sad, but grievous, conflict. Leaders, like Theodore Herzl, David Ben-Gurion, Vladimir Jabotinsky and Moshe Dayan, all knew it and said so. President Mahmoud Ahmedinejad of Iran sings from his own inflammatory version of the same song sheet, using his anti-Jewish version, threatening the existence of the State of Israel and its citizens, thereby terrifying the people who have the Shoah, or Holocaust, as part of their living memory. The situation has so deteriorated since 1897 that large sectors of Jews and Muslims throughout the Middle East are now fearful of the other and see violence as the only way to resolve the issue. Israel has become a world nuclear power and has the will to use that power if its security is threatened. The Iranian President in 2008 saw the very existence of Israel to be a sufficient threat as to require its extinction. His utterances might be perceived to be the primary, inflammatory statements in the entire conflict.

Both peoples have their genuine stories of violence by the other and therefore see the other as a threat to their own security. Both feel at risk before a hostile, bellicose neighbour. Both feel justified in their militant stance and the actions they take against the other. So the world sees an intransigent situation which resists any resolution. Ancient Israel was never without non-Jews in the land and there was a measure of co-existence, following the expulsion of Jews from Jerusalem in AD 135. It is true that small numbers of Jews had once lived peacefully in the region with their Arab neighbours for generations. This is no longer the case. As it now stands, Israel in the 21st century is a dynamic, virile, powerful nation, prepared for all possible threats, including pro-active violence, in the name of self-defence. And there are many threats to Israel's existence. But where does it all lead and how will the violence stop? Both sides have their truth and can make argument and counter-argument. To listen to the truth of the other has yet to be sufficiently undertaken and explored. Animosity, resentment and fear have been obstacles that have brought the impasse, producing cycles of violence, recrimination and justification.

Among the major inter-related obstacles are three issues of principle for those who claim religious affiliations.

i) How can the Jewish government of Israel automatically expect massive financial and military support, openly imported from its Christian supplier, the USA, while both combine to resist the rights of a democratically elected Islamic party, Hamas, to obtain arms to protect its people from Israel and the USA, which seeks its overthrow?

ii) Is it realistic for Palestinians to expect Israel to respond to overtures for peace, when there are repeated statements from Hamas and Hizbollah which threaten Israel's existence?

iii) Is it realistic for Israelis to expect Palestinians to be passive and to be partners for peace, when Palestinians exist behind the, so-called, "security fence" with a blockade of their borders, and with Israeli settlers taking control of lands which are not theirs and restricting the free movement of the people by Israeli army checkpoints?

All three claim that terrorism is inflicted on them by the other, while they are the ones at risk, thereby seeking to justify their actions against the other. For the sake of their children and grandchildren, the blame game has to stop and be replaced by genuine and permanent rapprochement.

Terrorism And Its Origins

Acts of terrorism can be likened to the sicknesses coming from disease-bearing insects, such as mosquitoes, emanating from the breeding ground of a swamp. The sickness of terrorist acts may be diagnosed, along with remedies for their treatment. However, unless the root causes of a swamp are recognised and dealt with, so that the swamp becomes a fertile area, then the diseases borne by the carriers will continue, and sickness and death will prevail. Terrorism in Israel and Palestine continues, partly because the root causes in the swamp are not sufficiently researched and remedied. The unspoken question for many may include, "Why the terrorism by both sides?" and this book is an attempt to answer that question. The book provides insights into the swamp, with its tragic, destructive elements. They are found as ancient texts and belief systems which have become volatile and poisonous, rather than health-giving and creative. The swamp needs to be understood as such and transformed into a source of life.

Although there are many definitions of terrorism, already described in one of my earlier books,[1] I hold that there are two basic types, i.e. state and non-state terrorism. The word "terrorism" cannot be confined to suicide bombers, horrific and repugnant though they are. Alan Dershowitz, Professor of Law at Harvard University, is one who argues strongly for the case of Israel in the Middle East conflict and controversy. While he rightly describes acts which he perceives as terrorism, he makes no mention of the causes of terrorism nor, crucially, does he consider the actions by a state which terrify a civilian population.[2] In particular, this could apply to the audacity of Israel's accusations against Hamas and the rocket attacks on Israel, as though there was no extensive provocation by Israel, in terms of its blockade, through border restrictions, on supplies of natural resources and other necessities, especially in Gaza. If Israel suffered a blockade by land, sea and air, to the accompaniment of daily incursions by hostile aircraft, one would understand any resistance it could muster. The difference between armed resistance against oppression on the one hand, as with French resistance by the *maquis* in World War II, and terrorism on the other, is not well-defined. Professor Dershowitz's silence on the filmed theft of Palestinian land and property, including even the removal and misappropriation of fruit trees, is a regrettable lapse of observation by a skilled professional. For him to leave aside, unquestioned, the notion of the Jewish claim under the Abrahamic Covenant awaits the application of other serious minds to a serious problem for all Jews and Arab Christians and Muslims.

Dershowitz seems to understand terrorism from only one limited viewpoint, that of the Israeli victim, for he shows no awareness of the Palestinian victims of state terrorism by Israeli forces and settlers. Nor does he show any awareness of the long-term privation of the Palestinian people which is caused by Israel on a daily basis. It is hard to believe that Israel would be passive under similar conditions. The issue is cyclical and interactive, and it is not the case that one side is the innocent victim and the other the oppressor. Although a recognised international lawyer of repute, Dershowitz ignores what amounts to an embargo on trade in both directions, as though there was no bellicosity in such policies. This means that there is a serious deficiency in any discussion of the subject when they are omitted from the debate. The issues are given coverage in the pages of this book.

One of the major contributors to the subject is Dr Viktor Frankl, a Jewish survivor of the Holocaust, more correctly called Shoah, who was a prisoner in Dachau and other concentration camps. His parents, brother and wife all died but he survived and went on to become the founder of the Third Viennese School of Psychotherapy, namely, Logotherapy. In one of his books he describes the state of daily terror in which Jews and others lived and either died or survived.[3] He argues that the pivotal place between the two alternatives largely depended on whether or not the individuals had a sense of meaning and purpose in their lives. He found that the State terrorism by the Nazis against the Jews and other groups could be better endured by those who had a will to survive and live. Such a strong mental state would also contribute to understanding the Jewish will to endure and survive in the Jewish-Arab wars which were to follow. This being the case, it could equally indicate, for some, the Islamic Arab will, not only to survive perceived Jewish State terrorism but to become dedicated to overcoming their oppressor by suicide attacks, which hold the promise of life and reward after death.

It was in the course of a sequence of numerous visits to Israel and Palestine from 1993 onwards that the people I met, unexpectedly and unintentionally, showed that the primary influences of the conflict were more than political

Zionism or security but, particularly, included that of the Abrahamic Covenant. This was taken from the Book of Genesis, in which it is written that God promised the land of Israel to Abraham and his people, the Jews, for their exclusive and eternal possession.[4] It is this promise that is known as the Abrahamic Covenant. The tragedy of the literal interpretations of the Genesis texts is that they miss the rich and timeless messages of religion, which are to do with inclusiveness, rather than exclusiveness, with harmony rather than alienation. There are many different types of truth, some scientific and empirical, while others are existential and more to do with meaning and significance. To hold the Genesis accounts to be historical and scientifically sound, rather than profound in religious and human terms is to miss the point. The literalist interpretations have turned out to be pivotal in identifying fundamental problems between Jews and others, and are particularly discussed at length in Chapter 4. For many religious Jews, the land of Israel is inseparable from their belief in that promise in Genesis, even if they do not examine the process behind their unquestioning acceptance of the literal accounts of the Abrahamic Covenant. There is, as yet, no exact agreement about what is meant by the Land of the Abrahamic Covenant. Some see it as encompassing the land between the River Euphrates in Iraq and the River Nile in Egypt, according to one passage in Genesis [5] and this is known as Eretz Israel. Others see it differently, including part of Lebanon within its compass but the final borders of the Land have yet to be determined by the State of Israel. Although it is beyond objective verification, Jews, and Christians too, have been prepared to argue and act through the centuries for the reality of the Covenant in relation to the land and the people. While there are Jews throughout the world who have no desire to move to the Land, they recognise the centrality of its religious meaning and importance for world-wide Jewry. Therefore, they are prepared to subscribe to it financially and to ensure that it is supported politically and militarily.

My fieldwork research of interviews pointed to a number of additional emerging themes, especially to be seen in the treatment of refugees, the settlements of the West Bank after 1967, the oppression of the civilian population in the occupation, and the failures of the attempted resolution conferences at Oslo (1993), Camp David (2000) and Taba (2001). The relationship between Israel and the USA was also seen to be strongly influenced by religion which meant that Israel was seen as especially favoured, to the detriment of the indigenous Arab population. The failure to resolve the problem over the decades does not show the major players in any great light, but rather in regrettable, inept, and even wilful, shades of grey.

The Intrusion Into The Present From The Past

The issue for many devout Jews and Christians is their insistent belief in the inerrant nature of the Hebrew scriptures, which must be upheld at all costs by those so persuaded. Many are untouched by the scholarship which offers insights into the way the biblical documents were collected by redactors after 536 BC and were thereby made available for transmission to subsequent generations. It will be seen that the view of the scriptures as literal history, recording the occupation and control of the land, and to be replicated in the present era at all costs, affects current political dealings. The outcome for such a belief is that, as long as the Abrahamic Covenant is left untouched, and that the Jews keep the land for themselves and no other, then all other matters are open for discussion. Consequently, the apparent divine designation of the land represents a logical block to the return of Palestinian land and refugees, or the establishment of a viable Palestinian state in what is seen by certain Jews as their sacred land. Not every Israeli or Jew holds that literalist interpretation of the Hebrew scriptures, although it is understandable that the ancient Israelites genuinely believed that what they were doing was from God. For people of the 20th and 21st centuries to be willing to believe and approve of such accounts presents difficulties in bringing about any resolution. For decades, there has been a sufficiently well-organised body in Israel, supported by many religious groups in the USA and Europe, who do so believe.[6] The outcome is all too visible: "Peace, peace, when there is no peace."[7]

Notes

[1] Whitfield G.V., *The Roots of Terrorism in Israel and Palestine: The Uses and Abuses of the Abrahamic Covenant* (Lexington, KY: Emeth Press, 2007).

[2] Dershowitz A., *The Case Against Israel's Enemies* (Hoboken, NJ., John Wiley & Sons, 2008), 182-183.

[3] Frankl V. E. *Man's Search for Meaning* (New York: Washington Square Press, 1985 edn.).

[4] Genesis 13. 14-17; 15. 18-21; 17. 1-8.

[5] Genesis 15. 18.

[6] The Westminster Confession of Faith, written in 1646, is still a foundation document and basis of belief for the Calvinist reformed tradition of Protestantism and includes the literal interpretation of the Bible.

[7] Jeremiah 8. 11.

Chapter 1

The Usual, Predictable, Suspects– The Over-Zealous

This chapter considers the perspectives of some of those involved in the front line of the struggle for peace with security and justice. The problems are complex because of the different interpretations of those involved and the lack of an agreed approach which could lead to any resolution. Aggravating the situation are the grievances of both Israelis and Palestinians who see themselves as victims and the other as their persecutor. In reality, both have had their share of being victimised and have been involved to some degree in persecution. Arguing from different positions, both hold to their right to the land and the outcome is intransigence, fear and misery. It is hard to avoid the accusation of being partisan when both peoples have their horror stories. The reality is that both have to find ways of being other than adversarial.

Mutual Grievances, With Accusations Of Persecution

Public apologies to Jews and Muslims are long overdue from Christians who have persecuted them through the centuries. Such is the controversial view of a retired professor of Jewish Studies in Israel,[1] which he presented to a gathering of scholars in Prague in 2006.[2] This call by Professor David Friedman was included in his basic question about what to do before Messiah comes. He further asked what was to be done until the day when Egyptians, Iraqis, Syrians and Israelis would all serve the one God and his Messiah. He gave at least two answers, drawn from two Dutch Reformed speakers at a previous reconciliation conference held only days earlier.[3] He referred to anti-Semitism in parts of the historic church, based on "replacement theology" whereby the church has supposedly replaced Israel in the eyes of God and, secondly, the wrongs committed by Christians against Muslims through the advent of the Crusades and colonialism. Both these historic wrongs needed to be examined. He stated, "Overall church compliance during the Crusades, the Inquisition and East European pogroms are the eyes through which Jewish people see the church today."[4] He also referred to the silence of the churches during Hitler's genocide. He argued that the church needed to affirm the existence of the Jewish state and to work on obtaining the forgiveness of the Jews.[5] "If you want to help effect a positive political change in the Middle East, first repent towards the Israeli and Arab peoples. Then issue a strong challenge to the Muslim nations to accept Israel as an equal nation."[6]

Friedman went further to discuss the problems and perils of Israel in the face of Islamic enmity. He was clear about the hatred existing in Syria and Iran towards Israel, and their support of Hizbollah in Lebanon. He held:

> We are in an actual state of war.... As long as we are threatened we will act like a threatened people. We will justifiably care first and foremost about the State of Israel surviving. A people bent on this very legitimate need cannot be expected by anyone to act altruistically. If you expect Israel to make peace with the PA,[7] understand that the Muslims' world hatred and unwillingness to accept us must change or it simply won't happen.[8]

In conclusion, Friedman stated an Israeli principle, shared by all threatened people, "We also know that we cannot make ourselves more vulnerable because the threat of us perishing has always been too close to us to ignore."[9]

A different picture is presented by the Palestinian, the Rev. Philip Saa'd, who refers to the deaths of thousands of Palestinians and the hundreds of thousands who have "been stripped of their lands and property, and are even now displaced." He sees the struggles as being perpetuated caused by three ongoing Israeli policies "the continuing occupation of the West Bank...the growing number of settlements in the Palestinian territories, and the severe oppression under which the Palestinians have been placed by the Israelis."[10] For Saa'd:

> The hostility and violence which have lasted almost one hundred years...were, and still are, motivated by religious convictions.... Each party [Jews, Christians, Muslims] claims the ownership of this little piece of land, and says it is theirs as a gift from God. These claims are, of course, according to their beliefs and interpretations.... They believe that God promised the land to Abraham and to his descendants 'the Jews'. Genesis 15. 18-20 and that this promise is unconditional and eternal.[11]

Included in his analysis are both the Muslims and the Christians who invaded Palestine because of religion and have been under a cloud of suspicion and enmity ever since. It is his belief that the conflict is made worse by the arguments of the different religious communities who hold diverse interpretations, especially when they are based on literal interpretations of the texts, rather than regarding them as spiritual in content and meaning. The end result is not humble agreement but divergence, with hostility and enmity. What is sacrificed by all sides is any notion of human dignity.

Ancient And Modern History, Persecution And Security

Issues of Biblical interpretation and history are intermingled and complex. The original conquest of the land of Canaan, as recorded in the Book of Joshua, can be interpreted in different ways. Some see the stories as a series of acts of violence, based on survival needs. This contrasts, however, with the traditional interpretation of a captive existence in Egypt, followed by a dramatic Exodus and decades wandering in the desert with the same leader, Moses, who was inspired by the conviction of religion. Whatever the realities of unrecorded history, the Jewish conquerors of Canaan acquired their religious rituals and substance over time which enabled them to become a viable minority movement. The people learned, by skill and guile, how to manage, preserve and then advance their distinctive culture, despite their internal divisions. The Jews thereby established themselves as a people, long before the State of Israel. Their unifying factor through the centuries, before and after the Diaspora, has been their religion, based largely on the Torah and the Talmud. Essential though it is, because of the pogroms and thereafter, the fundamental drive for security has not been their "unifying factor," as many secularists hold, so much as their religious faith and doctrine. The majority of Jews do not necessarily wish to return to Israel, or they would return without the encouragement of religious, racist, political and even criminal factors.

There is little doubt that the fears of Jewish extinction in the Arab wars of 1948, followed by the Egyptian threats in 1967 and the Yom Kippur War of 1973 leave Jews feeling more secure in their Diaspora than in the land of Abraham. But the price of Jewish survival continues to be immense. It may take many more years before future generations of Jews examine their paradoxical history in the 20th and 21st centuries. What began as a legitimate quest for security for Jews in the late 19th century has become a quest where the people they conquered, the Palestinians, are now one of the most deprived and oppressed people on the planet. What had been sought as a place for enduring safety and freedom, after the oppressions of the pogroms in Russia and the infamy of the Shoah, is now the scene of occupation, injustice and poverty, perpetrated by the Jews against the indigenous inhabitants of the land. A people who sought for understanding and justice for themselves have brought about despair in the people they have knowingly reduced to a minimal existence. Yet, paradoxically, Jews cannot be without fear of any rising Palestinian power in the future.

The paradoxes are also dilemmas. There is such a thing as shame that is not always immediate but sometimes comes with hindsight, as happened with the younger generation in post-Nazi Germany. Inevitably there was to be strife between Jews and Arabs after the Balfour Declaration of 1917 and the subsequent failure to interpret and activate the clear understanding of the civil and religious rights of the indigenous Palestinian population in 1917. The Bedouin proverb, "Beware of the Camel's Nose," is one that could be applied to the situation. It summarises a tale about the Bedouin, sheltering in his tent during a sandstorm, and the camel who asks if he could put his tender nose inside the tent for a short while for protection. There follows a lengthy story, of slow but steady intrusion as the camel fills the tent completely and the Bedouin is pushed outside. After the Balfour Declaration, this became the Palestinian experience. As yet, there seems little sense of Jewish shame because many, understandably, still live in the paramount mode of survival.

The issue of the Shoah, or Holocaust, and the land of Israel is one that has multiple problems. Professor W. D. Davies of Duke University argues that there is little doubt that the Shoah resulted in the perceived justification of the founding of the Jewish state.[12] The fact that the land had to be Israel and not Uganda or the Argentine, despite the land being occupied by Arabs for centuries, was due to a combination of sympathy for the Jews and a Christian background of solidarity with the right of Jews to the land of Abraham. The stories of Abraham in the Book of Genesis include the promise of that land to him and his seed, and are consistently, though not unanimously, taken literally by Jew and Christian alike. Davies acknowledges, "Probably, if not certainly, what the Shoah did was to make the connection between the doctrine of the Land and the necessity of a State in the Land unavoidably explicit."[13] He also writes, "The complexities, paradoxes and obscurities of the territorial theme cannot be sufficiently emphasised." [14] Separately, the guilt felt by European nations, particularly Germany, means that the shadow of the Shoah brings about a need to protect the Jews, lest they be allowed to suffer again without witnesses being proactive in their protection – despite Israel being one of the strongest military societies in the world. With hindsight, many Jews in Israel are contemptuous of the European Jews who walked passively to the Nazi gas chambers without resistance. Modern Israeli Jews are now prepared to use pre-emptive strikes and to fight any group which threatens them,[15] whether in Syria, Iraq, Lebanon, Egypt or Jordan, and even Iran. For their own reasons, Israel has possessed a nuclear capability since the 1960s, and their fears appear well-founded. Meanwhile, the problems in making peace continue to mount.

After 1947, there was bound to be further strife as the needs of the indigenous Palestinians were put aside by the Israelis and the withdrawing British forces. The UN partition plan was rejected by the Arabs because it gave the Jews control of 55% of British mandate Palestine, when before it had only 7% of the territory and despite the fact that Jews numbered one third of the population. This seemed grossly unfair but the Arabs under Husseini had supported Hitler, while the Jews had fought with the allies. It can hardly be claimed that the Palestinians were properly organised as a political entity at the time. Moreover, when the United Nations voted on the Partition in 1947, it made a decision which affected a country largely populated by Arabs. That decision did not represent the United Nations in their "finest hour," and would not be acceptable in the 21st century. Professor Gabriel Josipovici regards the UN decision to be: "a disaster for Jews and Arabs."[16] Palestinians found themselves continuing to receive thousands of people who were claiming the land as the original owners but who were almost entirely white people from European countries. For the Palestinians, after the defeat of the Arab forces in 1947 and 1948, the outcome, called the Nakbah, was a catastrophe: hundreds of thousands were made homeless and became dispossessed persons, more commonly known as refugees. After the Wars of 1948, 1967 and 1973, there were opportunities for rapprochement via UN Resolutions, 194, 242 and 338. Alarmed by the threats from Arab countries, Israel, instead of seeking ways for co-existence with Palestinians at an early stage, expanded its occupation and control, which went hand in hand with the reduction of quality of life for Arabs. Ignoring their oppression of Arabs, which was bound to bring resistance in many forms, Israel used the mantra of security against another Shoah. The outcome can now be seen, sixty years later, to be less than humane and more oppressive which, in turn, brings about the relatively puny, but frightening, responses of Arab terrorism, despite Palestinian experience of the overpowering force of Israeli state terrorism. The problems since 1947 in Israel and Palestine show no sign of being resolved and it is essential to consider issues that, at first sight, do not appear to be influential in the present intransigence. Israel is in control of the whole of the occupied West Bank and, despite talks about a future resolution, including a Palestinian state, there has been an impasse for decades. The shortage of enlightenment and self-awareness limits Israel's insight in perceiving that it is creating an environment of Arab resentment which, cyclically, feeds on its own paranoia. The outcome is a series of policies to take more Arab land, restrict any notion of Arab quality of life and to brutalise a population that is desperate to survive Israeli oppression, to the point of politicide,[17] i.e. the reduction of the national viability of the people, similar to the western colonisation of native lands in Africa, Australia, Asia and North America. This is a critical issue for the future, because the present is already without hope and in chronic need of change.

The question has to be raised about how many generations of Jews will pass through the planet before they are able to perceive differently, leave behind their inferiority and fear, and seek to follow their ancient prophets, "to do justly, love mercy and to walk humbly"?[18] Equally, it cannot be over-emphasised that there are sound reasons for Jewish fears because of threats of destruction from militant Arab voices in Iran, Syria, and Lebanon, as well as from within Israel itself by Hamas and Hizbollah. The ebb and flow of fear and retaliation, oppression and resistance are mingled and confused. Nothing seems clear and straightforward, each side being reactive and then, even more reactive. Critical questions for both peoples remain, as yet, unanswered and this is the mutual dilemma. Both sides blame the other instead of taking responsibility for their failures and their acts of violence, aggression and perceived terrorism. Both sides have their horror stories and yet find it difficult to perceive the total picture where both are persecutors and both are victims.

The policies and actions of the present religious Zionist movement have many motivations, including the natural quest for survival, as well as its commitment to Jewish religion and tradition. Although the separate religious groups may not be numerically larger than the non-religious sectors, Jewish belief systems have been passed on through the centuries by ritual, study and devotion so that even the non-devout would have understanding of their religion and history from their upbringing. Sensitivity by Israel, driven by its own diverse elements of superiority, fear and sense of destiny, is not a consideration when Palestinians are seen to be resisting Israel's possession of their land promised by God. In that case, any sign of serious opposition will be met by immediate and violent Israeli reaction. It would be an obvious, proactive strategy to render harmless any potential opposition by reducing its quality of life through measures of control. What many see as Israeli insensitivity, overreaction, disrespect, or provocation is, to the Israelis themselves, a blend of a divine mission and survival which overrules everything else. Ironically, this has led to its own entrapment in the contradictory behaviour of deliverance for itself and oppression of its neighbour. The issue of the people and the land is confused and complicated by the demands of those with a sense of divine mission.

The Land As Divine Mission And The Balfour Declaration

The Jewish view of divine mission supports the present occupation of land in excess of what Israel was given in the UN Partition Plan of 1947. Some are content with occupying the smaller portion of the land, but others, more extreme, are intent on gaining the larger land area, known as Eretz Israel, between the rivers of the Nile and the Euphrates.[19] Where this is the case, there is suspicion among Palestinians and others about the lack of agreed international borders. Certainly the land mentioned in the last verses of Genesis Chapter 15 is most indistinct. According to Davies: "The land was never defined with geographical precision"[20] and, in 2009, the borders still remained undetermined. It remains to be seen whether the first Jewish-Arab war of 1948 is really considered to be ended, or, using the words of the late Professor Tanya Reinhart of Tel Aviv University, it is, "Just the first step in a more ambitious and far-reaching strategy."[21]

As the influence of the Abrahamic Covenant is uncovered, it is important to bear in mind some basic considerations. It is not always understood that the Hebrew word for "Covenant" (*berith*) can also be the word used to describe an agreement, or relationship, between rulers and ruled. The Abrahamic Covenant assumes a three-fold belief in the existence of God, that he is just and that there was an historic person named Abraham with whom he initiated the relationship. If there is doubt about any of these beliefs, then the religious arguments cannot stand. If that is the case, those propositions for the existence of Israel have to be replaced by other, more sound, reasons. This is not the task of this chapter; instead it addresses the origins of Jewish belief as perceived by most Jews and which affect life in Israel, with special reference to terrorism. It was the principal of the Leo Baeck College in London who said, "It is not so much a matter of whether the accounts are true but that people believe them to be true."[23] Literal interpretations have serious political ramifications because, for some, they lead to the ideological determination to possess and control the land by whatever means are necessary.

Stories, like those of Abraham, that have been around for a sufficiently long period, can be taken symbolically rather than as matters of fact. Comparison with the tales of King Arthur and the Knights of the Round Table, with their accounts of chivalry, honour, and relationships, as well as dishonour, disloyalty and antagonism are well known. Professor Norman Vance[22] has described them as part of the medieval romantic stories, going back to Celtic times and brought together as a whole in the 15th century by Thomas Malory. The same might be said about the stories of the Abrahamic Covenant, except that the outcome, when taken as objective truth, has been far more devastating and costly in human life. For this reason alone, there is urgent need for a re-examination of the texts, with the disastrous applications that are based upon them. When people first meet the stories, perhaps as children, they readily assume them to represent events that actually happened, before realising that they could also be understood as a different category: literature, rather than history.

When one considers those Arthurian stories from Celtic mythology, their significance can be recognised as models of both chivalrous behaviour and value. To interpret them as inerrant accounts from history, however, leads to the quality of their meaning being diverted, rather than being respected for what they are. Although there are separate descriptions of the land in the Bible, many Jews argue that the ancient Biblical texts justify their occupation and control of Palestine. Such an argument from ancient writings would not carry weight elsewhere with other colonialist peoples and nations.

Some see similarities in the collection of ancient Jewish stories from four major traditions[24] and edited together after the Jewish return from Exile in Babylon in 536 BC.[25] As such the stories are acceptable for their beauty and as examples of major divine-human relationships, but they are hardly to be taken as inerrant, historical truths. More seriously for others, the belief in those accounts as being the word of God who gave the land to Abraham, and which must be taken at face value, is of paramount importance. The latter is the view of many devout Orthodox Jews and Conservative Evangelical and Fundamentalist Christians, as distinct from what is sometimes called "mainstream religion."[25] Where literalism and inerrancy of scripture are held as primary factors in faith and practice, the argument that Israel is the land of the Jews and no one else becomes the ultimate truth that must be upheld at all costs, whatever the price in human misery. That appalling price, being the logical consequences of such beliefs, provides sound reason for re-examination of them, rather than blind obedience to them.

There are a number of separate perceptions, beyond religious ideology. One, a basic tenet of the Israel-Palestine conflict, is offered by the Canadian moral and political philosopher, Professor Michael Neumann,[27] who states, "The central fact of the conflict is that Zionists sought sovereignty in Palestine." He argues that they did not simply seek a homeland, where they could feel safe after centuries of discrimination and persecution, but a sovereign state. It is apparent that the idea contained both nationalist and religious aims. From this possessive thrust followed the perfectly understandable Arab resistance. That notion of possession is extended by the Israeli peace activist, Uri Avnery,[28] who describes the core of the conflict as being nationalistic, but containing religious and social aspects. He holds that when Jews in Europe reacted against anti-Semitism, it was the religious and traditional motives that drew the Zionists to Palestine and not elsewhere.

There are other complex views about the nature of the possession of the land by Jews. Kathleen Cavanaugh, of the University of Galway,[29] suggests that the "Promised Land" narrative has been neatly placed to legitimise the choice of venue, when it is about land and the competing claims to that territory. She is not convinced that the point of safety would have to be this particular geographical location. It happens to be this special place, but she asks whether it is the religious significance that manifests the need of safety, or the historical backdrop that brought people there? She points out that Jewish claims to land, and the holy land in particular, are matched by Muslims who equally make their own claims, and this opinion had already been put to me during my interviews with Hamas in Bethlehem.[30] On the Palestinian side, the rise of religiously based political groups such as Hamas is, perhaps, better explained by desperation, rather than the Quran. The pull of Palestinian society towards Hamas, is probably better explained by their perception of what they consider to be the failures by the international community to adjudicate fairly, coupled with the perceived corruption of Fatah.

Cavanaugh perceives links between the nature of religion and political influence around the time of the Balfour Declaration and the British Mandate. The inextricable link with a religious manifesto comes not from either Jews or Palestinians but from the role of the British, in the form of Balfour, Sykes and Lloyd George during the mandate period. "They believed quite literally in the necessity of bringing the Jews home, in order for there to be the second coming [of Jesus Christ, which] was taken quite seriously…and was at the heart of British policy."[31] Moreover, the Grand Mufti, Haj Amin al-Husseini, was eventually to do the Arabs no favours by his support of Adolf Hitler as they became seen to be identified with Nazis before and during World War II. This was despite the proliferation of notorious Jewish underground groups who, in their quest for independence, fought against the British. Both sectors could be seen to be anti-British. The involvement of evangelical Christians in England since the early 19th century through the LSPCAJ had helped create the conditions for a sympathetic, supportive movement to ensure a favourable response to the Balfour Declaration in 1917.

There was also strategic, political and diplomatic influence on the part of the Jews, which was discovered through meticulous research by Professor William Rubinstein of the University of North Wales in 2000. In exploring the identity of a Jewish family, he discovered that the author of the Balfour Declaration, Leopold Amery, for his own undeclared reasons, was himself a "secret Jew" because his mother was identified as a Jew.[32] Although the Declaration was signed by Lord Balfour, it had come from the office of Lord Milner. Lord Milner had appointed Amery, who was his Private Secretary, to be political secretary to the war cabinet in 1916. Lord Milner requested Amery to draft the Balfour Declaration in 1917, which was put before the full cabinet and passed with only two small amendments. It was then sent to Lord Rothschild and committed Britain "to establishing a Jewish 'National Home' in Palestine. This momentous document was, in effect, the founding charter of the State of Israel, which was established thirty-one years later."[33] Amery was, thereafter, a significant influence in the development of the Jewish presence in Palestine. While never declaring himself openly as a Jew, he went on to establish the Jewish Legion which fought under British supervision later in the war. After the creation of the British Mandate, Amery acted as Dominion Secretary from 1925-1929 and Rubinstein writes: "During this period an amazingly wide range of the infrastructure and characteristic institutions of the future Jewish state came into existence."[34] His parliamentary career was one that was distinguished throughout, being evidently supportive of the Jews, but never publicly owning that belief.

The land issue is considered to be much less to do with religion, according to the view of journalist Danny Rubinstein[35] of Ha'aretz, and more to do with identity, history and culture. He asks where else is the Jewish culture physically set in geography, history, tradition and language but in the land of Israel? He agrees that the influence of the Bible as a document, which crystallises their ancient history, is seen to be significant, even by non-believers. He argues that as the Soviet Republic broke into separate nationalistic states, the Jews, who were part of a number of mixed races, had no identity in the new Russia. Thus, they came to Israel, not because of religion or Abraham, so much as their need for an identity. In Israel, as Jews, they had the right of return, a right which is only for Jews and not for Gentiles. This brings increasing animosity from the Palestinians who, along with the refugees, are prevented from returning to their homes if they should leave the country, even temporarily. This preferential treatment is an abrasive factor within Israel, where citizenship is provided for the Jewish Russians, and alienates even further those Palestinians who live in Israel and Palestine but are deprived of the same freedom of movement.

The Similarity Between The Conquests Of The Lands Of Canaan And Palestine

The thrust for exclusive possession and control of the land may be perceived differently by separate groups but it is not possible to remove the religious drive from the debate. When the Jews first entered the small territory of the land of Canaan in the time of Joshua, they believed that God had instructed them to take possession of the land and settle in it because he had given it to them. This instruction is contained in The Book of Numbers:

> Speak to the Israelites and say to them: "When you cross the Jordan into Canaan, drive out all the inhabitants of the land before you. Destroy all their carved images and their cast idols and demolish all their high places. Take possession of he land and settle in it for I have given you the land to possess.[36]

It has already been argued that the belief in those ancient accounts as being factual, historical truth, rather than ancient myth or legend, is strongly maintained still by many influential Jewish and Christian groups throughout the world. The background issue was probably one of Jewish survival. Joshua, who had endured the desert under Moses and then espied the fertile land at the oasis of Jericho wanted, and needed, its fertility. His military victory there,[37] was followed by the defeat at Ai, which offered greater security and which Joshua eventually subdued.[38] The cost to the inhabitants was extermination, perhaps caused by the mixture of Jewish military genius and aberrant psychosis, without regard for the potential consequences of Canaanite reaction.[39] One can now reasonably pose the question as to whether or not it is acceptable to inflict on Palestinians something akin to the dispossession and violence that was perpetrated by their forebears in Canaan.

It has been pointed out that there are variations in the definitions of the land promised by God to be possessed and occupied.[40] Davies points to the reality that, notwithstanding the actual promises that might have been understood,

> what is important is not the rediscovery of the origins of the promise to Abraham, but the recognition that that promise was so interpreted from age to age that it became a living power in the life of the people of Israel. Not the mode of its origin matters, but its operation as a formative, dynamic seminal force in the history of Israel.[41]

Naturally, when the Jews entered Canaan under Joshua, there were other people there in abundance, or there would have been no record of conflicts. Similarly, in the 19th century, when Herzl was committed to an independent and secure Jewish state, the land in mind had been populated by others for centuries – the Palestinians. The outcome has also been similar viz., the displacement of the indigenous population through warfare, followed by numerous political tactics of dispossession. The issue of justice for the Palestinians was not to be considered at all, because the primary issue was ideological, based on the drives of security and religion.

Decades after the events, some Jews already look back with some sense of shame at the colonial behaviour of their forebears, who are still alive and well.[42] The exchange of ideas had commenced in the context of European colonialism in Africa, but the discussion then extended to include the indigenous Indian tribes of North America. At one time they were described as the savages, rather than people protecting their hunting grounds and the herds on which they depended. The ideological policy of possession and control by incarcerating the people into reservations is, retrospectively, seen by many to be shameful. This feeling is now shared by those Jews who look with horror at the outworking of ideological policies aimed at possession of the land and resources of the Palestinians, in the name of security and religion.

There was support for the Jews over many years, beginning long before the Shoah of the 1930s and 1940s, because of the missionary-cum ideological work of the LSPCAJ in the 19th century, and which culminated in the Balfour Declaration of 1917. It was this Declaration which paved the way for the Jewish State in the Arab land of Palestine, following the expulsion of the Turks from the region in World War I. The Palestinian academic, Ghada Karmi, describes that process as:

> colonial and racist.... The idea that a foreign people could be invited into another land without the knowledge or permission of the native population would now be regarded as outrageous. But it still informs the Western approach to the Arabs in this conflict.[43]

It is the Jewish historian, Avi Shlaim, who has sympathy with that position when he points to the harsh realities of the situation. He refers to an oration in 1956 by Moshe Dayan at the funeral of a young farmer in a kibbutz. Having described the land taken from the Arabs he went on:

> What cause have we to complain about their fierce hatred for us? For eight years now, they sit in their refugee camps in Gaza, and before their eyes we turn into our homestead the land in which they and their forefathers have lived.[44]

The Israeli daily newspaper, *Ha'aretz,* in 2002, contained an article, quoted by Karmi, where a writer presses the point which is held by many in Israel:

> This land was our country when we were a small, isolated minority.... Absolute justice holds that the state of Israel is, and always has been, the only Jewish state, and this country has been solely that of the Jewish people.[45]

That statement, being based on biblical assumptions, is challenged by Karmi who expresses the views of many when she holds that a matter of religious belief, taken from the Bible, cannot be accepted as proof of anything.

Strangely, and disastrously, despite peace conferences and agreements, even as late as December 2007 in Annapolis, there has been no peace agreement to bring about two separate viable states with defined boundaries. Indeed, for some years there has been strong evidence of Israeli policies of debellatio[46] and politicide to undermine and reduce any potency for a future autonomous Palestinian state.[47] The future is waiting for civilised humanity to resolve this man-made crisis according to the United Nations Universal Declaration of Human Rights.

The contemporary situation is better understood when we examine the background to the impasse. The next chapter focuses on the major effect of the settlement movement, and those instrumental in making it a potent, dynamic force in the life of Israel and Palestine, the organisation known as Gush Emunim

Notes

[1] Friedman David, 'The Political Reality of Living in Israel, with a Suggested Path towards Reconciliation' in *Christian Perspectives on the Israeli-Palestinian Conflict,* eds. Wesley H. Brown & Peter F. Penner (Neufeld Verlag Schwarzenfeld, Germany: 2008), 69-70.

[2] "Christian Perspectives on the Israeli-Palestinian Conflict," held at the International Baptist Theological Seminary. Prague, 13-17 November, 2006.

[3] Dr Willem Ouwneel and Pastor Steven Meester. Friedman, 70.

[4] Friedman, 72.

[5] Friedman, 76.

[6] Friedman, 76.

[7] Palestinian Authority

[8] Friedman, 80.

[9] Friedman, 82.

[10] Saa'd David, 'How shall we Interpret Scripture about the Land and Eschatology? Jewish and Arab Perspectives' in *Christian Perspectives on the Israeli-Palestinian Conflict* eds. Wesley H. Brown & Peter F. Penner (Neufeld Verlag Schwarzenfeld, Germany: 2008), 107.

[11] Saa'd David, 108.

[12] Davies W. D. *The Territorial Dimension of Judaism* (Minneapolis: First Fortress Press, 1991), 120-121.

[13] Davies, 122.

[14] Davies, xvii.

[15] Davies, 121.

[16] Josipovici Gabriel. Private correspondence with the author, 13 May, 2009.

[17] Politicide is a term introduced by Baruch Kimmerling as the process of weakening a state so that it cannot be a social, political and economic entity. Kimmerling B., *Politicide*. London: Verso, 2006.

[18] Micah 6. 8.

[19] Viorst, 205.

[20] Davies, xvii.

[21] Reinhart T., *Israel/Palestine How to End the War of 1948* (New York: Seven Stories Press, 2002), 10-11.

[22] Rabbi Jonathan Magonet, Leo Baeck College, London. Interview, 21 December, 2004.

[23] Professor Norman Vance, Professor of Literature, University of Sussex. Interview, 21 May, 2007.

[24] The four major sources, or writings, are taken from the school of Higher Criticism which deals with the authorship and origins of the first five books of the Old Testament. These are known as J for Jahweh, E for Elohim, D for Deuteronomist, and P for Priestly. These have been edited together to form one complete document, known as the Pentateuch or Torah.

[25] They had different reference points and were written at different times for different people with different objectives. This book is not intended to enter into the debates and discussions between scholars over the years.

[26] The word "mainstream" is often used as a general, but imprecise, term to describe Protestant, non-conservative groups. See Victor B., *The Last Crusade* (London: Constable, 2005), 30, 36-37.

[27] Neumann M., *The Case Against Israel* (Petrolia, California: CounterPunch & AK Press, 2005), 30, 36-37.

[28] Avnery U., *Truth Against Truth* (Tel Aviv: Gush Shalom, 2005), 2. Uri Avnery was an elected Member of the Knesset and is Director of Gush Shalom, the Israeli peace movement.

[29] Correspondence with author, 16 November, 2007.

[30] Bethlehem, 18 March, 2006.

[31] Correspondence with author, 18 November, 2007.

[32] Rubinstein W. R. 'The Secret of Leopold Amery' in *Historical Research. Vol. 73, no. 181. June 2000,* 175 (Blackwell Publishers Ltd. 108 Cowley Rd.).

[33] Rubinstein, 184.

[34] Rubinstein, 185.

[35] Rubinstein D. Interview, Jerusalem, 17 March, 2006

[36] Numbers 33. 51-53.

[37] Joshua 6. 1-25.

[38] Joshua 8. 1-29.

[39] Joshua 9. 1- Joshua 10.43.

[40] Davies, 16-17. (endnotes) refers to Exodus 23. 31ff, Numbers 24. 1-10, Deuteronomy 11. 24 and Joshua 1. 2-4, unlike Genesis 15. 17-21, where the land is less extensive than Genesis 12. 1-3.

[41] Davies, 18.

[42] Piterberg G., *The Returns of Zionism* (London: Verso, 2008).

[43] Karmi G., *Married to Another Man (*London: Pluto, 2007), 5.

[44] Shlaim A., *The Iron Wall* (London: Penguin 2000), 101.

[45] Karmi, 64.

[46] *Debellatio*: A political process of debilitating a people after a conflict, or war, so that they cannot govern themselves and have to be governed by another, more powerful, neighbour.

[47] Kimmerling B., *Politicide* (London: Verso, 2006), 3.

Chapter 2

The Unintentional Jewish Agents in Terrorism in The 20th Century— A Dialectic Of Gush Emunim and the Settler Movement

Gush Emunim And Settlements

The analysts, observers and commentators, critics and apologists for Gush Emunim, the Bloc of the Faithful, are many. I have been stirred by what I have seen of its lasting influence in Israel and Palestine. The devotion and commitment of its activists may be seen as admirable but I find it hard to see their contribution as anything less than creative in the overall perspective of history. I have therefore looked to a wide range of writers who have researched and worked more closely in the field. Their contributions to the subject are included in this chapter. The analytic commentary of Gideon Aran is written by one who has studied the movement at close quarters.[1] He acknowledges that its objective is supra political and religious, being "the full redemption of Israel and the entire world."[2] When we have understood that objective, while not necessarily condoning Gush Emunim's actions, we are enabled to see beyond its tactics of violence and intimidation. It has its own interpretation of law and order, seeing itself as accountable to an authority higher than the state and, therefore, free to take political action against the state if, and when, it considers its own vision and ideology to be under threat.[3] Its commitment to safeguard what it sees as "sacred land" or, "sacred geography," involves the movement in the conquest of the land of Israel, regardless of occupants or law makers. Although comparatively few in number, Gush Emunim settlers have their own unique, exclusive, mindset and culture, in terms of family life, community, education and religious expression, the latter overlapping with political and military life. Authority within the community is governed by rabbinic, rather than statutory, authorities. Central to its life is the three-fold focus of the Torah, the land and the people, and the highest achievement is held to be the establishment of the settlements.[4] One part of its belief system, Aran maintains, is founded on "the biblical narrative concerning God's promise to the Patriarchs."[5] In turn, this is reinforced by the Law of Moses in the Torah and traditional Jewish law in the Halakhah, to which members give hours of study every day. What now follows will lead to questions about the political interpretations and ideological strategies that come from such study.

Originally conceived by Rabbi Abraham Kook,[6] Gush Emunim emerged from a religious root of Orthodox Judaism in the 1930s and became an unorthodox, dynamic, confident, assertive, spiritual-political organisation after the Yom Kippur War of 1973. It was to become a highly effective and disciplined extra-parliamentary pressure group which, for a while, changed the nature of political and religious life in Israel. As a religious grouping, it became a catalyst for dramatic change to the government policies through its pro-active strategy of settlements in the West Bank, which it considered to be the liberated lands of Judea and Samaria. Journalist, writer and scholar, Milton Viorst, supports Aran, stating that Gush Emunim was an organisation, formed "to satisfy Religious Zionism's territorial imperative…whose ideology assured them that annexation of the land was a greater duty than obeying the law. Gush Emunim became the vanguard of territorialism."[7] Holding religion as superior to, and more important than, civil or international law, Gush Emunim became a powerful movement, so that settlements expanded thereafter until, in 2007, the settlers of all persuasions were numbered in hundreds of thousands. Situated throughout the West Bank, including Jerusalem, they are subsidised by whichever government is in power, their activities facilitated by exclusive roads and services, and having protection provided by the Israel Defence Force.

History does not stand still and, between writing, publishing, purchasing and reading, things can change dramatically. As soon as something is up to date, it is overtaken by events and interpretations, subsequent to the original writing. Although the subject of Gush Emunim, the Bloc of the Faithful, and the larger settler movement has been addressed by a number of writers, there has been a shortage of comprehensive work on the damaging effects of settlements in general.[8] This chapter points to events which have had lasting negative influence in Israel and Palestine and, like the book as a whole, is written at a different angle from others I have consulted. The reality is that the Israel Palestinian conflict, whatever the outcome, will continue to be discussed, argued over and written about for decades – at least!

The ideological-cum-theological, stance of Gush Emunim is pivotal in any discussion of the occupation by Israel because it shows the embedded nature and origin of the settler philosophy and practice. Although perceived as obscurantist by some, that stance is nonetheless rational for its activists and supporters, and justifies the immoveable logic of its position. Depending on the perspective of the speaker, the movement can be described as a loyal servant of God or as a dangerous and disastrous component in Jewish and Arab life. After the wars of 1967 and 1973, the leaders of the settler movement embarked on a task which was far more than the acquisition of land and more like a sacred mission on behalf of the Jews and their God. Acting independently, according to its own ideological beliefs from 1973, it used the support of thousands of volunteers, together with the assistance of the State of Israel and its military machinery, to achieve its ends.

For there to be any appreciation of the difficulties involved in meaningful dialogue with its adherents, the belief system of Gush Emunim has to be more fully understood. Professor Baruch Kimmerling points to the contrasting positions of the Jewish and Arab communities. He sees the communities of Gush Emunim as deeply religious "to be run according to the laws of Halakhah and the judgement of rabbis... [with] the sublime aspiration of transforming the Israeli state into as Jewish a state as possible."[9] However, "For the local Arab population, the 'return' of the Jews, who thought they owned the country after 2000 years of exile, sounded ridiculous, unacceptable and dangerous."[10]

Although there is little by way of explanation of its belief system by either, the founder, Rabbi Abraham Kook, or leaders of Gush Emunim, Professor Ian Lustick[11] suggests that there is a systematic rationale for its ideology which was put forward and published by Professor Harold Fisch, the former rector of Bar-Ilan University.[12] Fisch is one who argues that Jews are not normal in quite the same way as other peoples, but unique, with a divine, unique destiny as God's chosen people.[13] This is interpreted to mean that normal laws of justice do not apply to Jews because, "God ordered us to be the people of the land of Israel."[14] The outcome of that kind of belief is that such Jews have different laws and a different accountability. They see Arab hostility as part of Israel's battle against evil on behalf of God and they demand that Arabs have three choices, to flee, to surrender or to fight.[15] Lustick reveals the distinction, held by one of the major, early settler leaders, Hanan Porat, between Arabs who live in the land as individuals but, who as a group or nation, cannot have any rights over it.[16] This means that talks about human rights and borders miss the point, for the struggle is between God and evil. Gush Emunim, like some other fundamentalists, therefore expect no concessions, and expect persecution, until the coming of Messiah. Peace with others is perfectly acceptable, as long as there are no concessions on land, because Israel has to possess the land for Messiah to come and then the world will realise the cosmic redemptive mission of God through the Jews.

The crucial nature of the theology of Gush Emunim lies in a threefold notion of God, the land and the people, without which there is no Zionism, for God created the land before the people.[17] This means that the land of Israel, for religious Jews, is holy and cannot be seen as real-estate to be traded for peace because it is set apart for God. This is not always understood by non-Jews. Nevertheless, this has been the settlers' ideological battleground for Israel since the Six Day War and shows the impossibility of any peace talks that refer to land, such as United Nations Resolution 242, which speaks of a return to the 1967 borders as they were before that particular War. An insight into the implacable, but logical, nature of Gush Emunim[18] is provided by their profound belief that the land is not for the Jews to give away.

Inevitably, there are other sides to this ideological, religious position, which may arouse discontent from a range of quarters. Jewish messianism, focused on the coming of the Messiah, has a number of elements, many doubtless noble, while others, very human and normal, are worthy of consideration because they are part of any natural human condition. Everyone seeks for acceptance, with a sense of personal worth and value, as distinct from being insignificant or, worse still, of being without esteem due to different kinds of misfortune. Therefore, it is normal to seek to feel "special," rather than to feel of low estate. The same dynamic can go for a people who feel at risk before greater odds. Instead of feeling "victims" they will seek for compensation by being "special" or carefully selected, over against others. In order to avoid any sense of weakness or shame, they may escape possible feelings of humiliation by having a protector who will save them because they are a specially chosen and unique people with a distinctive destiny before all others. It is not unknown for people to seek to possess a status that removes them from the humiliation they otherwise dread. It is predictable that those who feel the dread of inadequacy will seek for power and control over others and will regard this search as a mission, when it is actually their defence against the reality of being normal. This can be observed happening in many ways, not least in terms of both religion and international alliances. Could this rationalisation be an unspoken agenda for the Jewish condition in Israel, as a chosen people, on an exclusive land, with a divine and eternal destiny? Is there such a divinity who would make such an exclusive selection in his creation, or is the selection constructed by the people themselves who need that kind of reinforcement? Yet, what kind of deity is it who would be so discriminatory? And so militaristic? One can easily understand that those with such a mindset would be appalled at the notion of a deity being set at nothing, despised, humiliated, degraded and crucified, although it is part of the Christian tradition. Moreover, to have exclusive attachments to a particular piece of land, or even a particular place, may be understandable for a primitive religion, but such territorialism seems out of place in a modern world, other than as a place of appreciation, memory and reflection. These issues have yet to be properly discussed, but that particular discussion is not the primary task of this book.

There were a number of highs and lows for Gush Emunim, which may be viewed as watersheds in their story. The victory of the Six Day War of 1967 ignited their messianic aspirations and eventually led to the formation of one of the early settler groups, Elon Moreh in 1973, after the Yom Kippur War. In 1974, they mobilised and returned to their former village, Kfar Etzion, followed by others to establish a foothold in Hebron, which was to lead to the settlement nearby named Kiryat Arba.[19] Following the Yom Kippur War of 1973, religious groups like Gush Emunim took matters into their own hands by spearheading a settlement grouping, aided and abetted by senior politicians like Moshe Dayan, Yigal Allon, Ariel Sharon, Shimon Peres, Menachem Begin and many others. In contrast, the return of the Yamit settlement in Sinai to Egypt in 1982-3, as part of the Israel-Egypt agreement, was a serious blow to Gush Emunim. However, even more immense was the decision of the Israeli Supreme Court in 2005, in relation to the disengagement from Gaza, which emphasised that settlements were not permanent, but were a belligerent occupation.

The Background, Leading To Rabbi Abraham Kook And "Messiah's Donkey"

The story of Zionism in the 20th century is one of a gradual development of strategies which were to achieve some of the goals of Gush Emunim for the occupation and control of Palestinian land. Zionism began as a secular, nationalist movement and gradually brought round the majority of the religious communities to make it a conjoined secular and religious enterprise. What commenced as a quest for Jewish safety from pogroms and persecution had its origins in the writings of the founder of the Zionist movement, Theodore Herzl, who experienced virulent anti-Semitism as a journalist in Paris. After the Dreyfus Affair in Paris in 1894, he stated: "What made me a Zionist was the Dreyfus trial."[20] The historian, Professor Gabriel Piterberg holds that current Zionism has moved along similar lines to Herzl, becoming nationalism that is now theologically joined with colonialism, regardless of its outward appearance.[21] The outcome is revealed in the policies of the governments of Israel as they continue the diminution of Palestinians and their territory. Piterberg notes that in the war of 1948, there was ethnic cleansing of Arabs, which was typical of other settler nations, such as the Europeans who settled in America and South Africa, where displacement of native peoples was the norm.[22] The history of native peoples was described, not in their own tribal stories but through the accounts of settler colonialism by the European powers and those who came afterwards, as they removed or eliminated the indigenous people. In the case of Israel and the Arab population, Jewish colonialism is similarly exposed in the gradual swallowing up of Palestinian land through successive wars after 1947, so that Israel became a classic settler-state with its superstructure of laws and institutions. Evidence of racism and discrimination among Jews themselves was seen from the early days, not least in the kibbutzim where there was little room allowed, even, for Sephardi Jews from the Middle East.

The Labour movement in Israel might have been expected to be socialist, but such was not the case. The Israeli sociologist, Professor Gershon Shafir, writes, "The most distinguishing characteristic of the Jewish Labour Movement in Palestine was that it was not a labour movement at all. Rather it was a colonial movement in which the workers' interests remained secondary to the exigencies of settlement."[23] The reality was that there were two distinctive separate entities, creating a "dual society paradigm" of the Jewish settler community and the indigenous Palestinian community. Piterberg puts this paradigm down to the Palestinian presence, with their resistance being a consequence of the dynamics of the Israeli community/settler state, which became an ethnic plantation colony, based on the model of European control of land and employment of local labour.[24] This is further sharpened by Piterberg, who extends the insights of Shafir to suggest that, for the purposes of colonisation, instead of employing a local labour force, the settlers moved on to use Jewish labour to perform the work previously done by Arabs. The latter were not protected by any labour laws because they were increasingly prevented from joining the labour trade union institution, the Histradut. Racism deeply entered the movement of the working class, which had become part of the colonialist enterprise.

Although contested by the Left, the Histradut, whose general secretary was David Ben-Gurion, was intended exclusively for Jewish workers, with power kept from Arabs. When the Histradut came to consider the emerging union of railway workers in 1922, which might have included Arabs, it was not accepted – the formal title of the Histradut was, "The General Histradut of Hebrew Workers in Eretz Israel." The union had the opportunity to create its non-ethnic, solidarity grouping of indigenous Arabs with the Jewish workers. Instead, the leftist members were to be expelled from the union.[25] Arabs were never permitted to join the Histradut and to have joint representation in the corridors of worker power. This kind of racial and ethnic division, and exclusiveness, was also seen in the kibbutzim. Instead of being open to Jews from anywhere in the world, the kibbutzim according to Piterberg who highlights Shafir's insights, were controlled by the Jewish National Fund. Those responsible allocated land to Ashkenazi European Jews but hardly any to the Sephardi Jews from North Africa and the Middle East. Indigenous Arabs were completely excluded.

Because of the ideological differences and mutual contempt between the different Zionist factions, the secular-religious connection in the 20th century did not take place easily at first. The secular Zionist Jews defied the Orthodox for decades as they set up the Jewish National Fund, purchased land and settled communities in Palestine. Although Mizrahi Jews followed Herzl in 1903 in accepting Uganda as an alternative Jewish homeland to Palestine,[26] for the religious, Agudat Yisrael. (Torah-True Jews), this proposal of an African territory would never be acceptable because it was not the "holy" land that God had entrusted to the Jews for his eternal purposes. For decades, there was a separation between the various expressions of Jewish religious life but, when the State was formed in 1948, there was growing accommodation between the sacred and the secular. This was to change after the Six Day War of 1967.

It was the Rev. Abraham Isaak Kook who first discerned the strategic nature of the Zionist nationalist movement in the 1920s. Kook was the Chief Rabbi of Palestine and the initiator of what, decades after his death, became Gush Emunim, the leading settler movement after 1967. David Morrison's book gives a series of pen-portraits of the significant people who created the settlement of Gush Etzion and the academies for the study of the Torah, the yeshiva, and it provides his own description of one whom he sees as the original source of the movement, the Rev. Abraham Kook.[27] Born in 1865 in Russia, Kook went to Israel in 1904. However, he was in Germany during World War I having gone there for a conference, at the end of which he returned to become Chief Rabbi of the Yishuv, the Jewish community in Palestine. He visited the secular, often anti-religious, Jews who he saw as, "a representation of God's redemptive plan," but who he felt were mistaken in their wish to be the same as other people. He held to the conviction that all Jews had a messianic vision and not one that was secular, and consequently believed that even the secular and anti-religious were Jews nonetheless. According to Morrison, Kook was one who had reminded critics about the two Covenants in Jewish history, one with Abraham and the second with Moses and the Jewish people at Sinai. Kook pointed to the difference to show that, unlike Abraham, not all the people at Sinai were holy and pious men and women at all. Morrison shows the understanding of Kook about the differences between Jews at the time of the Covenant with Moses:

> those sinners whose souls are linked with love to those issues affecting all of Israel, the land of Israel and the renaissance of the nation of Israel, the souls of those sinners of Israel are more perfect than the souls of the religionists who do not have that feeling for the good of the majority and the building of the nation in the land.[28]

Two controversial academics, Israel Shahak and Norton Mezvinsky,[29] describe Kook's profound, but alarming, belief in the superiority of the Jewish soul, and the subsidiary nature of non-Jews, which attracted a significant, powerful following. The journalist, Gershom Gorenberg, draws out Kook's conviction of the role of the Jews thus, "The world's redemption depended on the Jews living in the land of Israel, and therefore the return of the Jews to their homeland was an expression of God's will. Secular Zionism [which commenced the return] was thus a stage in God's plan."[30] Although there was a great deal of opposition to Zionism from some in the Orthodox community, Kook had perceived that they had mutual interests with secular Zionists in obtaining the land of the Covenant. He discerned the secular Zionists as the servants of Jahweh, in similar vein to the Persian, King Cyrus, who restored the Jews to Jerusalem from Babylon in 536 BC after their Exile. Kook perceived them as "Messiah's Donkey,"[31] referring to the prophet Zechariah who foresaw the Messiah entering Jerusalem on a donkey. This description was not to be interpreted as disparaging, but a simple recognition of the part unwittingly played by the state. In similar vein, the secular Zionists would be the inadvertent vehicle for the eventual installation of religious Zionism, which would supersede the efforts of the secularists, in preparation for the Messiah. Kook may well have felt that the same might be true of the Balfour Declaration in 1917, which assured Jews of their land. Kook was in London at the time and "perceived it as a further step forward in God's plan for redemption. Confident of his interpretation, he worked to persuade Jews everywhere to build on Britain's offer."[32]

Kook is described in the Encyclopaedia Judaica[33] as both a religious mystic and prolific writer who saw the Return that was to come as religious because only in the land of Israel could people work out their religious life. Unlike most Orthodox Jews, Kook identified with Zionism and in 1921, as the first Ashkenazi[34] Chief Rabbi in Palestine, he focused on creating a yeshiva, or theological education system. In 1924, he established his first yeshiva, Merkaz HaRav, which was small and poorly funded but it managed to continue during his lifetime, until his death in 1935. He rejected the literal exegesis of the creation stories of Adam and Eve[35] because he sought a more profoundly mystical interpretation of creation and understood evolution to be compatible with Jewish mysticism. He saw piety as linked to morality and argued that Jews were chosen to further the divine goal of human perfection. He held that the people and land of Israel possessed a particular holiness, so that the relationship of the Jews to Israel was essential to the divine source.[36] Kook did not establish a following of any size in the inter-war years of the 1920s and 1930s as he was neither a member of the ultra conservative religious haredim, nor a secular Jew. [37] It was his small group of disciples from the Bnai Akiva youth movement, followed by their education in the Merkaz HaRav yeshiva under the leadership of Kook's son, Rabbi Zvi Yehuda Kook, who were to become the conveyors of his message in Gush Emunim.

The strategic influence of Kook and his son, who was to be the actual founder of Gush Emunim, is described by Milton Viorst.[38] He perceived that the elder Kook was not a typical, traditional Orthodox Rabbi but one who was able to perceive in the drive of Herzl, an initiative which would serve the purposes of God for the land and the people of Abraham. As Chief Rabbi, he saw the strategic nature of secular Zionism as connected to the ultimate objective of "the restoration of a holy state."[39] His vision was not fulfilled in his lifetime but Viorst points out that his theology of return had added a layer of religious mysticism to Zionist nationalism. When the time was ripe, after the Six Day War of 1967, the religious fervour came to be activated in turning the occupied Palestinian land, including Jerusalem, into the lands of Judea and Samaria.

Many of the convictions of the Kooks and Gush Emunim are focused on Biblical memory, calling Jews to be faithful to their memories and records of the past as God had provided for them.[40] This especially meant the promise of the land as their inheritance, despite almost 2000 years of absence during the diaspora. This assertion of Biblical memory is contested by Professor Michael Feige who argues against what he describes as the, "overarching principle that constructs the position of the movement vis-à-vis the rest of society and determines its critical positions vis-à-vis modern Israel." [41] There were special reasons for this focus on early religious stories, not least because it appeared to Gush Emunim that secular Jews had forgotten their history, traditions and religious responsibilities. Equally, Gush Emunim knew it had to provide a non-negotiable argument that the land was theirs by divine right and record, which excluded all others, particularly the Palestinians. Therefore, the land and the sacred places were seen by Gush Emunim followers as irreplaceable. They held that God had made a promise of specific land to a specific people, and this was enshrined in its mythical history, always to be remembered, defended and upheld.[42] Feige strongly criticises the claims of Jews, on the basis of the Bible, for their return to the Holy Land, and puts aside their use of the prophets, such as Ezekiel,[43] regarding the prophecy of the return of the faithful to the land of Israel. He writes:

A crucial point emanating from this idea is that Jewish history as such, and history in general, does not render political property rights in the present. In other words, the connection between the people and the land is meta-historical: it precedes history and constitutes it. The most authoritative memory is the commitment to the covenant that binds God to the people of Israel.[44]

Feige argues that history, normally understood as belonging in the past, is misplaced and that meta-history is what may yet be created. However, the Jews, by their interpretations, believe that they cannot resign to others their right to the land. He goes on to make the essential point about their use of the Abrahamic Covenant, "The most authoritative memory is the commitment to the Covenant that binds God and the people of Israel." [45] Feige thereby summarises the basic position of Gush Emunim, which was asserted by one of its outstanding leaders, Hanan Porat. Porat distinguished Gush Emunim from secular Zionism. He disagreed with David Ben-Gurion that Israel was the birthplace of the Jewish people with the counter argument that the Israelites were created outside the land, in the desert, and the land was to be given. "The uniqueness of the Jewish people is that its connection to the land is meta-historical. It creates history and is not derived from it."[46] Feige sums up the problem by stating, "For Porat, Zionism is qualitatively different from other nationalist movements because it is a religious return, based on divine logic…and is the most uncompromising component in the movement's ideology."[47] Gush Emunim activists see themselves making history in accordance with the covenant promises, and the Bible retains its importance as a record of events, particularly in the Torah and the prophetic literature.

Rabbi Abraham Kook And Professor Harold Fisch

Probably the strongest apologist and theorist for Kook, and therefore Gush Emunim, was Professor Harold Fisch of Bar-Ilan University.[48] In considering the work of Fisch, it can be argued that he used the views of others in order to develop his own theories. Although couched in terms of admiration, there is the sense that he wishes to use, even to take, their arguments and place them on firmer, if slightly different, ground.

Fisch decried the notion of Jewish assimilation, whereby the Jewish nation would become like other nations, because he saw its place as utterly distinctive and unique among the nations as the messenger and agent for God's redemptive activity for the world. He focused on the Abrahamic Covenant, seeing it as literal truth, beyond contradiction. Following the words of the prophet Isaiah,[49] he believed that through the "Zionism of Zion," the nations would ultimately turn to the God of Jacob because his law had been proclaimed from Jerusalem on Mount Zion.[50] He regarded those who tried to assimilate themselves into the cultures of other countries as doomed to failure, whereas the Jew who accepted his separateness could retain his self-respect and thereby live with dignity.

The Abrahamic and Mosaic Covenants were Israel's central myths for Fisch because through them the people became a Covenant people,[51] with both promise and obligation; the Jews were God's chosen people and they had to obey his commandments. The Jews were a people whom God would redeem and then entrust with the land of Canaan forever.[52] It was on this basis that the Jews had to reunite themselves to the land and be redeemed.[53] For Fisch, the Covenant rested on the distinctive relationship between God, land and people. "The land is holy because God chooses to dwell in it and chooses that we should dwell in it with him. Take away the theological dimension and Zionism itself turns to ashes."[54] At this point, Fisch turned to another prophet, Ezekiel:

> They shall dwell in the land where your fathers dwelt that I gave to my servant Jacob; they and their children and their children's children shall dwell there forever. My dwelling place shall be with them; and I will be their God, and they shall be my people.[55]

In the case of the Jews, there would not be a quest for real estate because, for them, their return would be in order to fulfil their divine destiny. Fisch perceived that, as they conquered the Arabs in the Six Day War of 1967, the victory was transformed into a dawning realisation for the Jews that expanded to love for the land.[56] The understanding Fisch saw in it, or gave to it, was that the underlying motive and passion of Zionism for the land was the covenant between God and his people.[57]

Fisch also took the views of Martin Buber to express his own interpretation to those who would part with some of the land of the Covenant for peace and those who would not. He takes the issue of the Uganda plan of 1903 in which land was offered to the Jews for them to develop it. When it was first presented, many were prepared to accept it but the "Zionists of Zion" successfully led the refusal of the offer in 1905. In his argument, Fisch argues his case for the "age old Covenant responsibilities and promises: 'For out of Zion shall Torah go forth, and the word of the Lord from Jerusalem'."[58] In other words, there could be no covenant loyalty in a non-covenant territory. This could not be contemplated at the time, even though it could have meant the immediate, if temporary, solution to the territory-less Jews, no displacement of the Arabs after 1948, and a place for pre-Shoah Jews to move and live. The situation of the indigenous Ugandans might equally have provided problems later in the century but, unlike the Palestinians, that was not the issue at the time.

This apparent obsession with a particular piece of land, based on selected verses of scripture, is given its own rationale from Jewish theology. The view of the land, held by Fisch and others in the settler movement was to unfold and lead to the torrid years of the post-1948, 1967 and 1973 wars, and thereafter. It shows the genuine belief of those who held a view of the sanctity of a particular piece of land to be of far greater ultimate importance, which would override every other consideration, even the lives of countless thousands of Jews and Arabs. Arguing that the state of Israel, "whose warrant for existence depends on biblical evidence,"[59] Fisch perceived, "proceeding in the land of Israel, is a *religious revolution*"[60] (his italics). He saw, "the Jew has really no escape from the Covenant; it is what determines his existence," and, unlike Christians, he has no choice in the matter. Fisch insisted that the covenant task of Israel was to be witnesses to, and servants of, the Lord. In this, he denied that the Palestinians had any right to the land of Israel because he saw their identity as one that was "invented" and which sought to destroy Israel. [61]

Writing in 1978, Fisch perceived Gush Emunim members as, "the chief representatives of an uncompromising Zionist Covenant faith...to the fore as the most revolutionary force in Israeli public life."[62] He saw the movement as distinctively separate from the Jewish Irgun terrorist group, and having no partnership with it. Gush Emunim, with its ideological, "covenant faith," created, as part of its military preparedness, intensive Jewish settlements along its borders. Seeing Israel's unique covenant mission as the alternative to political Zionism, he interpreted it as meeting the need of Israelis for something beyond secular ideals. The call to a return to first principles by the "religiously indifferent and the non-observant"[63] Jews was sounded by Fisch. In demanding spiritual rehabilitation, he stated:

> Without a fuller Zionism, one that includes in itself the mystery of holiness and the dream of salvation, it is difficult to see how the Israeli people can maintain themselves in the face of the ideological offensive directed against them.[64]

The logical outcome of Fisch's position became, for many, a point of reference.

Rabbi Abraham Kook And Martin Buber

Although, at one level, Kook was considered by some to be a fundamentalist and racist, at another he was admired for his Kabbalah mysticism, and capable of winning the respect of people, such as Martin Buber. Personally, and very differently, Buber sought: "A peaceful symbiosis of Jews and Arabs in Palestine as peoples having equal rights in a bi-national commonwealth."[65] He saw Zionism as "a sacred mission, a command to found a just society and to initiate the Kingdom of God."[66] For this to come into being, Buber is quoted as saying that politics must achieve "a lasting brotherly understanding with the Arabs in all areas of public life."[67] Buber took the view of the unity of the land and people of Israel from Moses Hess, which he saw as, "penetrating to the very heart of the Zionist idea."[68] Buber understood the difference between those Zionists who were prepared to accept the offers of Uganda or the Argentine, as a homeland for the Jews and he was aware of the difference between those who wanted a Jewish state anywhere, and those who had the spiritual and emotional attachment to the land of Israel because it was the home of Judaism for the fulfilment of its perceived divine mission. Kook was utterly singular and sought the realisation of the messianic hope in the resettlement of the holy land which was the land of the Covenant.[69] Buber understood the thinking of Kook to represent three inter-related levels of the regaining of Israel. Only in the land can the people achieve their own existence again and it is only there that work will be rediscovered as the free creative function of the spirit while, in order to regain its holiness, it needs the land. The three ideas had existed separately as political, ergonomic and religious concepts but it was Kook who saw their indivisible unity for the Jews. For Buber, it was Kook's belief in the unique sense of holiness that was his inspiration and drive, rather than any political gain or sense of superiority.[70] This belief did not come to fruition before Kook's death in 1935, but the gap between the secular and the religious was gradually to draw closer.[71] Yet, paradoxically, it was always to remain separate, as witnessed by the religious settler movements, which were distinct from those who were willing to trade land for peace in the peace process.

Gush Emunim Prior To The Six Day War Of 1967

In between 1948 and 1967, there had been no significant political moves by the religious parties, as long as they preserved and developed the agreements made with Ben-Gurion in 1948. The government granted privileges to the Ultra Orthodox Jews in terms of proportional representation and Sabbath observance, dietary laws, as well as the pivotal points in family life of birth, circumcision, Bar Mitzvah, marriage, divorce, death and burial. In 1967, however, in the period leading to the Six Day War, Israel felt fearful under threat of extinction. It was to the alumni of his father's yeshiva, Merkaz HaRav, that Rabbi Zvi Yehuda Kook spoke on the eve of Independence Day in 1967, referring tearfully to the divided land which separated Jews from many of their holy places such as Jerusalem, Hebron and Shechem (Nablus). Only three weeks later, however, Jewish troops had captured Jerusalem and the Six Day War of 1967 ended in the rout of the Arab forces. Ehud Sprinzak, of the Hebrew University of Jerusalem, and many others, have written about how this was taken as a Messianic deliverance, followed by a quickening of religious fervour. As such, it should not be forgotten that these were the lands, believed by the religious to be promised to Abraham by God. The victorious war that followed, which included the capture of that territory and the way his words were interpreted, meant that Kook was seen as a prophet by his people.[72]

What was to emerge was the metaphor, or model, of an "iceberg," introduced by Ehud Sprinzak when he described the submerged, out of sight, process of raising funds for Gush Emunim on a large scale, often from official bodies, but not obviously in the public view.[73] For its eventual success, it included the development of an expansive network of supportive contacts, with a strategy of influencing key people in decision-making processes of government. In ten years after 1974, Gush Emunim had created, by its success, a core of support, even from those who would not be members but who recognised its achievements. The movement offered "spiritual inspiration to its supporters and to provide a focus for political action when necessary."[74]

Gush Emunim In The Pre-Formative Years And Its Gradual Emergence

Some of the basic presuppositions in Jewish society, essential for the success of Gush Emunim after its establishment in 1974, are identified by Lustick.[75] Its crucial framework was its basic belief in the Jews as God's chosen people who would be his servants to fulfil his eternal purposes in the coming of the anointed one, the Messiah. Therefore, it would use any device to achieve those ultimate, spiritual objectives, whether to capitalise on the political work of the government or the evangelical work of the Church's Ministry Amongst Jewish People[76] and others, without being identified, or connected to any of them. Its goal was sacred and the means used were secular, by occupation and control. Although not everywhere the case, many Christian evangelicals had enabled the Jews to have respect and status, and took the lead in their return to Israel because of the Biblical promises of both the Abrahamic Covenant and the future appearing of Jesus Christ, whom they saw as the Messiah.. This is developed in Chapter 3.

Gush Emunim was not structured in any formal way until 1974, but there were a number of earlier actions by those who became its leaders. Afterwards, its belief system, ideological outworking, strategy and tactics became visible as it became a dynamic force for change. The slogan of Gush Emunim became, "The land of Israel for the people of Israel, according to the Torah of Israel" and is based on its reading of the Abrahamic Covenant.[77] Over the next few years, after the Yom Kippur War of 1973, it was to change the life of Israelis and Palestinians and make its mark on the world thereafter.

The ideological work of Gush Emunim began imperceptibly, but not unintentionally, as its leadership took form and shape in the religious educational system of the yeshivas which was based on the Jewish law of Halakhah. Gideon Aran and others have pointed to the energy and movement that appeared after the Six Day War of 1967.[78] In that war, through strategic, pre-emptive, air strikes against Egypt, which destroyed its military base, Israel moved from fear of its own obliteration to the capture of Jerusalem and the West Bank, which was seen as Judea and Samaria. The victory was seen by many Israelis as the logical extension of a militaristic, messianic act and that the newly conquered land had now to be possessed and controlled in its entirety. Aran notes the strategic conjoining of the professional, political and commercial expertise of secular nationalists in the Land of Israel Movement with the ideological, religious, visionary activists of what became Gush Emunim.[79] Aran is another of those who note the rise in the influence of the national-religious groups which had been nurtured in the yeshiva educational system for years, producing an elite corps of dedicated, idealistic, religiously focused, Talmudic-based younger generation of military age. These were reinforced by the Hesder yeshivas, which combined military service with religious studies, no longer being exclusive and separated from the political life of the country. They provided a backbone to the National Religious Party and were no longer passive in their attitude to the government, but ready to take issue and be militant in matters which they saw as a betrayal of their religious idealism.

With hindsight, it is possible to perceive that, after the establishment of the State of Israel in 1948, there were those who had a vision of a future Jewish state. One core group of adolescent, dedicated students, known as the Gahelet, formed "the Pioneer Torah Scholars' Group" which was distinctively different from the contemporary groupings of the time.[80] Drawn to the teachings of Rabbi Zvi Yehuda Kook and his father, Rabbi Abraham Isaak Kook, they discerned and created a form of political theology. This was to become the ideological masterpiece of Gush Emunim for many future generations. Gush Emunim's eschatological vision of the future foresees Israeli sovereignty over all the land of Israel[81] within its maximum biblical boundaries,[82] i.e. the River Euphrates in Iraq and the Brook in Egypt. From a 2000 year dream, it became transformed into a physical and political reality, never to be relinquished but to be fulfilled by any means through messianic, political activism which superseded normal politics. It became a fervent, active, militant religious nationalism, drawing from its established religious educational system of yeshivas which were based on the Jewish laws of the Halakhah.[83]

There is a wide range of Jewish religious communities, often difficult to understand in terms of their varieties and separate beliefs. Although having similarities, there are differences between the fundamentalism of the neo-Orthodoxy of Gush Emunim, and the pietistic Ultra-Orthodox groups of the Haredim. A particular definition of fundamentalist belief which they appear to have in common, is seen by Lustick as holding a three-fold thrust, namely, of uncompromising injunctions which could not be put aside, belief in direct contact with their source of transcendental authority, and active political moves to create rapid comprehensive change.[84] Unlike the Ultra Orthodox Haredim, the National Religious, or Sephardi Mizrahi movement, does not seek to be separate and exclusive. Instead they are more integrated into society, while maintaining their own special connection with their understanding of the Halakhah codes of Jewish law. Mizrahi ideology, with its Middle East background, involves a proactive stance regarding the land of Israel, in terms of preparing for Messiah, whereas the Haredim, with its European Ashkenazi background hold fast to the conviction that the Messiah will make his appearance without human intervention. Gush Emunim, while religious at the core, is not exclusive, as the Haredim, but includes secular nationalist parties in its commitment to the Biblical promises of land, based on, "uncompromisable, transcendentally valid imperatives."[85]

Gush Emunim And The State

In exploring the Gush Emunim interpretation of history, the former students of Rabbi Abraham Kook provided insights that were taken seriously by Ehud Sprinzak.[86] According to his students, Kook saw the Jews as part of the ongoing redemption process for all mankind, validated by a range of events, including modern Zionism and the Balfour Declaration of 1917. As such the movement was not exclusive, like the Ultra-Orthodox, but saw itself as part of the redemptive operation achieved through the offices of the sacred and the secular, all in the hands of divine influence. Thus Kook's followers could discern that influence through secular events of history, like the Six Day War of 1967, which were interpreted as unfolding Jewish history for the world's redemption in which Jews could, and should, play their part. Hence the Six Day War of 1967 was easily understood in the same dramatic terms as their redemption from Egypt through the Exodus. The consequence was the need to inhabit and possess the sacred land as of old, this time through exclusive settlements, regardless of any obstacles which might be raised to impede its Messianic intention. They could detect a chain of divine events from the establishment of Herzl's leadership and the First Zionist Congress of 1897 in Basel, which gave them a combination of confidence and determination to complete the divinely appointed task for Israel and the world. Sprinzak perceived that they saw their task as one that was logical and holy; a holy people, for a holy land, for a holy God. In this, Palestinians could be accepted as long as, in turn, they accepted Jewish control of the land and their laws.

In relation to secular authority, Gush Emunim saw the State as part of God's activity and to be respected, provided that it did nothing to subvert God's intention as they interpreted it, especially with regard to the land of Eretz, or Greater, Israel and the people. It was therefore logical that religious Jews would be part of the Israel Defence Force (IDF) and form part of its leadership. If religious norms, as Gush Emunim understood them, were not followed, then the movement had the responsibility to oppose the state by whatever means were needed. The land and the people of God took precedence over all other considerations, whether from the Knesset or any outside authority. This gives insight into the perceived failures of the Yom Kippur War of 1973, after which Jews who held these views saw the need to organise themselves differently and formally. This led to the formal establishment of Gush Emunim in 1974, known in English as the Block of the Faithful.

It was difficult to categorise Gush Emunim as an organisation. Sprinzak found that it did not fit in with protest, political or religious groups, even though it had parts of each within its modus operandi. Attention has already been drawn to Sprinzak who introduced the model of an "iceberg," so that what appeared visible to the outside viewer was one of political extremism. Submerged and out of view, however, was a far greater proportion of the population with a background of education in the religious academies and who were widely involved in the professions, as well as those who were highly trained Rabbis. Sprinzak held that, on the one hand, Gush Emunim had great respect for the State and its institutions because they represented the will of God.[87] However, on the other hand, the State does not have the same sense of sanctity:

The state is never mentioned as part of the 'holy trinity' – the Land, the People and the Torah of Israel...unlike the holiness of the trio which is absolute and eternal, the sanctity of the state is relative and conditional.[88]

The interpretation was that, should the government prohibit settlement construction, the prohibition was null and void because the preservation of the integrity of the Holy Land was a sacred obligation.[89] Sprinzak went further and indicated its disrespect for the rule of civil law, if that law does not carry through the conviction of Gush Emunim because: "Eretz Israel in its entirety belongs to the Jews by divine command."[90]

Rabbi Abraham Kook had seen beyond the old exclusivity of the Ultra-Orthodox Judaism and was ready to be strategically pragmatic in the fulfilment of his vision, without forfeiting any matters of principle. His son, Rabbi Yehuda Kook, more than thirty years after the death of his father, was able to hold to the vision, as he saw it, of the secular events of war having a spiritual relevance for the attainment of the Promised Land. Before his death in 1982, he had seen his followers convert the military conquests into the consolidation of his divine mission. As with other settler narratives, three intrinsic Gush Emunim perceptions emerged: the uniqueness of the settler nation, the exclusive primacy of Zionist privilege and the denial that the presence and actions of the settler-colonisers determined the structure and nature of society, namely the Matrix of Control as described by Professor Halper.[91]

Post 1967 – Martin Buber, Arab Obduracy And The Early Face Of Gush Emunim

The victory in the Six Day War of 1967 led to the expansion of Religious Zionism, including Gush Emunim, whose supporters, as distinct from the Ultra-Orthodox movement, interpreted the victory as a sign that the recovery of the land meant the imminent coming of the Messiah. This is at odds with the Ultra-Orthodox, who regard Zionism as a sin because true messianism is passive and the Messiah cannot be moved by the inclinations and manoeuvres of humanity, unlike secular and Religious Zionism which is proactive.[92] Having gained their State in 1948, the land became the most important factor after 1967 and it was clear that the different ideologies of the Orthodox and the Religious could coincide with secular Zionists. Martin Buber[93] argues that the possession of the land was not robbery and describes it as "the command from heaven...sincerely carried out. Where a command and a faith are present, in certain historical situations conquest need not be robbery." There was, strangely, a curious misuse of insight to justify the actions which had such destructive effects on an indigenous people for decades, as well as themselves as perpetrators, and this shortcoming still persists.

The obduracy of both Israel and the Arab states after the Six Day War of 1967 is shown by Milton Viorst and others. The Arab states adopted a defiant stand against Israel of, "no recognition, no conciliation and no negotiation."[94] Shlomi

Gazit, as head of the assessment department of IDF intelligence at the time, drew up a set of proposals, in preparation for a Palestinian state:

> The goal was a formal and comprehensive peace with all the Arab States, based on a nearly full withdrawal to the 4 June lines or, at the very least, stabilizing a *de facto* Israeli-Arab co-existence, while finding agreed solutions to the main problems that separated the parties.... We called for Israeli generosity based on the results of the war. Israel should not humiliate its defeated enemies and their leaders .... Among the recipients of our document were the prime minister, the minister of defense, the minister of foreign affairs, the chief of staff, his deputy and the head of intelligence. Unfortunately, not one of them responded to the document. No discussion was held, nor was any action taken.[95]

Religious and secular Revisionist Jews combined to resist any loss of the newly conquered land. Viorst[96] argues that, despite their smallness of numbers "Religious Zionism became, after the Six Day War, Israel's most dynamic political force." Following his father's substantial, preparatory work in the 1930s, Rabbi Zvi Yehuda Kook and his followers began to promote the strategy of settlements in the occupied territories.[97] Kook and his supporters reshaped the Orthodox understanding of the Halakhah, which was the application of God's words at Mt. Sinai, so that it served his religious ideology. "Not only did they insist the Law required permanent Jewish rule in the territories but they proclaimed its supremacy over secular law."[98] Although no longer young and healthy, Kook understood the tactic of combining religion with militarism and encouraged his followers to take positions of strategic influence in the officer cadre. He also strengthened his connections with the nationalist, secular Zionists, rather than the Ultra-Orthodox. One of his followers, Rabbi Moshe Levinger, was to begin the first settlement in Hebron in 1968 and, despite initial government opposition, his activists created a new Jewish town above the city, named Kiryat Arba.[99] Before this, in September 1967, there was an apparently innocent move by the former inhabitants of the village of Kfar Etzion, set between Jerusalem and Hebron, for them to be restored to where they had once lived before being evicted during the War of 1948, and this was later to be renamed Gush Etzion.

In their book on the building of settlements, the establishment of Gush Etzion has been described by Professor Idith Zertal and the political commentator, Akiva Eldar, as, "The crack in the dam"[100] and was achieved only a few months after the War. This contrasted with an earlier action, described by Sprinzak as "illegalism,"[101] when the Mughrabi Quarter, home to 135 Arab families and which backed on to the Wailing Wall in Jerusalem, was demolished by bulldozers while some inhabitants were still inside their homes. This was done without authorisation and "a paradigm had been created."[102] The border between the legal and the illegal had been broken down. Thereafter, "Insisting on the rule of law looked like hypocrisy."[103] The transgression of law, which was to become a feature of the settlement movement, had been given its precedent by its own government. International law was also involved. A memorandum, marked "Top Secret" dated 18 September, 1967, was sent to Prime Minister Levi Eshkol by the legal counsel of the Foreign Ministry, Theodore Meron, who was the government's authority on international law. It stated: "My conclusion is that civilian settlement in the occupied territories contravenes the explicit provisions of the Fourth Geneva Convention."[104] Eshkol knew early on that settling civilians in occupied land violated international law but he was already exploring his options for such illegalities, despite the Hague Regulations of 1907 which stated: "Private property cannot be confiscated."[105]

After the Six Day War of 1967, Palestinians lived under military rule, controlled by Defence Minister, Moshe Dayan, who had little accountability to anyone. His belief, although unrealistic, was that Israel had to make its presence in the territories permanent so that there would be no further warfare. President Lyndon Johnson had asked Levi Eshkol: "What kind of Israel do you want?"[106] He received no answer and Israel appeared to be uncoordinated in terms of any policy. On his own, in the occupied territories, Dayan "formulated a policy of 'invisible' rule," which became an "invisible occupation."[107] Gorenberg notes that, in April, 1968, the United States instructed its Embassy in Tel Aviv to remind the Israeli government of America's, "continuing opposition to any Israeli settlement in the occupied areas." Gorenberg goes on: "Even when under military control, they [the Israeli government] still violated Article 49 of the Fourth Geneva Convention."[108] Settlement building continued, despite this reminder, being built next to army bases on Arab land, expropriated for military purposes, which were permitted under the laws of occupation. The land remained, legally, with the original owners but the army had exclusive use of it for as long as it wished. The army was aided by the Nahal, the "Pioneering Fighting Youth" whose members combined military duties with working on the land in kibbutzim.

In the spring of 1968, those who were to become leaders in Gush Emunim began their struggle for the "City of Abraham" by becoming squatters in Hebron.[109] Their strategy was to be a model for territorial opportunism and expansion. Using small groups of dedicated activists, they became expert in direct-action strategies of violence, manipulation, confrontation and provocation. In celebration of the first Passover after the Six Day War of 1967, Rabbi Moshe Levinger led a selected group of families to stay at the Arab hotel in Hebron, named the Park Hotel. The town had great significance for Jews and Muslims because it was purported to be the burial place of Abraham, as well as the place where David was anointed King of Israel. At the end of Passover, however, the party refused to leave the hotel and thus commenced a strategy of territorial acquisition in the name of religion, which contrasted with the ethics of their 8th Century prophets, "To act justly, and to love mercy and to walk humbly with your God."[110]

Despite defying the existing government law, which prohibited Jews from living there, "Levinger explained that he was settling in Hebron in response to God's decree of Jewish sovereignty over the entire land of Israel…insisting he was subject to God's law alone."[111] In a few words, Viorst summarises, "… the government gave in…allowed Levinger not only to settle in Hebron but to establish a

Yeshiva there. It authorised his people to carry arms."[112] Soon afterwards, the government constructed a Jewish town named Kiryat Arba on the surrounding hills which became home for 5000 settlers and "religious Zionism, having defeated the government at Hebron, prepared further challenges to the mainstream's resolve."[113] One of the prime movers in the government who supported Levinger and the subsequent settlement at Kiryat Arba was Yigal Allon, a leading member of the government and of settlement expansion. Lustick describes what was soon to become Gush Emunim,

> The movement is a zealous spin-off of Zionism...following the 1967 War. Gathering strength during the 1970s it allied itself with Likud governments under Menachem Begin and Yitzhak Shamir, and helped entrench Israel's presence in the territories so deeply as to produce threats of civil war should that presence be removed.[114]

Between the Six Day War of 1967 and the Yom Kippur War of 1973, there was little in the public gaze, despite facts on the ground which ignored United Nations Resolution 242, of 22 November, 1967, requiring the return to the 1967 borders. Gorenberg, writing about the failures of international diplomacy which brought about a stalemate, states: "The stalemate was the soil in which settlements grew.[115] Meanwhile, the ongoing nurturing of leadership within the religious movement continued. The UN Resolution 242 had at least one fatal flaw which was exploited thereafter. The withdrawal by Israel from Arab "territories" was understood by the UK, Russia and the Arabs to mean "all the (occupied) Territories." This was afterwards denied by Israel, which argued that the absence of the definite article, "the," meant that it needed to give up only parts of the land and not all. This has remained a disputed issue since 1967 and is still unresolved, except that Israel has established itself almost completely in the territories. Because of the separate interpretations of the meaning of the language, there has been no successful move to resolve the issue since 1967. Meanwhile, the Israeli government acts as though the land belongs to Israel and proceeds with its occupation and control of the population and the resources of land and water. Inevitably, the Palestinians feel dispossessed and embittered. By the one-sided Israeli interpretation of UN Resolution 242, carried out against the UN arguments, and the failure of the international community to bring about an agreement, a viable Palestinian state seems unlikely.

The Labour government deliberately retained the land it had captured in 1967, as a strategic defence, despite the view of those who saw this as contrary to United Nations Resolution 242. The government's justification for this retention was not only as a protection against outside attacks but because there was an Arab population of more than half a million inside the West Bank.[116] This number was probably far more, in excess of two million. However, in 1967, "Land of Israel Movement" was established immediately after the Six Day War to ensure that the land belonged to the Jewish people and could not be relinquished under any circumstances. Its claim went further than any existing party, but summed up the old

Jewish yearning for their promised land. This was nurtured by Moshe Dayan who, in the election of 1969, insisted that the Labour party should retain possession of the West Bank through settlements and military occupation. [117]

For many, the Yom Kippur War of 1973 showed the loss of land which was considered to be holy. Hitherto, the secular state of Israel had been seen by some religious groups, as Messiah's Donkey, and being instrumental in the appearing of the Messiah (Zechariah 9.9). That perception was interpreted, used, and even taken advantage of as such. However, failures in the war, the loss of land and the threat of more loss, were to ignite the activists against the State. Gush Emunim offered Torah Zionism as a way of moving on from fading secularism in early 1973, and highlighted the perceived national decay during the Yom Kippur War. After the war, its belief system in 1974 offered a cutting edge, pruning the dead wood of secular Zionism which was prepared to surrender the holy land of the Torah. The pruning would allow the new, religious, vine shoots to prevail, and were to constitute the Bloc of the Faithful – Gush Emunim by name.

The Explosion Of Gush Emunim After The Yom Kippur War

Gush Emunim, was formally created to repossess the land in February 1974 by religious Zionist Jews attending a conference at the kibbutz, Gush Etzion. Reference has previously been made to Aran who traced its beginning, over twenty years earlier, to the early 1950s when a group of mature students, named the Gahelet, followed the spirituality of the late Rabbi Avraham Kook and made his son, Rabbi Yehuda Kook, their religious leader.[118] Subsequently, their passion and devotion took them to positions of leadership and responsibility in what was to become Gush Emunim

The Yom Kippur War in October, 1973 had resulted in a stalemate during which the power of the Israeli army was seen to be vulnerable and inefficient in many ways. Following internal disquiet within the civilian population there was a powerful, proactive move for a change in the national focus by the religious. Rabbi Kook and his followers called for Israel to move into its Biblical borders, especially the West Bank, now to be renamed Judea and Samaria. Lustick writes that, for Gush Emunim, the coming of the Messiah "cannot be completed if parts of the land are relinquished, or if parts of the land are left unsettled by the Jews." [119] There is a simple logic, therefore, in their adamant refusal to contemplate any move by the government either, to allow a return of refugees, or a return to the 1967 borders. United Nations Resolutions to that effect are plainly impermissible, therefore, because, for Gush Emunim, their task was always one of the redemption of the land in preparation for the Messiah and the "authentic expression of Judaism."[120] Secular Zionism, as "Messiah's Donkey,"[121] had but paved the way for militant, ideological, religious Zionism.

Those who were to become leaders of Gush Emunim made connections with other groups, notably the Land of the Israel Loyalists, which consisted of a range of veteran members of previous activist, underground and military groups.

Numerous problems existed between the different groups and included questions about the extent of Eretz Israel and whether it reached to the Nile in Egypt, or to the Brook in the centre of Sinai at Wadi El-Arish.[122] What they had in common, however, was the primary task of settling the land, exclusively for the people of the land, and not giving their promised land back to the Arabs. The movement was eventually to move beyond the secular nationalism of the Land of Israel Movement, and Gush Emunim's focus became a matter of messianic redemption and was accountable only to God.

Initially, Gush Emunim members were active among demonstrations and protests against what was seen as American pressure to give back the "Land," through arrangements with Syria and Egypt about the Golan and the West Bank. Based on religious commitment to Eretz Israel, there was a dividing line between those who believed both the Jewish people and the land to be holy, and those who would not see the belief through to its logical conclusion. Under the policy of settlements, known as "Hitnachalut," Gush Emunim set up what began as outposts of squatters, which could be temporary until they were made permanent.[123] This was to become a regular strategy for settlement creation whenever there was governmental opposition. It became a long drawn-out battle of wits, during which Gush Emunim was able to refine its strategies, methods and tactics in obtaining pressure groups to demonstrate in such ways, including violence, so as to persuade the government to yield possession of the land to the settlers, but not the Palestinians. This was accompanied by plans to establish settlements and after two initial, temporary setbacks for the Elon Moreh group at Sebastia, there was success at Ofrah, close to Ramallah, in April, 1975.

Prior to these events and during the winter of 1974-1975, a small "work brigade" of four people had worked quietly at Ba'al Hatzor, north east of Ramallah, which was to become the settlement of Ofrah. Led by Yehudah Etzion, they commenced the construction of a fence but from April they were regularly joined by small groups of volunteers to renovate an abandoned Jordanian military post at Ein Yabrud.[124] What was disguised as an ordinary civilian work camp at a military base became a ruse to allow for overnight sleeping arrangements. On 20 April, 1975, a group of men and women moved into houses on the site and quietly took up residence. They were there to stay. What happened afterwards indicates the capacity of the movement to work swiftly and effectively. A generator and a water tanker were among the gifts provided by different groups of volunteers, with water, electricity and primary services being installed and paved roads constructed.[125] By December Ofrah had been recognised as a civilian settlement and was entitled to official government support. It was a small group but had the effect of establishing a pattern for the future and became a symbol of religious vision and tenacity.

In this they had been passively supported by the Defence Minister, Shimon Peres, who instructed that they were neither to be helped, nor hindered. In their book, Idith Zertal and Akiva Eldar refer to Danny Rubinstein who had written in 1982 that there had been unrecorded meetings with officials behind the scenes.[126]

With no official obstacles to prevent them, they were allowed to pursue their ambitions. Aided by Yisrael Galili, the settlement adviser of Peres, in May, 1975, Ofrah had become another, officially unacknowledged, Gush Emunim fact on the ground with buildings and services. This was despite the criticism of William Scranton, the US representative to the United Nations, when he addressed the Security Council on May 23, 1975, saying,

> substantial resettlement of the Israeli civilian population in occupied territories, including East Jerusalem, is illegal...under the Fourth Geneva Convention and the presence of these settlements is seen by my government as an obstacle to the success of the negotiations for a just and final peace.[127]

What was absent was a clear government policy so that officials could respond to a set of given criteria, in the absence of which, individuals would respond differently. There appeared to be a growing inconsistency, in terms of aims and objectives, by the government in relation to Gush Emunim. Depending on who was involved, and in control at the time, government ministers supported, or opposed the settlers. Sometimes they used the army to protect the settlers and, at other times, they used the military to oppose them. For itself, Gush Emunim had a corps of dedicated adherents, but they were increasingly able to call on assistance from a wide body of volunteers and to deploy them with great effectiveness.

Another Gush Emunim success, following that at Ofrah, was in December 1975 at Sebastia, near Nablus, the ancient capital of Biblical Israel, formerly called Shechem. Assisted by Ariel Sharon, it was settled by the Elon Moreh group and was the first of a succession of settlements which followed as they took a site, settled it, and then moved on to another and then another. There are different accounts of how it came about but an outline of events can be seen. The spiritual significance of the Elon Moreh settlement in Samaria was its proximity to Shechem which was the place where Joshua confirmed the Covenant with the Jews after their conquest of Canaan and where the bones of Joseph, the son of Jacob the patriarch and Rachel, were buried.[128] It took until December 1975, after eight attempts at settlement and successive, violent confrontations led by Rabbi Levinger and prevented by the army, before a compromise was reached. In fact, it was a victory for the settlers, because Rabin gave in to their pressure and the intense public support they received. The settlers, consisting of thirty families, were allowed to establish themselves temporarily in Kadum, a nearby army base. After much prevarication, seventeen months later, a new settlement named Kedumim was established on 17 April, 1977, near the military base where the settlers had lived since the festival of Hannukah in December 1975. Rabin lost the election a month later to Menachem Begin and the settlement was still there at the turn of the century.[129] There were to be many more "Elon Morehs."

Gush Emunim Strategy From 1974

Gush Emunim had established three core principles of elaborate and defined ideology, focused objectives and gifted, committed membership recruited from throughout the country. The leadership worked out its strategy of objectives for achieving control of the land and its tactics of how to achieve them, using small groups and large mass rallies, with propaganda and publicity. It was an exciting, civil warfare as it appealed to three primary interests of nationalism, religion and security in one united ideology which satisfied all three. In particular, it had a dynamic, attractive, idealist energy that was different from the kibbutzim of earlier years and was now focused on reclaiming their Biblical lands in occupied territory. Above all, it was different from the old ways and zealously looked to the future with vast spiritual ambition. It created settlement groups of 12-20 families who would meet and be recruited and then instructed in the ways of settlement creation and team cohesion.

Its propaganda included portraying themselves as heroic Israelis with the highest ideals, intent on keeping the land of Abraham in the face of the oppressive state, plus lectures, marches, festivals and rallies and appealing to Jewish idealism. It had a successful strategy of total, evangelical, religious ideology, supported by many in the Knesset and with wide media coverage. In the years from 1974 until after the defeat of Rabin in the 1977 election, Gush Emunim was the spearhead of the differing Zionist groups. Its tactics were simple but planned meticulously. It was able to mobilise massive public resistance to any peace project, noticeably in August, 1975 during the shuttle diplomacy of Henry Kissinger, when it constructed, "a festival of anarchic ferocity" in the midst of the Sinai II agreement between Israel and Egypt.[130] It would either work quietly with low-key, invisible innocence, as earlier at Ofrah, or work violently with direct action on a large scale to wear down government resistance, as later at Sebastia in November, 1975.

The result was more to do with anarchy than democracy, with theft of land continuing under another name. The government had lost its way and in May, 1977, Menachem Begin was elected to form a new government.

With the benefit of hindsight, one of the questions which arose in the research of David Weisburd and Albert J Weiss asked: which of the two were deviant, Gush Emunim, the state or both?[131] In his foreword to their book, Albert J. Reiss presented the historic Jewish claims to sovereignty in the captured territories of 1967, as perceived by Gush Emunim, and argued that the State must recognise those claims as legitimate, even if the means used are deviant.[132] Weisburd and Weiss found it extremely difficult to define this community empirically, since Gush Emunim had never established any official membership lists, although in its Amanah settlements there was a clearly identifiable group of settlers after 1978 which identified with the movement.[133] Weisburd and Weiss saw that the effect of the 1967 War was to revive traditional religious and secular ideologies for the establishment of Jewish sovereignty in the captured land and Gush Emunim was one of the spearheads that emerged. They had found that the Gush Emunim youth who were born after 1948, were seen as a religious elite trained in the religious academies and ready to take leadership roles in their country. Some had studied under Rabbi Zvi Yehuda Kook, who was Dean of the Merkaz HaRav Yeshiva in Jerusalem and who had great influence on many. The elder Kook had argued that the secularists, unwittingly, were helping to bring about the messianic redemption of the Jews. His son had similarly impressed on his students that they lived in a truncated Land and that the Land was larger than the State of Israel.

Weisburd and Weiss points to the difference between other Orthodox rabbinic authorities and Rabbi Yehuda Kook, because the latter felt that the land could not be traded, and to prevent this they should be ready to sacrifice their lives because the land was more sacred than life. Kook had passed to his students a normative perspective about the land, as distinct from the government which was ready so to trade and, accordingly, was the body which was deviant.[134] It became clear, from Weisburd's and Reiss's interviews with the Gush Emunim activists after 1974, that Kook with his ideological teaching was the leading mind of the strategists and activists. Rabbi Moshe Levinger was a case in point. Following Kook, who said that withdrawal from the West Bank was forbidden, he insisted that the government did not have the right to make a law that a Jew cannot make Aliyah,[135] stating: "No government has the authority or right to say that a Jew cannot live in all the parts of Israel."[136] He argued that they saw themselves as acting against the political deviants in government, and that religious Gush Emunim represented Jewish loyalty. Although the Likud government and Gush Emunim had much in common after 1977, they did not hesitate to disobey Likud when they thought it wrong and undermining of their beliefs. Compromises could sometimes be reached between the two very simply as settlements were placed inside army camps, the settlers working as civilians, with accommodation and services fully supplied.[137]

Governmental Attitude Change After The Likud Election In 1977

Following the election of the right-wing Likud government, there were a number of quandaries, especially because right-wing politicians had been supportive of Gush Emunim in many of their activities. Now, in government, Likud wished to govern and were less inclined to have a combustible, freelance group of activists, answerable to no one but themselves. The settler groups would have clearly known and profited from the absence of a normal, formal structure of leadership, constitution, decision-making process, with accountability, regulations, and all that makes for progressive management procedures.

As the activities of Gush Emunim became apparent, it could be seen to those outside as having what might almost be regarded as a cavalier approach to its organisation. This would be misleading because within the movement it was efficiently and effectively organised. It was clear about its aims and objectives, having sound tactical and strategic awareness, coupled with political and public skills for acquiring financial backing, public support and political influence. Even as late as 1994, Professor Gideon Aran was able to write of Gush Emunim: "Curiously, despite the movement's propaganda efforts, GE has never published a binding and systematic program."[138] He acknowledges an, "amateurish position paper...published during GE's early days...shelved a short time later...GE's only unequivocal and comprehensive statement of faith in over twenty years." His summary includes, "its objective is the full redemption of Israel and of the entire world...its right to full sovereignty therein...[including] settlement throughout the Land of Israel."[139] Lustick describes the outcome of the separate, state settlements: "But, as they were always meant to be, the settlements planted in the territories by a succession of right–wing fundamentalist governments have proved to be dangerous obstacles to the consummation of a peace agreement."[140] Both Aran and Lustick could write in the 1990s, about both types of settlement, with the benefit of hindsight.

It has been made clear that Gush Emunim had its own clear ideology, with specific targets and a dedicated leadership. However, they also relied on support from a range of people, as well as the media and their public, including politicians. But the question might have been: "Who would influence whom; would the settlers influence the politicians, or vice versa?" Likud and Gush Emunim had used each other to achieve their mutual ends but Gush Emunim had the upper hand when it came to militancy. Their activists were unafraid to take on the government because they appealed to the higher court of religion, which justified the righteousness of their cause over Labour or Likud. While not necessarily approving in any way, this ultimate religious ideal was understood by every Jew, even non-believing, secular settlers, to have its own code of honour and respect.

Gush Emunim And Likud Until 1987

The relationship between Gush Emunim and Likud is described by Lustick as: "symbiotic," Gush providing an ideology of "ultra-nationalism and active messianism."[141] He writes: "The world view of Jewish fundamentalism is based on myths of Jewish chosenness, mission and territorial sovereignty similar to those that shaped Jewish politics before the Roman expulsion."[142] Zionism had already created a Jewish political presence in Israel, followed by military events in 1967 and 1973. These were followed by the dedication and success of elites who linked traditional Jewish dreams and objectives to affect strategic elements in sufficient number in Israel and beyond. The anticipated, and hoped for, expansion of settlements had not been achieved by 1984, despite government financing of jobs and services.[143] This was to change under Ariel Sharon.

Likud was to become conjoined with the twin pillars of the Abrahamic faith and Zionist vision. Politics and religion attracted visionaries and dreamers (Joel 2. 28-32) on a massive scale, bringing an energy and dynamic that was in line with Jewish prophecy of the last days and the triumph of Israel over her erstwhile enemies. The governments of Likud gave financial and military support to the settlers of Gush Emunim, as the settlers themselves worked with the determined passion of religious idealists and ideologues. Opinions are divided as to whether the Likud was more interested in the political, economic and security interests than the religious. It seemed, when it was not in government, that it was ready to support Gush Emunim and its religious ideology, for its own ends. After its election, the focus was more materialistic, although unwilling to be dismissive of their former activist colleagues.

The latter day perspective of retired Major-General Shlomi Gazit, writing in 2003, gives an insight into the changes which took place in the settlement system. The first explosive intervention of Gush Emunim, particularly after its establishment in 1974, set a revolutionary pattern for the rush for Palestinian land in the name of Judaism. The drama of bellicose manipulations of the state systems by Gush Emunim, in order to take the lands promised by God to Abraham for his people as part of world redemption, shook the Labour government establishment to the core. Part of its success was due to the political assistance of many, especially the Likud Party and, within it, the National Religious Party. When Likud, under Menachem Begin, was elected in 1977 it opened the gates of settlement reform and expansion.[144]

The demonstrations by Gush Emunim were no longer necessary to persuade the new government because Likud created its own settlement policy. This was the Mattiyahu Drobles's Settlement Plan for defence, using settlements as buffers and as warning and defence positions to respond to attacks, both from the East and within the territory. It consisted of three strategies: the seizure of land for settlements, subsidised housing for new settlers, and exclusive roads for settlers to assist commuters to travel to places of work. In contrast, the settlement work of Gush Emunim was on a much smaller scale. The person selected to implement the Likud policy was the Minister of Agriculture, who controlled the Israel Land Authority, Ariel Sharon. His strategy was to establish settlements in principle, no matter how small, and to let them grow, and not the other way round, thereby creating facts on the ground.[145] Professor David Newman made the point,

> In the case of Gush Emunim, the personality who became their champion was Ariel Sharon...were it not for Sharon they might have remained an unofficial movement, unable to receive the development budgets from the ministries of Agriculture, Housing, Education, Defence and Religious Affairs.[146]

In 1977, without including Jerusalem, there were 5,000 settlers in the West Bank but at the end of Sharon's time in office six years later, the number had increased by a further 27,000 settlers.

Aran records that after the Likud victory in 1977, Gush Emunim "immediately embarked on a massive settlement campaign [to which] Menachem Begin reacted negatively [and] a bitter conflict ensued."[147] Both sides had positive and negative feelings for the other, each wanting to give and take, with the other giving ground on either freedom to operate, or control by the state. In July 1978,

Gush Emunim produced a "Master Plan for Settlement in Judea and Samaria" and called for the long term settlement of 750,000 Jews in Judea and Samaria by the end of the century. Newman was sceptical about the realism of such a demand, calling it, "a highly fictional plan."[148] Their roles had changed; Gush Emunim was no longer the revolutionary movement, against the government, and the government was no longer conciliatory on the land issue. The Likud government established settlements without Gush Emunim, fully serviced and supplied with electricity, security, road systems and subsidised housing. The movement was losing its primary role to the government:

> From 1977 until the end of 1984 two Likud governments poured more than $1 billion into Jewish settlements in the West Bank and Gaza Strip and various support activities. In the West Bank alone nearly sixty new settlements were added. The number of Jewish settlers in predominantly Arab areas of the West Bank increased from a few thousand to over 38,000. Sweeping land requisitions and zoning restrictions were implemented to provide a land reserve for future settlements.[149]

A year after his election, Menachem Begin had to respond to his part of the Begin-Sadat agreement of 4-17 September, 1978, known as the Camp David Accords, and facilitated by President Jimmy Carter.[150] In signing those Accords, Prime Minister Begin "reconfirmed a specific commitment to honour UN Resolutions 242 and 338, which prohibit acquisition of land by force and call for Israel's withdrawal from occupied territories."[151] This included: "withdrawal of Israeli military and civilian forces from the West Bank and Gaza and the recognition of the Palestinian people as a separate political entity."[152] In 1995, this was the kind of agreement that led to the assassination of Prime Minister Rabin. It is conceivable that Menachem Begin signed the Accords without any intention of carrying them through, or perhaps he could not resist the pressure that was to come. This was not unusual. In his sociological study, David Weisburd notes how the Begin government drew back from implementing in full the Camp David Agreement of 1978 between Egypt-Israel.[153] Modern commentators, who see similar shortcomings in subsequent agreements in the Oslo Accords of 1993, may, in the future, see parallels with agreements made at Annapolis in December 2007. Whatever the reasons, the agreements were not honoured, except for the evacuation of part of Sinai. At the time, for Gush Emunim, the Accords amounted to treachery. The Sinai town of Yamit became the symbol of resistance for not only Gush Emunim, but all their associates, as the "Movement to Stop Withdrawal" became a lengthy, ideological struggle. It was only in April, 1982 that the IDF removed the settlers and their supporters, despite a lengthy series of protests. For the first time, it appeared that the effective strategies of Gush Emunim had lost their earlier potency before the public.

Some writers, including Aran and Weisburd, have suggested that this was the beginning of the demise of Gush Emunim. Certainly some events would indicate that to be the case, but its influence is far from finished, despite Rabbi Levinger's belief that Gush Emunim no longer existed.[154] There were two factors which may well have had a deleterious effect on its influence; one was Jewish terrorism and the other was materialism. Between 1981 and 1984, there were terrorist attacks on Arabs, for which members of the Jewish community were imprisoned. There were also attempts to destroy the mosques on the Temple Mount and Arab buses in the rush hour, but these were intercepted and prevented by Israeli security forces. The malcontents who were charged consisted of twenty-seven people, many of whom were involved with Gush Emunim. The outcome was a deep division within the movement because while many deplored the violence, those who were ideologically committed saw such acts as the logical extension of their beliefs. The movement was to slow in its influence and others were to take pre-eminence.

Quite separately, the initiative of the Likud government in building settlements was able to attract a different kind of settler and one who was less ideological and more materialistic. In the early days of Gush Emunim, the settler was seen to be a pioneering hero, struggling on behalf of God to occupy land to prepare for his appearing as Messiah. The settler was ready to endure hardship and primitive forms of survival in order to achieve that goal in the face of state opposition and violence. Instead, the Likud invited settlers to live in a pleasant state-subsidised bungalow or house, complete with garden, electricity and water, protection of the IDF, provision of a road system and within commuting distance to work in nearby towns. Not everyone was prepared to be a pioneer, living in primitive conditions, because they wanted a less demanding and pleasant environment in which to live and bring up their families. The materialist values were not compatible with the idealism of the religiously driven settler. While some settlements contained elements from both traditions, in the 1980s most were different from each other.

The differences in the settler movements began to be nudged apart by the government in 1979, when it established a new organisation, Yesha Council, which gradually became significant in size and lasting influence throughout Israel. Each settlement in the West Bank (Judea and Samaria) and Gaza was represented on the Council by its delegates and was utterly different from Gush Emunim, which was largely controlled by an "in-group" of older, established rabbinical figures. In July, 1982, the government was joined by the ultra-right-wing Tehiyah party, which was led by Professor Yuval Ne'eman who became head of the settlement committee. In two years, he approved eighty-two settlements, often making the decision himself.[155] Between its election in 1977 and the end of 1983, the Begin government had approved one hundred and three settlements, compared with twenty-two during the period 1967-1977. By 1984, dozens of new settlements were built on Palestinian land which had been obtained, allegedly, by chicanery and unscrupulous deception, largely conceived by close personal associates of Ariel Sharon, the Defence Minister in the Likud government.[156] Although prohibited from buying Arab lands, corrupt Israeli and Palestinian land dealers were exposed in the Israeli press as they lured elderly, illiterate Palestinians into selling their land, acquiring some 31,000 acres of land in the West Bank.[157] The death of

Rabbi Yehuda Kook in 1982 had left a gap which could not be filled by another individual with the same authority and respect, both within and outside the movement. This was to have a significant effect on the arguments between separate groups about the nature of the Temple Mount and the construction of the Third Temple to fulfil messianic aspirations. Meanwhile, Gush Emunim had established its own organisation of religious settlers, "Amana," a few years earlier in 1976 but it represented only its own ideological group of like-minded, religious people. They are zealous rebels with a cause and have a discipline to go with it. Its core values are maintained as the threefold focus of the Torah: the Lord, the people and the land, which assumes the ultimate destiny of God's Covenant of the land, as the call to take it and create the security to retain it until Messiah appears. Politics is the natural, ideological expression to flow from that religious passion. Peace was more than political and only concurrent with the three-fold unity of God, the land and the people, and was thereby, an all-enveloping process.

After The Intifada Of 1987

The Intifada of 1987 led to fundamental questions being asked of the religious settlers, which required interpretative rigour. Which rabbinic interpretation was to take precedence in an argument and if so, which one of the many available and frequently pressed forward? There were problems of sacred history which involved different interpretations of the Torah and halakha. Moral and ethical questions arose about the land and whether it should be held at any price or with a compromise. Capital questions were asked about whether or not there is a difference between the punishment of a non-Jewish murderer and a Jewish murderer? Aran points to questions being raised about doctrinal and practical issues for Gush Emunim, including issues of the distinction between Jewish and non-Jewish blood.[158] For the leadership, the issue was always subjected to rigid religious disciplines and not for any human considerations. Despite the questions, by 1988, Gush Emunim had established over 130 settlements.[159] Backed up by a strong and effective educational programme, it created a religious elite of informed, dedicated and trained leadership. Politically, it could depend on the support of an unofficial lobby, drawing from five separate parties, including members of the Knesset and Cabinet ministers.[160] Gush Emunim, despite having no formal membership, had a strong organisation which could call on support if, and when, it so decided. Its primary support was drawn from the Ashkenazi section of middle class, educated Jews rather than the Sephardi Jews, although both groups were seen to support the political parties which focused on issues of land.[161]

There were meaningful similarities between the settler movement of Gush Emunim and the traditional Kibbutz movement at the founding of the state in 1948, both seeing themselves as pioneers for the land and the people at different stages of recent history. The Government had consistently supported Gush Emunim and its policy of building and expanding settlements, despite the latter's opposition to any compromise on land. Despite attempts to stop settlement building by President George Bush and Secretary of State, James Baker, from 1989, they were repeatedly misled and outwitted by Shamir and Sharon.[162] By 1990, despite the changes in the settler movement as a whole, Gush Emunim remained the most militant and effective protagonist in the battle over the territories. The costs of the settlements for subsidies and infrastructure services created a deficit of $500 million in the budget of the Ministry of Housing and Construction in 1991.[163] For Aran, writing before the Madrid conference of 1991, the emphases of Gush Emunim seemed at a crossroads as to whether it was in decline or whether there would be an upsurge. It had reached a height of influence and, as it seemed to decline at the turn of the century, the advent of the suicide bomber and the rise of Hamas changed the situation.

Religion, The Covenant And The Land

There is little doubt that both Ultra-Orthodox and Gush Emunim show the priority of their religious belief over anything else, including laws of State or United Nations Resolutions. Once religious commitments are first satisfied, especially the Mosaic Law, based on the Abrahamic Covenant, other matters can be considered. This belief and conviction was to become increasingly significant in the life of Israel. Although many are driven by fear of consequences for breaking the Law, or desire for reward for keeping it, others are driven by the focus on ultimate values and the sense of destiny in being part of what they perceive to be the intentions of God. This may be perceived as the major part of the drive of Gush Emunim. Although their actions may be interpreted as callous, bellicose, even sadistic, that is to miss the point of their drive which is of loyalty in a separate spiritual dimension. It does not justify their behaviour but, despite its perceived objectionable nature, it may help to explain it.

There are other Jewish groups[164] which adopt a different, less obscurantist, stance and represent a significant view in Israel and the wider Jewish world.[165] They argue that the Palestinians have a real grievance because their homeland for over a thousand years, was taken without their consent and mostly by force during the creation of the State of Israel. Gwyn Rowley, offering what he called a "reconstructionist approach," viewed "peoplehood, or nationhood, rather than religion as the central aspect of Judaism." In a devastating sentence, he holds that the triple Covenant relationship between God, the people and the land had been replaced by "idolatry of the land."[166] At the same time he recognises that, for Gush Emunim, Eretz Israel is the land for the Messiah which, if sustained, would lead to further conflict in the future. This had similarities to Haim Be'er, quoted by Michael Feige, who claimed in 1982 that Gush Emunim was "a Canaanite phenomenon ... that in consecrating the land, unwittingly promotes a fetishism of place – not unlike the Canaanite pagans of ancient days. This may result in the forsaking of other, more spiritual and profound, Jewish principles."[167] According to Feige, Be'er had affinities with the National Religious camp and was alarmed at the "harmful deviation of Gush Emunim." He was one of a number of critics of the movement, mentioned by Feige. He also included a member of Peace Now, Shulamit Hareven, who saw the movement as a reflection of the right wing whose political claims are commonly robed in religious language:

> Gush Emunim is not a religious group by any definition. It holds no different ritual, has no different beliefs, and does not demand of its members any special behaviour or change of personal characteristics, Gush Emunim is a political group.[168]

Settlements After Gush Emunim

Writing in 1988, during the Intifada, before the Madrid conference in 1991 and the Oslo Accords of 1993, Lustick describes Gush Emunim and shows the growing resentment by Jewish fundamentalism of moves for peace. This, logically, was to lead to the "righteous" killing of Rabin, seven years later, in 1995. A system of creeping annexation was still made possible, not so much with new settlements, but through new Israeli laws and administrative practices in the West Bank, which were prejudicial and contrary to Palestinian interests. In 1992, Rabin had said that settlement building would stop, except in Jerusalem and the Jordan valley, but settlements continued because they were considered "vital to Israel." By the time of the Oslo Accords in 1993, the Palestinians in the West Bank were governed by military law which was part of Israeli civilian law. Worse was to come for the Palestinians because, at Oslo, Arafat had agreed to the settlements and the construction of by-pass roads. Thereafter, settlements were built at will by Israel. Gazit put it down to Israeli opportunism and Palestinian naiveté.[169] The days of Gush Emunim's enterprises after the Yom Kippur war may hardly have been necessary, but they had done their work. Netanyahu, Barak and Sharon had still to come. Subsequent history has shown the failure of the Oslo Accords, including the assassination of Prime Minister Rabin in 1995 by an Orthodox Jew.

The West was largely unprepared to acknowledge the power of fundamentalism, of which Gush Emunim was but one grouping. For many, the movement was central to life in Israel, and understood by a people taught their religion, even if not practised in the same way. It became, and retains, a disproportionate influence in Israeli life by virtue of its ideology and its capacity both to mobilise and use extraordinary, even fanatical, methods of violence and publicity to achieve its end over the state. It was argued by Lustick, in 1994, before the murder of Rabin "the Jewish fundamentalist movement, and the settlers in the territories who have been its spearhead, have 'emerged as the greatest obstacle to meaningful negotiations towards a comprehensive Arab-Israeli peace settlement.' "[170] Milton Viorst describes the massacre of Muslims at prayer in Hebron by an American Jewish doctor, Baruch Goldstein, from the settlement at Kiryat Arba in February, 1994, soon after the Oslo Accords. Afterwards, his friends said that he believed that: "Jews could preserve their hope of redemption only by stopping the peace process."[171] What followed was the creation of a pilgrimage shrine on his burial site which became a place of veneration for settlers, including rabbis, to celebrate his actions and who saw him as a martyr.

Despite being a minority, religious, ideological movement, in his later research into the work and influence of Gush Emunim, the journalist, Robert Friedman,[172] had also given forewarning of its power in 1994. He describes how the Likud party was formed and elected in 1977, influenced by the collaboration of the secular, revisionist party of Jabotinsky with the religious settlers of Gush Emunim.[173] One outcome was the growth of settlements in the occupied territories, seen by Yitzhak Shamir as the land of Israel and not Palestine. For Gush Emunim, any relinquishing of the land would prevent the coming of the Messiah. Friedman, writing after the Labour victory in 1992, warned what might happen if Likud were to be re-elected in any future election. He had already described the settler movement as: "Far more than a massive construction project, it is a marriage of Jabotinsky's militant secular nationalism and Gush Emunim's messianism."[174] He thought that any peace moves which threatened the settlements, could lead to settler violence and civil war.[175] He concluded by warning that if Israel did not end its occupation: "Zionism, the national liberation movement of the Jewish people, will be debased by the Zealots."[176] Following the murder of Yitzhak Rabin, Israel had re-elected the Likud party, with Binyamin Netanyahu as Prime Minister.

The Legal System

The demography of the land changed and was to accelerate even further so that by 2001, there were 200,000 settlers in the West Bank. Robert Fisk notes that in 2001, the International Committee of the Red Cross had regarded the installation of the population of an occupying power into occupied territories as illegal.[177] Meanwhile, the conflict over language and the use of the word, "occupied," as distinct from "territories," has continued and the word "disputed" is still commonly used and not the word, "occupation." To achieve this, a number of legal stratagems were implemented at speed. One major device was that land designated by the military governor for "military and security needs" could be appropriated because placing military units for defence was not in violation of international law.[178] Israel's High Court of Justice was not authorised to rule in actions outside the State borders and, if it was for a military operation, it was beyond the rule of law. The issue of security was a deciding factor for the Israeli High Court, if it was so advised by the IDF.[179]

According to Oliver McTernan, the writer and activist, some view the lives of Jews and Palestinians as more important than the land and can envisage the exchange of land for peace.[180] This was reinforced earlier by Davies[181] who quotes Michael Broyde and Emmanuel Rachman "the overwhelming majority of halachic scholars, including those in Israel and the Diaspora, agree that the sanctity of life is a higher value than the inviolability of land ownership."[182] They, in turn, take material from J. D. Bleich: "it is halachically legitimate to barter 'Land for peace' if doing so will preserve the lives of the inhabitants of Israel."[183] Davies quotes Broyde and Rachman again: "The weight of rabbinic authority is that Jews are under no religious obligations to retain all, or any part, of the land of Israel if such retention will involve loss of life."[184] He concludes: "Within the fullness of religious traditions – the prophetic and the halakic – the doctrine of the Land is, then, hedged against inflexible absolutism."[185] Separate writers use different spellings from each other!

It appears that there were differences of opinion in Israel in relation to settlements, whether religious or state. Davies holds that Gush Emunim has used its own misuse and misinterpretation of halakha to advocate its position and it has carried sway with a significant section of the population over a number of years.[186] It has garnered religious support on the strength of its arguments from a wide constituency, but contrarily, there are also significant groups which oppose their position. Against the common background of hostility, hate and fear, Davies notes that both Israel and Arab communities developed similar characteristics.[187] He points to terrorism by both sides, the manipulation of education for political purposes, connections between religion and nationalism and a paralleling between the Palestinian and Jewish Diasporas.

Despite any arguments to the contrary, there is little accountability for government decisions because the military invokes the argument of security to justify any action it seeks to take and enforce. An exception to this rule was made when the Court decided that the grounds of security did not exist in the contentious issue of Elon Moreh and the settlers were evacuated.[188] The government resolved the problem in the future by not settling on private land but only state and public land. Strategic settlements were still built, even on small areas, or islands, in Arab areas, which then had to have security boundaries and exclusive roads.[189] A sophisticated, cynical, opportunistic, state settlement system took over completely from Gush Emunim as different sets of rules were imposed and established.

Ariel Sharon – Politicide Rather Than Debellatio

Unlike the policy of debellatio, which is to debilitate a country so that it cannot function and can be taken over, the policy of politicide aims to destroy the political and national viability of a whole country. The term was coined by Professor Baruch Kimmerling to describe the gradual extinction of " the Palestinian people's existence as a legitimate social, political and economic entity [by] a range of social, political and military activities." [190] This policy was instigated and carried through by Ariel Sharon, after his election in February, 2001. This became possible through Operation Defensive Shield which, although planned much earlier,[191] was directly triggered by the suicide bombing in Netanya, during the Passover festival in March, 2002. Under the pretext of attacking terrorism, the Palestinian infrastructure was systematically destroyed, while the American Secretary of State, Madeleine Albright, called for Palestinian restraint! Most of the Palestinian attacks took place in the Occupied Territories (95%), targeting settlers and their military guards, although those that took place in the Israeli cities received the greater media coverage.

For decades, since 1967, Israel had a policy of not annexing the West Bank, apart from Jerusalem, which would have involved issues of civil rights, including electoral rights. Instead, it had a range of measures to exercise civil control, as described by Gazit and others. The policy of settlement construction and extension continued unabated as it established the "facts on the ground" which increasingly would make any viable future Palestinian state all the more unlikely. Knowing this to be the case makes the policy all the more cynical, as elsewhere there were ongoing discussions about such an intention and possibility. The disengagement from Gaza in 2005 and the removal of a few small, isolated settlements in the West Bank involved the gesture of removing 9,500 settlers into Israel but, at the same time, the government retained its immense settlement blocks in the West Bank with 400,000 settlers.[192] The evacuation from Gaza was ideologically impossible for those religious who felt unable to leave their settlements, despite government orders, because the land was given by God to Israel to hold until the time of the Messiah. After Annapolis, and in the absence of Sharon, settlements were still expanding in 2008. Even the so–called Security Wall is seen by many as a land-grab, creating ever more, "facts on the ground."[193]

The Beginning of a Conclusion – "Let No One Say They Did Not Know"

One can understand how people can be fearful and therefore take initiatives to protect themselves. What becomes obvious in this chapter is the malevolence and hatred which both Israelis and Palestinians can exercise against each other. What is difficult for those outside to appreciate is the duress under which people live. However, there is a significant number of Israeli Jews who are appalled at the bellicose acts of their fellow citizens against their Semitic neighbours, the Palestinians. In his book, Professor David Shulman[194] has recorded a personal account of some of the antidote to the poison of inter-community hatred between 2002 and 2006. As he describes in detail, the settler violence, ranging between the poisoning of farm animals, to brutal attacks on Palestinian farmers, the destruction of their crops, and the theft of their produce, one wonders at the mindset of such violence and the hatred it reveals. As Halper has described, there is a Matrix of Control on the Palestinians,[195] but that does not account for those Israeli settlers who are proactive in making life unbearable for the indigenous people. Even more than that is the state structure which fortifies such acts of violence, and includes an Israeli Defence Force that stands back and allows criminal deeds to be perpetrated before their eyes.

As late as October, 2008, two separate Israeli organisations, Rabbis for Human Rights (RHR) and B'tselem, reported on attacks by settlers on Palestinian farmers gathering their olive crops. These included the destruction of trees and crops, stone throwing and the beating of farmers. The article included a photograph of a Palestinian photographer being assaulted by settlers.[196] RHR reported that although they called the security forces for protection, they did not arrive.[197] This, despite it being the responsibility of the army to protect farmers on their lands.

It has been a simple matter to describe Palestinian suicide attacks against civilians as acts of terror, for so they are. The outworking of Gush Emunim, aided and abetted by the Israel Defence Force, with state policies and government bureaucracy, can be seen to be essentially the same. It can be asked whether the Matrix of Control, and the violence against the civilian population in the West Bank and Gaza, are acts of state terrorism. One can include questions about theft of land, oppressive checkpoints, creation of Bantustan-like enclaves, restricted freedom of movement, lack of human rights, politicide and debellatio.

The contents of this chapter, from the world of Gush Emunim, partly support the position of Davies who holds:

> it is not the main religious elements in Israel that constitute the chief obstacle to Israeli-Palestinian coexistence and peace. ... It is mainly the secularist, nationalist leaders of the Jewish state, like Ben-Gurion, Begin, Sharon and others, who have elevated the claims of the Land above all else.[198]

This is not entirely the case at all. It was an eminent, international Jewish leader who said to me in November, 2000: "If it takes another thousand years to achieve, we will have all the land of Eretz Israel as well."[199] The pre-eminent, ultimate focus was the land of Abraham and nothing less would suffice.

Quite naturally, one must ask about the mindset of civilians and settlers. One may also enquire about the legislators who create rules which are biased against the Palestinians. In the end there is the voting public to be asked who, by their apathy, are not only silent but, also, passive. Ultimately, the questions have to be theological, or within political theology. What kind of God is it who allows his people to commit such acts in his name and for his sake? Such misuse and abuse of power does not honour the religion, or its adherents, or its deity. It is very likely that God has been falsely portrayed by those who claim to be his devoted adherents. One has always to understand that there will be people of a fanatical persuasion, but what does it also say about those who permit atrocities, as though they are not themselves involved as witnesses and observers? What kind of brutal or passive behaviour is tolerated by their friends, parents and grandparents? These questions are already raised in the Preface of this book. Already there are Jewish teenagers with guns who do not hesitate to use them and then feel proud of what they have done. Equally, there are Arab teenagers who are ready to become suicide attackers and then feel proud of what they have done. As important is the role of the international community which, by its passivity, gives silent licence for the acting out of violence against a weaker Palestinian people, with inevitable reciprocity.

Driven by fear, the quest for security and religious ideology, Israel is perceived to continue its expansion in the land. The control of Palestinian life continues, with settlements and exclusive road systems, supported by the State and the Israel Defence Force. Palestinians live in areas which are increasingly reduced in size and cut off from each other. A Separation Wall is still being erected on Palestinian land, despite the condemnation of the International Court of Justice. Unemployment, poverty, and malnutrition are in abundance and lead to resentment and bitterness throughout, causing violence, leading to counter-violence. This is where the situation has arrived in Israel and Palestine, in which Gush Emunim can be seen to have been an, "Unintentional Agent" in Israeli-Palestinian state and non-state terrorism.

"Let no one say they did not know." [200]

What now follows in the next chapter is an account of the early influences for the return of Jews to what they see as their Promised Land. Generations earlier, in the 19th century, a Christian evangelical missionary organisation set out to convert the Jews to Christianity. After its early years, it became formalised in 1809 as the London Society for Promoting Christianity Among the Jews (LSPCAJ). This body gradually developed to bring about public sympathy for the Jews in the British Isles. It expanded into the movement to enable the Jews to return to what they saw as the Land promised by God to their forefather Abraham. The ultimate goal of the Society was to work for the return of Jesus Christ, whom the Jews should recognise as their Messiah, and the final judgement by God and the end of the world. Following that chapter, it leads naturally to Chapter 4 and the examination of that promise to Abraham, known as the Abrahamic Covenant, and subsequent Covenants.

Notes

[1] Gideon Aran, 'Jewish Zionist Fundamentalism: The Bloc of the Faithful in Israel (Gush Emunim),' in *Fundamentalisms Observed* eds. Martin E. Marty & R. Scott Appleby (Chicago: University of Chicago, paperback edition, 1994), 265-344.
[2] Aran, 290.
[3] Aran, 299.
[4] Aran, 309.
[5] Aran, 316.
[6] Also known as Rabbi Avraham Kook.
[7] Viorst, 205.
[8] Exceptions to this shortage are noted in this chapter.
[9] Kimmerling B., *Politicide*. London: Verso, 2006, 37-38.
[10] Kimmerling, 20.
[11] Lustick I. S., *For the Land and the Lord: Jewish Fundamentalism in Israel*. New York: Council on Foreign Relations Press, 1988. 73.
[12] Fisch H., *The Zionist Revolution*. (London: Weidenfeld & Nicolson), 1978.
[13] Genesis 15. 18-21. "The Lord made a covenant with Abram and said 'To your descendants I give this land, from the river of Egypt, to the great river, the Euphrates - the

land of the Kenites, Kenizzites, Kadmonites, Hittites, Perizzites, Rephaites, Amorites, Canaanites, Girgashites and Jebusites.' "

Also Genesis 17. 5-8: "Your name will be Abraham, for I have made you a father of many nations. I will make you very fruitful; I will make nations of you, and kings will come from you. I will establish my covenant as an everlasting covenant between me and you and your descendants after you for the generations to come, to be your God and the God of your descendants after you. The whole land of Canaan, where you are now an alien, I will give as an everlasting possession to you and your descendants after you; and I will be their God."

[14] Lustick 76, quotes Shlomo Aviner, 'The Moral problem of possessing the land', *Artzvim* Vol. 2, (1982), 11.

[15] Lustick 78, quotes Zvi Yehuda Kook "Between the People and the Land," *Artzvi*, Vol. 2 (Spring 1982), 19.

[16] Lustick 79, quotes Hanan Porat, "Policies towards Arabs of the Land of Israel," *Artzvi*, Vol. 4 (Spring 1986), 10.

[17] Genesis 1. 1-28.

[18] Lustick, 88-90.

[19] Kiryat Arba is the ancient name for Hebron. Genesis 23. 2.

[20] Piterberg G. *The Returns of Zionism (*London: Verso, 2008), 8. Dreyfus was a Jewish army officer who was tried and imprisoned on fraudulent charges in the 1890s and eventually exonerated, but the case revealed the vulnerability of Jews to persecution.

[21] Piterberg, 30.

[22] Piterberg, 54 ff.

[23] Shafir G. & Peled Y., *Being Israeli.* Cambridge: CU 2002. 37.

[24] Piterberg, 64.

[25] Piterberg, 70-73.

[26] Lustick, 27.

[27] Morrison D., *The Gush (*New York: Gefen Books, 2004), 121ff.

[28] Morrison, 148.

[29] Shahak I. & Mezvinsky N., *Jewish Fundamentalism in Israel. (*London: Pluto, 1999), ix-x.

[30] Gorenberg G., *The Accidental Empire* (New York: Times Books, 2006), 22.

[31] Zechariah 9. 9.

[32] Viorst M., *What Shall I do with this People?* (New York: Free Press, 2002), 195.

[33] *Encyclopaedia Judaica* 1971 edn. Vol. 10 Article on Rabbi Abraham Kook, 1182-1187.

[34] Ashkenazi Jews were those who came largely from Europe.

[35] Genesis 2. 7 - 3. 24.

[36] *Encyclopaedia Judaica*, 1182–1187.

[37] Viorst, 195-196.

[38] Viorst, 192-201.

[39] Viorst, 196.

[40] Isaiah 46. 8-9; Psalm 137, Jeremiah 31.

[41] Michael Feige, *Space, Place and Memory in Gush Emunim Ideology.* 2. Private paper sent by the original writer to the Rev. Geoffrey Whitfield, 13 December, 2007.

[42] Genesis 17. 2-8.

[43] Ezekiel 36-38; 43.

[44] Feige, 3.

[45] Feige, 3.

[46] Porat H., 'Eye in eye they shall see the return of the Lord to Zion' *Ptachim* 32: 3-12. 1988. *I am looking for Anat.* Beit-El. Translation from Hebrew in Feige, 4.
[47] Feige, 4.
[48] Fisch H., *The Zionist Revolution.* (London: Weidenfeld & Nicolson, 1978).
[49] Isaiah 2. 2 -3.
[50] Fisch, 5.
[51] Leviticus 26. 12.
[52] Genesis 17. 4-8.
[53] Fisch, 20.
[54] Fisch, 20.
[55] Ezekiel 37. 25-27.
[56] Fisch, 21.
[57] Fisch, 23.
[58] Fisch, 80.
[59] Fisch, 121.
[60] Fisch, 135.
[61] Fisch, 152-153.
[62] Fisch, 166.
[63] Fisch, 168.
[64] Fisch, 169.
[65] Buber M., *On Zion: The History of an Idea* (London: Horowitz, 1973) x. Originally published in 1952 as *Israel and Palestine – the History of an Idea.* Paradoxically, later, he also saw the Israeli victory in the Six Day War of 1967 in sublime, spiritual terms.
[66] Buber, vii.
[67] Buber, ix.
[68] Buber, 111.
[69] Viorst M., *What Shall I do with this People?* (New York: The Free Press, 2002), 38.
[70] Buber, 147ff.
[71] The two factions became formally connected in the 1948 government when the religious parties, though small, were given responsibilities by Ben-Gurion. Israel was not a religious state but it consistently made concessions to the religious bodies. After the War of 1967, this rapprochement was to become entrenched, with exclusive rights and an exclusive destiny, led by the son of Rabbi Kook, Zvi Yehuda Kook, who became leader of the settler movement, Gush Emunim. The logical consequence of belief in Divine sanction, particularly after the Six Day War of 1967, meant that settlements for the religious would continue to expand and that previous inhabitants would be dispossessed, until the task of possession was completed. The end to achieve an exclusive Jewish state justified all the means involved. This is discussed more fully in the next chapter.
[72] Lustick, 36. "Taken from the text of notes to the address of Zvi Yehuda Kook, published as 'This is the State of which the Prophets Dreamed,' *Nekuda.* No. 86, 26 April, 1985, 6-7."
[73] Ehud Sprinzak, 'The Iceberg Model of Political Extremism' in *The Impact of Gush Emunim* ed. by David Newman (Beckenham, Kent: Croom Helm Ltd.), 1985, 27ff.
[74] Sprinzak, 41.
[75] Lustick, 17ff.
[76] Formerly the London Jews Society (LJS) and the London Society for the Promotion of Christianity Amongst Jews (LSPCAJ).
[77] Genesis 15. 18-21 and Genesis 17. 4-8.

[78] Gideon Aran, 'Jewish Zionist Fundamentalism: The Bloc of the Faithful in Israel. Gush Emunim,' in *Fundamentalisms Observed* eds. Martin E. Marty & R. Scott Appleby. (Chicago: University of Chicago, paperback edition, 1994), 265-344.
[79] Aran, 273.
[80] Aran, 270.
[81] Aran, 268.
[82] Genesis 15. 18.
[83] Aran, 274.
[84] Lustick Ian S., *For the Land and the Lord, Jewish Fundamentalism in Israel* (New York: Council on Foreign Relations Press, 1988 edition 6).
[85] Lustick, 8.
[86] Ehud Sprinzak, 'The Iceberg Model of Political Extremism' in *The Impact of Gush Emunim* ed. by David Newman. Beckenham (Kent: Croom Helm Ltd., 1985), 27-45.
[87] Ehud Sprinzak, 'The Politics, Institutions and Culture of Gush Emunim' in *Jewish Fundamentalism in Comparative Perspective* ed., by L. A. Silberstein (New York: Routledge, 1993), 121.
[88] Sprinzak, 122.
[89] Sprinzak, 123.
[90] Sprinzak, 125.
[91] Halper J., *Obstacles to Peace.* Bethlehem: PalMap of GSE, 2004, 12ff.
[92] Rose. 2005, 31.
[93] Buber M., *On Zion: The History of an Idea (*Edinburgh: T&T Clark, 1985), 49-50.
[94] Viorst, 191.
[95] Gazit. S., *Trapped Fools* (London: Frank Cass, 2003), 141-142.
[96] Viorst, 192.
[97] Viorst, 197ff.
[98] Viorst, 11.
[99] Viorst, 201-202.
[100] Zertal I., & Eldar A., *Lords of the Land (*New York: Nation Books, 2007), 15.
[101] Attributed by Gorenberg to Ehud Sprinzak. Gorenberg G., *The Accidental Empire* (New York: Times Books, 2006), 45.
[102] Gorenberg, 45.
[103] Gorenberg, 340.
[104] Gorenberg, 99.
[105] Gorenberg, 101.
[106] Gorenberg, 127.
[107] Gorenberg, 129-131.
[108] Gorenberg, 143.
[109] Aran, 268-269.
[110] Micah 6. 8.
[111] Viorst, 202.
[112] Viorst, 203.
[113] Viorst, 204.
[114] Lustick Ian S., *For the Land and the Lord; Jewish Fundamentalism in Israel* (New York: Council on Foreign Relations Press, 1994 Edition), ix.
[115] Gorenberg, 169.
[116] Newman D., *Jewish Settlement in the West Bank.* Occasional Papers Series No. 16, eds. John Dewdney & Heather Bleaney (University of Durham: Centre for Middle Eastern & Islamic Studies, 1982), 17.

[117] Gorenberg, 199.
[118] Aran, 270.
[119] Ian S. Lustick, 'Jewish Fundamentalism and the Israeli-Palestinian Impasse', in *Jewish Fundamentalism in Comparative Perspective* ed., by L.A. Silberstein (New York: Routledge, 1993), 114.
[120] Lustick, 115.
[121] Zechariah 9. 9.
[122] Aran, 278.
[123] Newman, 28-29.
[124] Gorenberg, 311-318.
[125] Zertal & Eldar, 37.
[126] Zertal & Eldar, 36.
[127] Gorenberg, 343.
[128] Joshua 24.
[129] Viorst, 207.
[130] Gorenberg, 322.
[131] Weisburd D., *Jewish Settler Violence* (Pennsylvania: Pennsylvania State Univ., 1989).
[132] Weisburd, ix.
[133] Weisburd, 138.
[134] Weisburd, 20-22.
[135] "Aliyah" means the "ascent" or "going up" to Jerusalem as the diaspora Jews return to Israel.
[136] Weisburd, 35.
[137] Weisburd, 38.
[138] Aran G., 'Jewish Zionist Fundamentalism' in *Fundamentalisms Observed*, eds., Martin E. Marty & R. Scott Appleby (Chicago: Univ. Chicago Press, paperback edition, 1994). 290.
[139] Aran, 290.
[140] Lustick Ian S., *For the Land and the Lord, Jewish Fundamentalism in Israel* (New York: Council on Foreign Relations Press, 1994 edition). xi.
[141] Lustick Ian S., *For the Land and the Lord, Jewish Fundamentalism in Israel* (New York: Council on Foreign Relations Press, 1988 edition), 8-9.
[142] Lustick, 153.
[143] Lustick, 157ff.
[144] Gazit S., *Trapped Fools* (London: Frank Cass, 2003). 267.
[145] Gazit, 268-270.
[146] Newman, 76.
[147] Aran, 280.
[148] Newman, 37.
[149] Lustick, 40-41.
[150] Carter J., *Palestine Peace Not Apartheid* (New York: Simon & Schuster, 2006), 221-230.
[151] Carter, 48.
[152] Carter, 48.
[153] Weisburd D., *Jewish Settler Violence* (Pennsylvania: Pennsylvania State Univ., 1989), 43.

[154] Aronoff M. J., 'The Institutionalisation and Co-optation of a Charismatic, Messianic Religious-Political Revitalisation Movement' in *The Impact of Gush Emunim* ed. by David Newman (Beckenham, Kent: Croom Helm Ltd., 1985), 60.

[155] Zertal I., & Eldar A., *Lords of the Land* (New York: Nation Books, 2007), 97.

[156] Zertal & Eldar, 99.

[157] Friedman R. L., *Zealots for Zion* (New Brunswick, N.J., Rutgers University Press, 1992), 74-75.

[158] Aran, 287.

[159] Lustick Ian S., *For the Land and the Lord, Jewish Fundamentalism in Israel* (New York: Council on Foreign Relations Press, 1988 Edition), 10.

[160] Lustick, 10.

[161] Lustick, 11.

[162] Zertal & Eldar, 114-115.

[163] Zertal & Eldar, 113.

[164] Avnery U., *Truth Against Truth* Tel Aviv: Gush Shalom, 26ff.

[165] This point was strongly made in a personal note from Rabbi Pete Tobias, dated February 16, 2009.

[166] Rowley G., 'The Land of Israel: a Reconstructionist Approach' in *The Impact of Gush Emunim* ed. by David Newman. Beckenham (Kent: Croom Helm Ltd., 1985), 125-126.

[167] Be'er H., 'Gush Emunim-Canaanites who wear phylacteries,' in *Gush Emunim: History, Sociology and Theology.* Paper 8, by Michel Feige, sent to the Rev. Geoffrey Whitfield, 13 December, 2007.

[168] Hareven S., 'Sociological model against reality' in *In the Diaspora. Bitfutzot HaGola* 1977, 79/80: 104-108. in *Gush Emunim: History, Sociology and Theology.* Private paper 8, by Michel Feige, sent to the Rev Geoffrey Whitfield, 13 December, 2007.

[169] Gazit, 281-285.

[170] Lustick, Ian S., *For the Land and the Lord.* (New York: Council on Foreign Relations Press, 1994), xi.

[171] Viorst M., *What Shall I Do with this People?* (New York: The Free Press, 2002), 237.

[172] Friedman R. I. *Zealots for God* (New Brunswick, N. J.: Rutgers University Press, 1994).

[173] Friedman, xxxiii-xxxvi.

[174] Friedman, xxxvi.

[175] Friedman, 248.

[176] Friedman, 249.

[177] Fisk, 526-527.

[178] Gazit, 271-272.

[179] Gazit, 274.

[180] McTernan, 117-118.

[181] Davies W. D. *The Territorial Dimension of Judaism* (Minneapolis: First Fortress Press 1991), 125-126.

[182] Michael Broyde & Emmanuel Rachman, *Midstream* 36/2. 1990 11 on "Halacha and the State of Israel."

[183] Broyde & Rachman, 12.

[184] Broyde & Rachman, 11, footnote 4.

[185] Davies, 126.

[186] Davies, 126.

[187] Davies, 125, footnote 11.
[188] Gazit, 278.
[189] Gazit, 279.
[190] Kimmerling B., *Politicide* (London: Verso, 2006), 3.
[191] Kimmerling, 154.
[192] Kimmerling, 224-225.
[193] Shulman D., *Dark Hope* (Chicago: University of Chicago Press, 2007), 144ff.
[194] Shulman, 12.
[195] Halper J., *Obstacles to Peace*. Bethlehem: PalMap of GSE, 2004, 12-20.
[196] 'On the Agenda', in *B'tselem Update 30 October 2008*. www.btselem.org
[197] Rabbis for Human Rights *info@rhr.israel.net* 31 October, 2008.
[198] Davies, 126.
[199] The identity of the person is not a crucial issue for this position because it is not an isolated belief.
[200] Shulman, 12.

Chapter 3

The Early, Unintentional, Christian Agents, 1800-1845: The London Society for Promoting Christianity Among The Jews

When I was working in Bethlehem, at a time when tourists were very few, there was a noisy altercation between a street seller and a group of pilgrims over a transaction. It happened outside the entrance to the centre where I was involved and I attempted to bring some light to a very heated discussion. However, the seller forcefully turned on me and accused me of being like those Englishmen who started all the trouble by bringing the Jews back to Palestine. His anger was apparent and I felt his poverty and his fury at what he saw as ignorance and injustice by the English. Of course, he was right. The British had enabled the Jews to return who, later, took his land and his livelihood. The return had begun with an English missionary organisation in the 19th century and which is still operational, almost 200 years later.

This chapter describes the early years of that traditional, evangelical organisation, which, without necessarily intending it, became one that had serious ideological ramifications for the futures of Israel and Palestine. Eventually called Church's Ministry Among Jewish People (CMJ), it passed through a number of phases in its early years.[1] The reality is that the CMJ first created an evangelical missionary organisation in order to convert Jews to Christianity. It then became focused on the Second Coming of Christ, to bring about God's reign on earth and to encourage Jews to enter their crucial part in the salvation story as they understood it.

What follows covers the period from 1801, until it was firmly established in Jerusalem in 1845 through the establishment of an Anglican Bishopric. By that time, it was clearly part of the English Establishment, both ecclesiastical and political. Its focus was evangelical, over all else, but the involvement of politicians at the heart of government meant that it had international influence which was to stand it in good stead as it expanded. Although it had political influence and created a swell of support for Jews, leading directly to the Balfour

Declaration of 1917, it would be shocked, hurt, and offended to find itself described as an "Unintentional Agent" in Terrorism in Israel and Palestine. Nonetheless, throughout the 19th century, it was at the forefront of the promotion by Christians of the needs of the Jews. However unwittingly, its objectives fitted in well with those of Gush Emunim and the religious Zionists in Israel. Both are driven by the dynamic of the literalism of the Abrahamic Covenant, whereby God gave the land to the Jews for their exclusive possession and, for both, this is their mission. They are therefore in the mainstream of Zionism, although their ethics would be very different in terms of violence towards another people. That being the case, their Christian and Jewish beliefs would not at all be consonant. The outcome, nonetheless, has been state and non-state terrorism in Israel and Palestine. This chapter tells the story of the establishment of what is now, Church's Ministry Among Jewish People.

As part of the London Missionary Society (LMS), formed earlier in 1795, it commenced its work among Jews in London in order to convert them to Christianity. The leadership broke from the LMS in 1808 and created an independent organisation for a few months until, in 1809, it became the London Society for the Promoting of Christianity Among the Jews (LSPCAJ). After 1809, supported by the beliefs of the leading, influential evangelical, the Rev Charles Simeon, it took a lead in initiating the return of Jews to what is now the land of Israel. This innovative development was in order to prepare for the Second Coming of Jesus Christ and the judgement of the world by God, as the evangelicals understood it. After 1815, the Society was to move into the political arena, as its form was shaped by forerunners of what emerged as Christian Zionism. Powerful structures were to be put in place that, with hindsight, will be seen to have been partly instrumental, decades later, in bringing about the Balfour Declaration of 1917, and developments thereafter.

During this early period, the focus of their missionary zeal, i.e. the Jews in London, was one of a people in poverty. Even worse, the Jews in Palestine were not only poor, but oppressed and exploited by the Ottoman authorities. Nonetheless, there were Jews who were prepared to make their home in the land, some out of piety and others who had been there, subsequent to their expulsion from Catholic Spain in the 16th Century.[2] The Jewish communities differed from one another, notably the Ashkenazi Perushim and Hasidim from Northern Europe who awaited the Messiah, and the Sephardi who were Middle Eastern. Unlike the Ashkenazi, who studied the Torah and Talmud, but did not work, the Sephardi community had a different culture and was prepared to work and trade. Each community depended on outside financial support from the Jewish diaspora by what was known as the haluka, or distribution, which was organised by the rabbis. The Jews were taxed in a number of ways by the Ottoman authorities, largely decided by the local ruler.[3] Their resulting poverty meant that they lived in dire conditions, which undermined their health. This made them vulnerable to the Christian missionaries who were to come with offers and inducements of financial help for converts and providing medical and educational resources, and even consular protection. It was not until 1827 that the English Jewish philanthropist, Sir Moses Montefiore, discovered their plight and, by creating clinical medical resources, began to do for his people what the Christians were doing as part of their evangelical mission. He also found that the poverty and hunger were not helped by the haluka, which was controlled by the rabbis, and he sought to deal with that dependency by instituting work projects to make them self-sufficient.[4]

In its work among the Jewish constituency, it was known as the London Jews Society (LJS) and was influenced by its normative Christian beliefs about the land and the people of Israel, which were taken from its literalist interpretations of passages from the Old and New Testaments. Its focus was simple and logical: God had entrusted the land of Israel to his people, the Jews, through the Covenant with Abraham. In seeking the return of Jews to Israel, it hoped to bring about the coming of the Messiah for the Jews and the Return of Jesus Christ for the Christians. It began as part of a wave of evangelical zeal, reinforced by fascination with the prophecies about the end of the world. Through its work, it helped to create a Christian constituency that, by the end of the nineteenth century, was sympathetic to, and supportive of, Jewish aspirations for the land of Israel. Its spiritual, or sacred, message had extended into becoming one that was also secular and political.

Nineteenth century missionary zeal became a strategic influence on the population of the UK as it became educated about the Jews and the Abrahamic Covenant so that many evangelicals accepted that the land was the natural inheritance of the Jews. Christians became sympathetic to, and persuaded by, the early days of Zionism, which was a logical development of their own belief system. By 1845, the Society had achieved its ecclesiastical and political underpinnings, through the appointments of an Anglican Bishop in Jerusalem and a British Consul, together with strategically placed people of influence in the English establishment like Lord Shaftesbury. By that time it had reached a watershed in its development as a successful organisation. The work of CMJ provided a fertile, public, ecclesiastical and political base in the UK to support future Jewish aspirations in the twentieth century for land and statehood. The period after 1845 is not examined here, apart from pointing ahead to the influence of the Society in later events. As an organisation, it still operates in Israel and the UK in order to fulfil its primary tasks. It cannot be said that, at any time, there was a drive to establish a State of Israel but, in due course, that was to become a logical by-product of its work. The Pogroms were still to come, bringing with them the rise in Nationalism and Zionism, leading to the Balfour Declaration of 1917 and the establishment of the State of Israel in 1948.

In the 19th century, the issue of the return of the Jews was based not so obviously on the Abrahamic Covenant, but on the prophecies concerning the end of the world. These were outcomes, or derivatives, of the Covenant rather than the foundation, without which there could have been no subsequent story. The urgency for the conversion of mankind, especially the Jews, included the fear of the end of the world and punishment at the final judgement, rather than the quest for a familial relationship with a God of creative grace. Thus, it is seen that when evangelical preachers made their appeal to convert the world and to restore the Jews to Israel in time for the Second Coming of Jesus Christ, few would include the bedrock of their faith by referring to the Covenant. When they did so, it was in a restrictive, literalist fashion of later exclusive demarcation and land possession. This is presently acted out by many involved in modern day Christian Zionism and Gush Emunim. The major drives of the Society, however, were the conversion to Christianity of the Jews and, according to Biblical prophecy as they understood it, their restoration to the land of their ancestors. Subsequently, scholars give accounts of the early influences, which show that the Society gained an impressive following of support that took powerful ecclesiastical, diplomatic and political forms.

The 18th Century Christian Backcloth

Two separate, pivotal factors contributed to the birth and growth of the LJS. One was spiritual and the other educational. In the mid-18th century, the Evangelical Revival, led by George Whitefield and John Wesley, brought about an immense response in England. It led to the creation of the non-conformist denominations, beginning with the Methodist Connexion and leading to the Baptist and Congregational Unions. Church-going increased, after a long gap since the days of the Puritans, and numerous non-conformist chapels were built. There was a focus on evangelism in the UK and this was to lead to missionary work among the "heathen" towards the end of the century. It also led to a mission through Sunday Schools to educate people in Christian knowledge, faith and practice. This included the Bible stories, which were taken literally and introduced people to the history of the Jews as God's chosen people. It also introduced the thoughts of eternal issues, of life and death, of reward and punishment, of heaven and hell, and of fear and condemnation at the final judgement. Dr Ghada Karmi describes the process of religious education in schools and churches as, "saturated with the texts, stories and themes of the Old Testament in which allusions were made to Zion, to Israel, to places in the Biblical Palestine and to the Jewish people."[5] She describes it as a system of "indoctrination." There can be little doubt that those who were taught the stories of the Bible received them with sympathy and respect, rather than criticism which was to come.

At the time of the creation of the Society, belief in the Bible was largely based on a literal interpretation, before the later scholarship of Higher Criticism changed this emphasis in the 19th century. This school of Biblical study had commenced in Germany and analysed the Old Testament in particular, separating the various sources which had been linked together by scholars of an earlier age. The findings of the research meant that the first five books in the Bible in particular were seen, not to be one continuous historical account but a combination of different writings, each of which had a different focus and were written with different aims. What followed was that the stories were held to be more important for their meaning and spiritual illumination, rather than as a historical record. This development created immense difficulties within Christendom and, especially, its evangelical and fundamentalist wings, including LJS.

It is argued here that the early quest for the LJS was that, as the spiritual children of Abraham themselves, they sought to bring the Jews into their understanding of both Jesus as the Messiah and the restoration of Jews to the land of Abraham, in fulfilment of prophecy. Its understanding of the covenant with Abraham came from separate texts. The first, which described the territory, was as follows,

> To your descendants I give this land, from the river of Egypt to the great river, the Euphrates – the land of the Kenites, Kenizzites, Kadmonites, Hittites, Perizzites, Rephaites, Amorites, Canaanites, Girgashites and Jebusites (Genesis 15. 18-21).

The second was personal between God and Abraham,

> When Abram[6] was ninety-nine years old, the Lord appeared to him and said. "I am God Almighty, walk before me and be blameless. I will confirm my covenant between you and me and will greatly increase your numbers." Abram fell face down, and God said to him, "As for me, this is my covenant with you: You shall be the father of many nations. No longer will you be called Abram; your name will be Abraham, for I have made you a father of many nations. I will make you very fruitful; I will make nations of you, and kings will come from you. I will establish my covenant as an everlasting covenant between me and you and your descendants after you for the generations to come, to be your God and the God of your descendants after you. The whole land of Canaan, where you are now an alien, I will give you as an everlasting possession to you and your descendants after you, and I will be their God" (Genesis 17. 1-8).

These texts, taken literally, were the foundation of that overall concept of the covenant, and respected as the basis of the earliest LJS evangelical mission. So much so that the covenant was taken for granted and did not always need to be specified when the subject was raised: it was accepted as a "given." Although not necessarily his own theological position, Goldberg writes, "For the rabbis who viewed history through the ineluctable prism of three key archetypes (God, Torah and Israel), every event was evaluated according to…those theological motifs. That God had chosen Israel was a given."[7] For Reformed Judaism and LJS, quite separately, there was a common basis of belief that was understood, and repetition was hardly necessary. Thus, the terminology used by LJS varied from the need to evangelise the Jews, to assure their return to the land in order to fulfil prophecy, and the logic of the promise of the land to Abraham. This meant that its focus on the people and land of Abraham was the pre-eminent basis for developing strategies for the planning and operation of evangelism and the Return. What had begun in England as a basic evangelical enterprise to convert the Jews, moved on in stages to incorporate social applications in terms of meeting their material needs in London. It then moved further to wider ideological issues as it encouraged the restoration of Jews to the land of their forefathers. This was to extend to the establishment of ecclesiastical and diplomatic structures in the development of its mission. It will be seen that, in the early days, the society lacked the skills that would be required for any completion of their vision, but the early initiatives were to lead to an organisation of substance.

The notion of the return of Jews to Israel was not new. The accounts of the Biblical stories had come into the public sphere through the translation of the Bible into English in 1611. In his tracing of the quest to convert the Jews, Christopher Hill writes, "The conversion of the Jews and the spreading of Christianity to all nations were necessary conditions, without which the Millennium (the reign of Jesus Christ on earth) would not take place."[8] He refers to the first book in English on the subject of the return of the Jews to Israel, written in 1621 by Sir Henry Finch MP, entitled, "The World's Great Restauration. [sic] and the Calling of the Jews" in which he called for a restored Israel.

According to the historian, Yaron Perry, "The main tenets of faith that had taken hold among the Protestants in the 16th century stated that the Second Coming of Jesus Christ was imminent and his advent would herald the utopian epoch of the Millennium."[9] What Perry and many others miss out, but to which others, like Pragai, refer, is the primacy of the Abrahamic Covenant, without which there would be no promise of a specific land to a specific people. Perry's lengthy description of what became the London Jews Society in 1809 and then the London Society for the Promoting of Christianity Among the Jews, while covering the rest of the century, fails to consider this fundamental factor. The emphasis on the Abrahamic Covenant has not been omitted by the diplomat, Michael Pragai[10], although he does not specifically identify the early organisations. He acknowledges that Christians had "known of the many prophecies about the return of the Jewish People to the land of their forebears, and of their restoration there as a Nation on the land originally promised to them and contracted for in Abraham's Covenant."[11] Goldberg writes, "For Jews of whatever background, religion and history are inextricably linked. The culturally and geographically disparate Jewries of the world share by way of a common identity a religious heritage stretching back to the first patriarch Abraham."[12]

This issue of the veracity of the Abrahamic Covenant has already been considered in Chapter 1 and there are two points that are important to raise again at this juncture. One is the issue of the historicity of the text and the other is its interpretation. Where the Genesis text is taken as historical, inerrant fact, rather than as a religious document intended to convey a message, there are difficulties in trusting its reliability for factual accuracy. Where the text is taken without a context of other accounts, but interpreted in literal terms and isolated from wider issues, there arises the impasse of contrasting interpretations. This leaves aside the issue of the beliefs of those with a different theistic perception, as well as those not holding one at all, disbelieving any view of an external divinity. Therefore, those who take the passages in Genesis, without a wider context and as an inerrant account of history, will logically believe that Jews alone are those entitled to exclusive possession of the land. This was part of the mindset of those in LJS who argued for the return of the Jews to take exclusive possession of the land, until the coming of the Messiah and the Second Advent of Jesus Christ. The view, taken from the school of Higher Criticism, that the texts are an edited collection of separate religious documents and available for consideration, learning and guidance, is viewed with disfavour and even hostility, by many of an evangelical persuasion.

One effect of a literal interpretation of the Bible was to introduce religious people to belief in divine retribution rather than a rich, creative relationship with the divine. Influential and well-known preachers like the Rev. James Bicheno and the Rev. Thomas Scott are seen to be representative of many who would emphasise the condemnation of the entire human race and the need to convert the unbeliever, or risk eternal punishment themselves. It was a time of apocalyptic belief in the prophecies of the Bible about the end of the world, with the separation of the "saints" for their reward and "sinners" for their punishment. Any forthcoming punishment at the end of the world would be avoided if the commandments were obeyed and the Jews restored to their land. In this, the LJS became a light for many, especially because the French Revolution and the religious political upheaval in France had made people wonder about how the world was going to end. "There were recurrent fears of French invasion"[13] and British military regiments were on watch on the Sussex coastline.

The violence in France had a particular effect on the evangelicals in England and, "in the field of Biblical hermeneutics."[14] When papal power was overthrown in 1798 as French troops entered Rome, the upheaval was felt throughout Europe. This was associated with movements, prophesying the end of the powers of the Roman Catholic church. Timothy Stunt writes,

> There was a growing number of expositors who maintained that the millennium had not begun in the reign of Constantine as Augustine had suggested, but that, on the contrary, its commencement was necessarily still to come. An era of millennial expectation and promise had been born, but in times of crisis, the message proclaimed by its heralds could acquire troublingly apocalyptic overtones.[15]

There was evidence for this in the years before the creation of the LJS. The Rev. James Bicheno, the famous Baptist preacher, interpreted the French Revolution from 1789 to 1793 as ushering in the close of world history. In a sermon of 1791, published in 1799 and subsequently thereafter entitled, "The Signs of the Times in Three Parts,"[16] he urged that the Jews should be restored to Israel, because the Jews had been given the "promised land" of Abraham as their possession forever. He argued from St Paul (Romans Chapter 11) that the Jews would be redeemed and that they would be restored to herald the Return of Jesus. He asked, rhetorically, whether Britain should not work to accomplish divine aims and use its power to end the exile of the Jews and restore them to their homeland. Bicheno referred to "the fulfilment of prophecy" and made his argument on the basis of, "our scriptures are of divine authority."[17] This was before the days of critical analysis, and the scriptures were taken as having supreme authority among many Christians, almost with the force of law. His works were reprinted many times, pointing to the fact that they were not only read, but in great demand and having influence. He was held in high regard and his standing as a preacher is evidenced by his regular appearance in that role.

James Bicheno continued to exert influence on the church-going public as he pressed for the restoration of the Jews to Palestine, publishing widely under that very title.[18] In his introduction, he sought to "lay a strong foundation of scripture authority for the restoration of the Jews and scriptural prophecies." He wrote, "The seed of Abraham...evidently chosen and set apart by God for special purposes to a people for himself to show forth his praise. Nor was the Covenant which God made with them to be in force for a short period but was to be an everlasting Covenant."[19]

> I will take you as my own people, and I will be your God. Then you will know that I am the Lord your God, who brought you out from under the yoke of the Egyptians. And I will bring you to the land I swore with uplifted hand to give to Abraham, to Isaac and to Jacob, I will give it to you as a possession. I am the Lord (Exodus 6. 7-8).

Bicheno referred to others who spoke of the Return of the Jews, "that the Jews will in God's good time be converted to Christianity and upon their conversion be restored to their native city and country." Bicheno not only based his words on prophecy, but also warned of the dire consequences, if they failed to heed the warnings, which brought strong pressure on those who were vulnerable to such insistence. In the same Report of 1815, Bicheno identified himself as a supporter of the Society as he gave a series of six "friendly addresses" to Jews in January, 1815 at the meetings of the LSPCAJ.[20] He addressed them as: "Ye children of Abraham and of the Covenant" and sought to persuade them of the truths of Christianity.

The work of Don Lewis[21] on Lord Shaftesbury refers to the influence of a number of others. In 1796, Charles Jerram, an Anglican ordinand, wrote a Cambridge University prize-winning essay: "The Grounds Contained in Scripture for Expecting a Future Restoration of the Jews." Taking from Genesis 17. 8, Jerram drew the conclusion that by an everlasting possession being promised to Abraham: "The claim of the Jews to the land of Palestine will always be reasonable."[22] In particular, Lewis refers to a contemporary of Bicheno, the Biblical commentator, the Rev. Thomas Scott, who wrote: "Commentary on the Bible," published in London in 1810. Lewis writes: "It was undoubtedly his commentary that did the most to popularise the notion of a Jewish return to Palestine among its countless readers throughout the English-speaking world in the 19th century."[23] Lewis writes that Scott looked "to the ultimate conversion of the Jews and their restoration to Palestine and was an early supporter of the LSPCAJ."[24]

In 1810, the Rev. Thomas Scott preached a sermon to the nascent LSPCAJ from Zechariah 8. 23, entitled: "The Jews a blessing to the nations and Christians bound to seek their conversion to the Saviour."[25] He said: "The descendants of

Abraham, Isaac and Jacob would, in every age, be the most distinguished and extraordinary people on earth.[26] Like Bicheno, Scott spoke of: "the scriptures (I speak especially of the Old Testament) are indeed the infallible Word of God."[27] From this, he urged the Society to acknowledge: "The accomplishment of the prophecy has laid us under obligations to the Jews which exceed all calculation,"[28] and argued that Christians owed it to the Jews to seek their conversion. Evangelicals were persuaded in good conscience thereby to support this missionary call and the LJS grew in both support and influence.

The Early Years Of The Church's Ministry Among Jews

The origins of the work among the Jews can be traced as far back as the late 18th century with the early missionary movement. The first missionary society in Britain was the Baptist Missionary Society (BMS), formed in 1792, which pursued its work in India. The records of the London Missionary Society (LMS),[29] formed in 1795, show how its work was influenced by the example of the BMS and referred to the writing of the first Baptist missionary, William Carey, in 1788. Carey's letter: "Enquiry into the obligation of Christians to use means for the conversion of the heathen," can be considered the foundation letter, or document, for overseas missionary work.[30] Richard Lovett's history of the LMS describes the growth of interest and commitment to overseas work within the Congregational Union until the formation of the LMS in 1795.[31] In the following years, this missionary work extended to include the work of converting the Jews to Christianity.

There were a number of stages in the early development of the LJS. In a sermon by the Rev. Ray of Sudbury, preached on 14 May, 1800 to the LMS, he declared: "I am aware of those strenuous and well-intended efforts which have been lately made for the conversion of the Jewish people: and suffer me to exhort that ye be not weary in well doing."[32] This was to be followed, on 1 December, 1801, when Joseph Samuel Christian Frey, signing himself, C. J. Frey, wrote a letter asking to work amongst the Jews in the East End of London,[33] following which he commenced his training as a missionary. In 1802, the LMS directed Frey to the Rev. David Bogue of Gosport for training.[34] Lovett recorded that Frey commenced to work for the LMS with Jews in London in 1805 in Jewry Street Chapel and Sion Chapel.[35] Later, on 24 February, 1806, it was formally resolved that Frey should extend that work and lecture and preach in The Jews Chapel, Spitalfields.[36] It was to take time before it moved to Palestine, but the work among the Jews had commenced.

Evidence of ongoing support for its work among the Jews is contained in the LMS records of 1805-1807.[37] They contain a sermon (No. III) to the Missionary Society, made on 15 May, 1806 by the Rev. David Bogue of Gosport, stating: "It is the duty of Christians to seek the salvation of the Jews."[38] He refers to the call of God, "To illustrate and enforce the obligations which lie upon you to seek the eternal salvation of the posterity of Abraham."[39] This kind of encouragement reinforced the concept of missionary work among the Jews at an early stage. Frey understood his evangelistic task needed to have a broader scale than preaching only. He planned a "House of Industry" in which Jewish enquirers could be taught a trade so that they might work and support themselves, rather than become financially dependent on the Society. He also envisioned residential accommodation for children and resources for their educational development.

There was a series of problems, which arose early on concerning the details of the work and the expenditure of LMS funds. On 23 March, 1807, the Directors of the LMS referred the problem to its "Committee for Jewish Affairs."[40] On 27 April, 1807, the Committee passed: "a motion that the Jewish Mission be entirely separated from the Missionary Society, consideration of which was finally postponed for three months."[41] Meanwhile, it was resolved, on 7 May, 1807, not to support destitute Jews "unless in the opinion of the Committee, after enquiry, the persons applying appear to have embraced the Christian faith or are sincerely desirous of obtaining instruction therein."[42]

As part of its responsibility, the LMS formally established the "Jewish Auxiliary Committee" on 2 October, 1807, "to assist Mr Frey." A paper, dated 19 October, 1807, in the CMJ archives referred to weekly meetings in early September and October, enabling Frey to report back to the Committee on the progress of his activities. Two days earlier, on 17 October, 1807 Frey had written to the LMS with a plan for a Free School for Jewish children.[43] This was an approach with which the LMS was neither familiar, nor comfortable, if it was to give its support and approval. Despite that, the minute book of the LMS General Committee of 4 August, 1808:[44] "Recorded that a society be immediately formed which shall be called The London Society for visiting and relieving the sick and distressed [spelt 'dishesfed'] and instructing the ignorant especially such as are of the Jewish nation."[45] This was to lead to the breaking point the following March. The London Society represented an extension of the LMS, beyond the anticipated work of evangelism, and expanded into a broader ministry, which included relief and education. Elsewhere, the LMS was intent on directing its efforts overseas, rather than in England.

Throughout the early support and encouragement, the practicalities of the work were not clear to all those with responsibility for the LMS. On 20 October, 1808,[46] the minutes "regret the declining state of the Jewish affairs under the care of the Missionary Society" (i.e. The LMS). Strains between the officers of the LMS and the missionaries in the East End of London were to the fore from an early stage. Frey followed with another request on 28 November, 1808, proposing apprentices, employment and a charity school.[47] According to the entry, the Directors had not planned such schemes unless the Mission to the Jews separated from the mission to the heathen. In the same correspondence, Frey suggested such a scheme might be viable and urged that funds should be raised, offering himself as a director with an increase in salary.

During 1807 and 1808, there had already been a number of differences of opinion within the LMS and the nascent LJS. Lovett wrote:

> It is evident that considerable divergence by this time existed between Mr Frey on

the one hand and the Directors on the other, as to the right method of working the mission to the Jews. On December 19, 1808, the Board reaffirmed its strong desire to carry on Christian work among the Jews.[48]

At the same time, it drew a boundary between their view and the proposition of Frey that poor children should be taken from their parents, stating "in order to maintain them in a charity school, and to educate them as Christians, is ineligible."[49]

The next few months were to be pivotal for the direction and development of the work among Jews in Palestine and Israel. Frey resigned from the LMS on 10 January, 1809, and it was minuted on 23 January, 1809.[50] This is recorded in an undated paper, entitled: "Please to take notice,"[51] and refers to his separation from the LMS. There are relatively few papers in that particular archive but there is one, dated 1 March, 1809, which refers to the formation of the new London Society (for the conversion of the Jews).[52] This followed the previous agreement on 4 August, 1808 for the London Society to be formed. This shows that for many months, it had been possible for the LMS to continue with its work among the Jews, but this was to prove abortive. On 25 March, 1809, after leaving the LMS, Frey wrote to George Burder, Secretary of the LMS, referring to adverse publicity and false accusations being made in public about him.[53] In the same box of papers, a further letter of 8 April, 1809 from the newly formed London Society shows a correspondence indicating ongoing disagreement and acrimony with the LMS.

There were ongoing tensions in the work which Frey was undertaking and on 1 May, 1809, he and his associates changed the name of the Society to the London Society for the Promoting of Christianity Among the Jews. By so doing, he publicly detached the work among the Jews from the LMS and it became a society that was to be supported by voluntary contributions. As well as pursuing the evangelical commitment to conversion, the new Society leased or purchased buildings for its school, church, and accommodation facilities. These two emphases, which created tension within the organisation, were extremely expensive and it will be seen that, eventually, the Society went into debt and could not continue without changes in its planning and management structures. The work among the Jews in London, prior to its focus and drive to move to Palestine, was extensive and expansive nonetheless. In that period, it was to establish itself firmly in the forefront of missionary work, with important support from strategically situated persons of high rank. This was to bode well for its future development and assisted in its emergence as a progressive and visionary enterprise which captured the imagination of others.

Among the first steps of the newly formed London Jews Society,[54] it communicated to its former parent body, the LMS, on 23 May, 1809, and referred to the active and organised move to convert the Jews. In its "Report of the London Society," The Committee of the London Society, recommended:

It is their duty, and ought to be considered their privilege, … that his kingdom may indeed be set up in the hearts of all mankind; and more especially in the hearts of his once chosen and highly favoured people – the Jews...the London Society is justified in appealing to the wisdom and judgement of the Missionary Society ... that the time is come, when Christians ought to make some exertion for promoting the knowledge of the truth, as it is in Jesus, among God's ancient people. [55]

The change from being a section of a missionary society, to one that was independent, had happened in a relatively short space of time. With the LMS being more cautious about the wider concept of material relief, Frey and his supporters had swiftly, and successfully, founded the LSPCAJ, following the earlier agreement on 4 August, 1808.

The new society quickly gathered significant support from the nobility, including HRH the Duke of Kent, and was able to expand its work in the East End of London.[56] The ability of the Society to attract that kind of support from people with a great range of influence was to stand it in good stead for many decades to come. In the Report of the London Committee of the London Society to the second half-yearly meeting of the LSPCAJ on 27 December, 1809, the list of vice-presidents included the names of the Earl of Crawford and Lindsay, Lord Robert Seymour, Lord Calthorpe, and William Wilberforce MP. The Report noted some growing concerns and problems between Anglican and Dissenting ministers. Later, the Report[57] reflected its social concerns in its rules which included a call for a monthly committee meeting in Jews Chapel, namely: "The Object shall be the temporal distress of the Jews, as well as their spiritual welfare."[58] Each report was to carry an extensive list of subscribers, including their names and the amount contributed.

In an undated paper in the archives, the new London Society published an address from its London Society Committee, including the aims of the society regarding the conversion of the Jews. There was still ongoing difficulty between the LMS and the LJS on 18 September, 1809. One letter in the archives is from a clergyman, offering "a peace maker between Frey and the Directors of the Missionary Society."[59] In the minutes of the meeting on that occasion, sent out on 26 October, 1809, the Directors of the LMS declined the invitation of LSPCAJ, aka The London Society to meet with them regarding their separate mission to the Jews.[60] It appears that the LMS directors wished to avoid further alienation and wrote that the LMS Directors "cannot admit they are calculated to 'excite prejudice' against Mr Frey or the London Society [as has been stated by the Committee of that Society]."[61]

The Second Half Yearly Report for the LSPCAJ, dated 27 December, 1809, contained information showing the growing support and encouragement being given to this young missionary enterprise. The Rev. Andrew Fuller of Kettering, Northants, a founder member of the BMS in 1792, reinforced the evangelical commitment of the LMS. Under the list of Quarterly Lectures, entitled, "Demonstration Sermons, or Sermons demonstrative of our Lord Jesus Christ as the true Messiah," Fuller preached, "to a great number of Jews" on 12 November, 1809.[62] The same report referred to their focus, "to confine their instructions, and direct their attention, to one object alone: *that Jesus Christ is the true Messiah* [Italics taken from the *Report"*][6]. In a later part of the Report, it narrated from the earlier event:

> Mr Bogue's Sermon, entitled, "The Salvation of the Jews, preached on the 15th of May, 1806," by which they exhorted the Jews and Christians to unite: "... and with one heart and hand, combining their exertions for making the God of Abraham, Isaac, and Jacob, known to all the kindred of the earth.[64]

In the Third Report to the Committee of 6 June, 1811,[65] the committee included three lords, three earls and a baronet. Showing its ongoing social concern, it reported on an increase in the number of children attending its school, as well as employment created through spinning and printing. Its evangelical focus was being sustained as it reported on its object of convincing Jews that Jesus was the Messiah, which although Christians took for granted, Jews needed greater proof. Its summary recognised the range of needs of the Jews, including their spiritual and physical needs and work and sustenance, as well as conversion. Similarly, in the Fourth Report of 21 May, 1812, during which time the work had developed under Frey, the resources that were proposed included a chapel, a boys' school, a girls' school, a printing press, a factory, and a place of safety for Jews and Jewesses, called an asylum. It continued to emphasise its primary task as "to limit themselves to the simple object of convincing their Jewish brethren, that Jesus is the Messiah, the Saviour of the world."[66] The Report gave enthusiastic praise to Frey for his work and lectures, which were attended in great numbers.

Once Frey had finally moved on from the LMS, he pursued his mission to the Jews. What he had outlined in a proposal in 1812 came to fruition on 7 April, 1813. The historian W. T. Gidney describes the development of what was called, "Palestine Place," when on 7 April, 1813, 20,000 spectators attended the stone laying ceremony in East London. The land was taken on a 99-year lease and eventually it included a church, two separate schools for boys and girls, the Operative Jewish Converts Institution, a Missionary College and staff residences. On 9 September, 1813, the Hebrew Christian Association was formed, entitled, "The Children of Abraham" with 41 members. This was followed on 16 July, 1814 with the building of a church for Jews.[67]

The Jewish Repository of 1814[68] records how the London Society had developed in influence as it contained a lengthy list of auxiliary groups from around the country. This created a serious burden for the Society because of the expenses incurred in the cost of travel and hotel accommodation for those involved. In its report of the Sixth General Meeting, held on 6 May, 1814, it included reference to the inclusion of HRH the Duke of Kent as Patron of the Society. Moreover, although late for the meeting, he had hurried to be able to take the Chair, which had been temporarily taken by William Wilberforce MP.[69] Also present was the Rev. William Lewis, who was to exercise a significant and stabilising influence a few years later. At this meeting, the highly regarded preacher, the Rev. Charles Simeon, impressed on those present: "I do conceive the Jews never had that attention paid to them which they ought to have had, and to which I think they have the greater claim, from the regard which the Most High bears upon them."[70] Simeon went further, urging forward the work of the Society in terms of facilitating its further steps: "I only make this observation; let those who are graven on the palms of Jehovah's hands be graven on the tables of our hearts."[71] While the Duke and Wilberforce expressed their support for the conversion of the Jews, the Duke expressed his aversion to proselytism, although others were less reluctant. The discussion turned to the methods that might be used and the focus became the recognition by Jews of Jesus as the Messiah.

The Move To Bring About The Return Of The Jews

A year earlier, in 1813, Simeon had preached a sermon on the subject of the restoration of the Jews, based on Amos 9. 11-12, entitled: "The future restoration of the Jews and their union with the Gentiles in one universal church."[72] He declared: "Nor have the Jews been so brought back to their own land as to be driven from it no more. It is to such a restoration of them that the prophet refers." The influence of such a profoundly respected preacher as Charles Simeon was to have a significant effect for many years. The biographer, Arthur Pollard, writes:

> The strongest evangelistic interest of Simeon's later life was the conversion of the Jews. He looked for a full and imminent restoration of God's chosen people. He preached for it diligently, "... From 1813, his correspondence was studded with it. Simeon at home worked as a kind of one-man general staff, preaching for the Society, recruiting workers, spreading propaganda, collecting funds, advising on overall strategy. Simeon's authority and influence ... [on Shaftesbury and Wilberforce]... was tremendous."[73]

From his close connection with Simeon, William Carus, his personal assistant and biographer, was able to write in similar terms.[74] He details his advocacy work, travelling and preaching throughout the country for the Society and conducting an extensive correspondence from 1815, over many years.[75] Simeon conveyed a strong sense of urgency for the restoration of the Jews: "Also ... the time for the conversion of the Jews was near, I would undertake, not only to show, but to prove, and that to demonstrate, that those signs were at this moment in actual existence."[76]

The connection of the Jews with Abraham, the founder of their faith, continued to be made explicit. The Jewish Repository, Vol. II, refers to an important year for gathering support to encourage its growth. On 23 July, 1814, the famous preacher, the Rev. Thomas Scott preached a sermon, which conveyed his public support for the Society. Then followed the occasion on 1 September, 1814, when: "... the Society, called The Children of Abraham, held their first anniversary meeting at the Jews Chapel, Spitalfields."[77] The same month, the Bishop of Norwich, the Rt. Rev. George Horne, wrote, "The Case for the Jews," arguing that: "... As the chosen seed of Abraham, they had an exclusive indefeasible [original spelling] right to the favours of heaven."[78] He commended the work by saying "from the Gentile church, may go forth, those who shall cause Israel to return to it. Blessed time! Delightful prospect." He then brought into the discussion, a further significant step, namely the prophetic material of the Return of Jesus Christ and the coming of the Messiah. The Bishop continued, saying: "... we may...contribute towards the preparation of our elder brethren, the once beloved and highly favoured seed of Abraham...when their and our Messiah ... shall return in glory."[79]

There had already been a growing movement to convert the Jews earlier that summer, between the Sixth General Meeting in May, 1814, and the events of September and October. The same Jewish Repository of the LSPCAJ included the substance of a sermon given on 27 August, 1814 by a Baptist academic from the Baptist Academy in Bradford, the Rev. William Steadman. Entitled, "The Importance of the Conversion of the Jews," he said: "Let me only remind you of the state of the scattered seed of Abraham, and of the claims they have to our benevolent exertions."[80] Referring to the obligations of his hearers to the Jews, he called for: "The most earnest desire for their conversion ... then, in its fullest and most glorious extent, shall the blessing of Abraham come upon the Gentiles." He went on to praise the LSPCAJ, announced his support for its work and encouraged his hearers to do the same.

Meanwhile, however, leading laymen were moving away from the Society, not least, the Duke of Kent. A number of costly initiatives had been taken at Palestine Place in Bethnal Green, which impoverished the Society with serious debts, which could not be met. The Society had established a church building, schools for boys and girls and an institution for converts, as well as its separate training college for missionaries.[81] The historian, W.T. Gidney, described the expansion of the Society and, despite the growth of the work and the supporting base, it had over-reached its ability to manage itself with due diligence. Even more problematical was that it was intended that the newly opened church in Palestine Place would be serviced by both Anglican clergy and Dissenting ministers. This caused serious ecclesiastical discontent because Dissenters were not allowed to preach from the same pulpits as ordained clergymen. Gidney noted that on 11 February, 1815, the Dissenters resigned, with further differences over financial remuneration and contributions.[82] A fundamental change in the structure was essential for its survival. This was to happen in 1815 when the debts of the Society were largely met by a wealthy jurist named Lewis Way.

The Move From Non-Conformity To Anglicanism

In his history of the Society, Gidney refers to the story when, in 1811, Lewis Way supposedly learned of the will of a Jane Parminter who declared in it that a particular wood of oaks, which Way had admired while riding in Devon, should not be cut down until the Jews had returned to their land. Gidney[83] records that in 1882, the will was found not to include that passage and may have been based on legend and not history. Nonetheless, Lewis Way became a dedicated supporter of the Society from 1815, rescued it from its crippling debts, and supported its growth thereafter, until his death in 1840. His financial input provided the release from its obligations so that it could move forward afresh. On 28 February, 1815, presided over by HRH Duke of Kent, the General Committee affirmed the decision of its working committee on 21 February, 1815, to take control of the Society. The LJS thereby became a Society: "To pursue the great design for which it was initiated ... in the salvation of Israel."[84] The Society became part of the Church of England, the Dissenters left, including Joseph Frey,[85] and the Rt. Hon. Thomas Baring, MP, became President.[86] This was not without serious problems. When Baring was to become President, he found that the Society was in debt for the amount of £14,000 and, because of it, he would have to withdraw and not identify himself with such an organisation.[87] Almost immediately, Lewis Way gave him a gift of £10,000 and a further £4,000 was rapidly raised to clear the debt. It appeared that the Society was removing itself from the difficulties between Frey and the London Missionary Society and establishing itself on firmer ground, with a more measured leadership.

Early on, because of his connections, Way was able to promote the cause of a homeland for the Jews. He undertook a journey to meet Czar Alexander I of Russia, "who shared an interest in Jewish restorationism."[88] Together, they travelled to the Peace Congress of Aix-la-Chapelle in 1818 and obtained a non-binding agreement from the gathered heads of state, which supported the concept of such a homeland. The death of the Czar in 1825 meant that the decision was not taken forward at the time but it remained as an early marker in the process of restoration. Carus records that Simeon did not forget, referring to: "The protocol, drawn up by the five United Sovereigns at Aix-la-Chapelle, declaring their approbation of the great objects of our Society, and their determination to promote the civil and religious advance of the Jews in the respective dominions."[89]

During this period, the LJS was not alone in drawing attention to the increasing interest in the Jews, as related to prophecy and the return of Jesus Christ. In particular, although not published in full until 1828, the influential work of the historian, George Stanley Faber, was being written between 1818-1820, predicting the imminent return of Christ to be as early as 1864.[90] He wrote: "Jews ... will be collectively brought back to the land of their fathers, that there, they will still form a separate people, and there ... they will be reckoned up among the nations of the earth," concluding: "Therefore, the nation shall not pass away until the day of final retribution shall arrive."[91] He argued for the synchronisation of the Restoration of the Jews and the national conversion of Israel: "The conversion of the Jews is constantly described, not as succeeding but, as preceding and effectively producing the general conversion of the Gentiles."[92] Faber reconciled the literalism of the Old Testament and the New Testament to account for the end of the world and argued that the Jews would be restored and employed as part of the final Day of Judgement.[93] Taking from Ezekiel,[94] Faber describes "the Israelites as employed, either literally or figuratively, in burying the bodies of their enemies during the space of seven months, knowing Jehovah their God from that day forward."[95]

The Move Beyond London To Palestine

A number of steps can be perceived, after the new society was formed in 1815. Until then, the work among the Jews had been focused on the East End of London. It was to move to Palestine and the small communities of Jews living there, often living in dire circumstances of poverty and ill health. There were inevitable difficulties for the Society because of the lack of knowledge and experience of the territory, to say nothing of the problems of communication over the long distances and the unfamiliar physical conditions that affected the health of those involved. Attempts were made to work in the region but they were unsuccessful and had to be concluded until the Society became better organised. Although the CMJ missionary, John Nicolayson, first visited Jerusalem in 1826, with a view to establishing the missionary station there, it was not until his move to Jerusalem in 1833 that a strategy began to be considered and worked through, which focused on the central core of work in Jerusalem. It will be seen that this was to be fortified by diplomatic input, which resulted in a consulate in 1838 and a Prussian-British policy in 1841 to create a joint bishopric.

Before that time, there were separate attempts at developments between 1812 and 1826.[96] Tibawi refers to letters to the Society in 1812 from a Dr. Cleardo Naudi in which he prompted the notion of working for the conversion of Jews in the Levant, including Palestine. Naudi writes: "Your society has appointed me one of its foreign directors" and goes on to refer to the "Restoration of the Jews."[97] Subsequently, the Jewish Expositor recorded that, in 1817, Naudi specifically recommended that missionaries should be sent by the LJS to the North African coast and on to Jerusalem. He had discovered that many Jews had returned there: "As if the time of their restoration was at hand ... It will promote the restoration of our fellow creatures in those unhappy regions."[98] The enlargement of the Society continued in 1819 when Joseph Woolf joined the missionary staff.[99]

Perry discloses in his endnotes that a number of people in trusted positions in the Society turned out to be of questionable character.[100] Apart from Joseph Frey,[101] who left for America under a cloud in 1816, there were also difficulties with Melchior Tschoudy[102] in 1820 and 1821. Although Tibawi gives no record of his work for the Society, Perry records his dismissal from the Society in 1822, followed by his becoming destitute in 1826.[103] In the correspondence between the London Committee and Malta, Dr. Naudi and the Rev. William Jowett commented on the frustrations in their relationship with Tschoudy, which was not at all smooth. They did not have any confidence in a future working relationship because he did not respond to their requests for information on which they might make decisions. In particular, they had asked him to provide a number of forms for the Society, but they had not been forthcoming.[104]

Around the same time, Joseph Woolf (sometimes also spelt Wolfe and Wolff), a converted Jew, offered himself to the Society and, according to Perry, was a resounding success.[105] Tibawi viewed his input differently, seeing his work as having "negligible results."[106] He acknowledges that there were leading members of the Society who were sufficiently impressed with his reports, that they contemplated establishing a mission in Palestine and Syria. When Lewis Way and the Rev. William Lewis went to survey those possibilities in 1823, he writes that they were not so persuaded, despite being keen advocates of the Society. Lewis, not knowing Hebrew, found his attempts to open a missionary outpost frustrated and left in 1824.[107] The failed attempt by Lewis Way to rent premises in Lebanon for training and respite purposes introduced the Society to its unpopularity in the area when the authorities refused to allow the Society to use the buildings.[108] In spite of Tibawi's reservations about the worthwhileness of Woolf's input, those on the ground at the time appreciated his contributions. Gidney gives several pages to his involvement,[109] writing of his conversion to Christianity at Palestine Place and his theological training under Charles Simeon before starting his missionary work in 1821.[110] Lieber gives a lengthy account of his work as a converted Jew who began in Jaffa in 1821 and took on a roving role until 1829.[111] Woolf was still involved in the work of the Society in 1842,[112] and in the period between 1846 and 1849, Gidney records that he addressed the Annual General Meeting of the Society.[113]

A different set of accounts concerning the individuals involved is given by Don Lewis. He writes that the LSPCAJ had been active in Palestine, through Tschoudy in Nazareth since 1821, and through Woolf in Jerusalem for three months during 1822.[114] In fact, its commitment had been earlier, although it took time before it became organised with any consistency. Gidney states that Lewis Way was impressed by Woolf who, being of independent means, was also gifted and even charismatic.[115] He made relationships with a number of leading Jews until his health declined in 1823 and he had to recover in Lebanon.[116] By 1830, Woolf and the LJS parted company because Woolf moved on to concentrate on other work outside the Society. Woolf was capable of creating warm relationships with some, but others were not so impressed and Nicolayson had reservations about his attitude to authority.[117] Nonetheless, he is seen by his peers to have "cleared the way."[118]

One outcome of Woolf's brief visit in 1822 was a decision by LJS to establish a permanent mission station in Jerusalem under the leadership of William Lewis.[119] On taking up his position in December 1823, he became involved in Jewish problems with Ottoman officials and had to intervene on their part. He thereby became respected for his making known the problems of Jews, which was to lead to a political-diplomatic involvement.[120] It was William Lewis in 1824 who first proposed the establishment of a British Consul as a means of protecting Jews who were not part of the Ottoman Empire. He was seen as a protector of the Jews when they were being discriminated against by the Muslims. This not only enhanced his status among the Jews, but his despatches brought home to his British readers, the serious plight of Jews in the region. This was to create not only a respect for the work of the Society but a sensitivity within the Christian public about the mistreatment of Jews in Palestine. It can be argued that, both politically and relationally, William Lewis grounded the work of LJS so that it could be seen in terms of justice and mercy, and he repeated his call for a consul in 1825.[121] Eventually, this was to become of crucial, strategic importance for the advancement of the Society under its various titles.

Beginning In Jerusalem – At Last

Following an outbreak of violence in Jerusalem, caused by the imposition of greater taxation, Lewis was withdrawn from Jerusalem and was replaced by Dr. George Dalton. Because of the violence, Dalton was moved to Beirut until it was over. On his return to Jerusalem in December, 1825, he was taken ill and died only a few weeks after his arrival.[122] John Nicolayson[123] arrived a few days before the fatality and thereafter had a roving role, moving first to Safed and then being based in Malta, from 1828 until 1832.[124] This gap was partly because of the hostility of the Jews in Jerusalem, the plague in the area and the instability caused by the tension in the Ottoman community due to its friction with Russia.[125] The arrival of Nicolayson in Jerusalem in 1833 was to mark a significant change in the work of the Society.[126] The LSPCAJ was not properly established in Palestine until after Nicolayson made Jerusalem his permanent base. From the early work of Frey in 1805, it had taken 28 years to get to that point.

Nicolayson's journal from March, 1832 to December, 1833 shows the length of time consumed by slow and laborious transport as they travelled from Malta to Jerusalem via Beirut. Despite the conditions and threat to his health, and that of his companions, it showed him to be a man of endurance and commitment.[127] Perry notes that he ended the series of missionary explorations in different places and established the permanent base in Jerusalem on 22 October, 1833.[128] This proved to be another of many watersheds for the society. Nicolayson saw the need for a church to be built, and the property of the Society to be extended, and he set about the task. Despite the many disagreements, complications and restrictions, the building work commenced in 1840, but was not completed and consecrated until 21 January, 1849.

Moves For Political And Ecclesiastical Reinforcement

A stronger structure was created in the 12 years after the arrival of John Nicolayson in 1833, until the death of the first bishop in 1845. This came about partly because of the input of people like Lord Shaftesbury, who enabled the Society to establish a permanent structure and raise its standing within the political and ecclesiastical establishment of the United Kingdom. The role of people who occupied strategic positions of influence was to be crucial in the future development of the Society. For LJS the period was one of anxiety because in the year that Nicolayson arrived in Jerusalem, it lost one of its major supporters through the death of William Wilberforce. Three years later, in 1836, Charles Simeon also died. These were significant losses in the support base of the LJS and into the breach stepped Lord Shaftesbury, the future stepson-in-law of Lord

Palmerston. The LJS was in need of persons of influence and Shaftesbury was already involved in the organisation to take forward his profound belief in the restoration of the Jews. Shaftesbury was influenced by a leading clergyman, Edward Bickersteth, who held strong convictions about both the return of Jesus Christ and the restoration of the Jews to Palestine.

For many years there had been great excitement and controversy about the return of Christ, the judgement of the world by God and the place of the Jews in the scheme of history. This was known as "millennialism," which was the thousand-year period of blessedness in the world and preceded the judgement of the world by God. There were a number of positions, where proponents would emphasise the texts that suited their beliefs and then argued passionately about their convictions. What they had in common was a fascination with the judgement of the world and where they differed was centred on the time of the return of Christ, whether before or after the millennium. The precise place of the Jews was not clear, except that they had to be part of the conditions that made the return of Jesus Christ and judgement possible. This led to the intention to convert them to Christianity and to facilitate their return to the land of Abraham, where Christ was to return in person.

Shaftesbury took pleasure from the fact that his stepfather-in-law, Lord Palmerston, was supportive of the Jews, including their physical return to the land.[129] The subjects of eschatology, the Second Coming of Christ and the final judgement of humanity were common themes for evangelicals and Shaftesbury was one of many.[130] His own biographer, Edwin Hodder, goes into detail about Shaftesbury's convictions:

> Shaftesbury ... never had a shadow of doubt that the Jews were to return to their own land, that the Scriptures were to be literally fulfilled, and that the time was at hand. ... His study of the prophetic scriptures led him to associate the return of the Jews with the Second Advent of our Lord and this was the hope that animated every other.[131]

Hodder describes Shaftesbury's relationship with his stepfather-in-law and his desire to associate Palmerston with his own spiritual mission. In a letter, dated 25 September, 1840, Shaftesbury wrote to Palmerston of the: "desire and expectation entertained by the Hebrew race of their return ultimately to the land of their fathers."[132] As though to appeal to the strategic and financial implications, rather than those of idealism or religion, Shaftesbury went on: "The cheapest and safest mode of supplying the wastes of those depopulated regions ... disconnected as they are from all the peoples of the earth, they would appeal to no national or political sympathies for assistance in the path of wrong."[133] Such a statement was to sound strange for many in the following century.

Barbara Tuchman, the historian, gives further details, referring to Palmerston's initiative with his Ambassador to Constantinople on 11 August, 1840, to suggest to the Sultan that Jews be encouraged to return to Palestine.[134] The Editorial/Leaders columns of *The Times* of 17 August, 1840 covered the issue of the return of the Jews in some detail:

> And there are, we feel assured, none who will not rejoice if, in co-operation with the advancing spirit of government and society in the East, they should again raise, in the ancient seats alike of their glory and of their humiliation, a breastwork against the further encroachment of lawless tyranny and of social degeneracy.[135]

The article continues and refers to Shaftesbury:

> A noble lord who has given attention to this matter and ... 'in the belief of an approaching restoration of the Jewish polity, and that no lasting solution of the eastern crisis can be expected till this takes place.' ... It is for the Christian philanthropists and enlightened statesmen of Europe to consider whether this remarkable people does not present materials which, when collected and brought into fusion under national institutions, might not be advantageously employed for the interests of the civilisations in the East.[136]

Tuchman makes two significant points which indicate that Shaftesbury was a child of his time and entrenched in the evangelical tradition of interpretation of the time. One was his belief in the literal understanding of the Bible as the inerrant Word of God. The other was his belief in the Second Coming of Christ, for which the Return of the Jews was the pre-eminent condition. In the period following so soon after the Evangelical Revival, the literal view of Scripture was widely known and accepted by the large, church-going public.[137] There was no known alternative position to be considered until the advent of the school of Higher Criticism.

The Growth Of Political Influence

The involvement of Shaftesbury and Palmerston, was to be of significant influence over the years.[138] Tibawi writes: "Shaftesbury's belief, founded upon a study of the prophecies in the Scriptures, was that 'everything seems ripe for their [the Jews] return to Palestine', this return being seen in a Christian missionary, not a Jewish national sense."[139] Earlier, in 1837, following a previous initiative in 1834 by John Farran, the British Consul in Damascus, Palmerston decided to go ahead and create a vice-consulate in Jerusalem. This move was to have immense political significance because it raised the profiles of both the CMJ and the Jewish people in the eyes of the government and the public. Although Lewis designates him as the British Consul General in Syria and stationed in Damascus, he acknowledges: "Virtually nothing is known of John William Perry Farran whose name does not appear on the first *Foreign Office List,* published in 1852."[140] In 1837, William Tanner Young was appointed as Vice-Consul and took up his post in 1838, which was extended in 1839, under the instructions of Palmerston, to include responsibility for Jews.[141] The international consequences were rapid as, within five years, Prussia, France, and the United States established consulates, followed by Austria in 1849.[142] The influence of LJS had reached unintentional, but significant, international proportions.

As early as 14 March, 1839, Young: "... advocates the scheme of the LJS for a Protestant church."[143] This despatch concluded with a reference to those whose views Young felt were entitled to consideration: "The one is the Jew unto whom God originally gave this land for a possession, and the other the Protestant Christian, his legitimate offspring." [144] Clearly, the new Vice-Consul was prepared to be proactive, rather than passive in his work, so that the position was influential and not a sinecure.

Young did not originate the idea of a church in Jerusalem because Nicolayson saw it as one of his early priorities. In 1835, he presented to the Society the concept that such an explicitly religious resource was essential to the work and worship of the Society.[145] At the time, the impasse, due to the Islamic law that prohibited such a project, included the principle that a foreigner could neither own property nor construct buildings. This meant that the initiative had to wait until political influence could be brought to bear. Rather than wait altogether, Nicolayson pursued his visionary task in the quest for suitable land. He and the Rev. William Lewis, who was stationed at Smyrna, worked together in 1836 on ideas for the church. Lewis encouraged Nicolayson, emphasising the need for a cleric to conduct the services on a regular basis. At the twenty-ninth Annual General Meeting, on 5 May, 1837, approval was given in London for the building of a Hebrew church in Jerusalem, namely, Christ Church.

The Vice-Consul, William Young, gave encouragement for the construction of the building but the Consul-General, Patrick Campbell, was sensitive to the need not to antagonise the authorities.[146] New places of worship were not permitted for either Christians or Jews. Nicolayson was more of a free agent than the Vice-Consul, who had to work within the restrictions of his diplomatic role. He was therefore free to go about his business in an unorthodox manner, simply by renting a house and conducting services in one of its rooms. He went further by purchasing land and disused houses, not in his name but in that of a go-between, until it was transferred to the LJS.[147] The building work went ahead, despite official local opposition, and the digging of the foundations began in December, 1839. [148]

In the course of this activity, Nicolayson also saw the need for a hospital, largely because of the year-long plague in Jerusalem between 1838 and 1839. Perry, taking from Nicolayson's journal,[149] records that in 1838, Nicolayson was to write to the Society for such a project, in the context of: "... the claims of Abraham's descendants in Jerusalem." Internationally, there were tensions in Europe because of the Turkish-Egyptian conflict between 1838 and 1840, which, temporarily, limited the horizons for development, even of a medical facility. When the hostilities ended, the international and ecclesiastical processes involved in the bishopric took pre-eminence over the hospital until the arrival of Bishop Alexander in 1842.

The Ecclesiastical Development – The Bishopric

The political and diplomatic structure of a British Vice-Consulate within the

Ottoman jurisdiction had been accomplished in 1837 and the next development was one of a bishopric in Jerusalem. Geoffrey Finlayson[150] points to the influence of Shaftesbury in the project, not least because of his close relationship with Chevalier Bunsen, the man chosen by the Prussian monarch as envoy to bring the project to fruition. The King of Prussia, Frederick William IV, was the brother of the Emperor of Germany and obviously had great influence. He instructed his envoy, Bunsen, to take the place: "By the side of the primitive church of the East and in the presence of the Roman church."[151] Throughout the hiatus of the hostilities between Turkey and Egypt, during which all Europeans left Jerusalem, Nicolayson remained in place. Negotiations had been taking place in London, with Shaftesbury acting "as an intermediary with the Archbishop of Canterbury, with Palmerston and with Peel, the new Prime Minister."[152]

Finlayson pointed out that Palmerston's interests included the strategic advantages of such an appointment, which would add to the political and economic effects of the vice-consulate. The historian, Henry Smith, described some of the events that led to the Act of Parliament on 9 December, 1841, that brought about the joint Anglo-Prussian bishopric.[153] Palmerston, Shaftesbury and Bunsen agreed that the first Bishop should be a former rabbi, the Rev. Professor Michael Solomon Alexander of King's College, London, after it had been declined by Professor Alexander McCaul.[154] Despite the opposition of the High Church party, the Oxford Movement,[155] a protestant evangelical was appointed to the bishopric. In a rapid series of events, a British Vice-Consulate had been established, a church was planned and an Anglican Bishop appointed, although yet to be consecrated. The move had signs of being not only ecclesiastical but political. The fact that a Bishop of the Church of England had been appointed, despite having neither a church, nor a cathedral, nor a diocese, added to the status of LJS, as well as its work among the Jews. It was also to lead to similar moves by European heads of state to take a greater interest in their churches in the region. Bishops from national churches might well be able to communicate with each other, unofficially and in privacy, over matters of state on behalf of their states.

The CMJ Archives record the permission given eventually to build the church in Jerusalem: "The Ottoman Porte has officially promised the English Ambassador that the Turkish authorities at Jerusalem are to be instructed forthwith not to oppose the erection of a church on Mount Zion in any way."[156] This was followed by the appointment of the "Bishops of the Church of St. James at Jerusalem," noting the involvement of Palmerston and King Frederick William IV of Prussia. The CMJ records show that at his consecration, Bishop Michael Solomon Alexander said: "What the friends of Israel longed, and prayed, and laboured for, was not simply the conversion of a few individuals, but the resuscitation of the Jewish people, the resurrection of the Jewish church."[157] Professor Ronald Clements argues that, for the Society, the appointment of the Bishop was strategically important in terms of their larger task of conversion of Jews and their involvement in a world-wide mission.[158] Against a backcloth of suspicion by the Orthodox and Catholics and, especially, the target group, the Jews, little was directly achieved in terms of converts however.

When the Bishop eventually arrived in Jerusalem in 1842, he brought Dr. Edward McGowan with him to establish medical work and a hospital.[159] A medical project had previously been started in December, 1838, but only lasted for just over a year because of personality clashes between the doctor, Albert Gerstmann, and Nicolayson.[160] In his first report of 26 February, 1842,[161] McGowan referred to the poor conditions for both patients and practice, with a dilapidated house and an under-equipped, dangerous building in which to do their work. He described his vulnerable team as: "our little community." In his conclusion, he said, "I believe it to be the most effectual preparation for preaching the gospel with success." He immediately embarked on plans to obtain a suitable property and to build a hospital. Lewis writes, "In December, 1844 the LJS opened a twelve-bed hospital in Jerusalem"[162] which was in a rented building. Lewis also writes about the opposition from the rabbis, fearing the ulterior motives of the evangelicals, but for the people it was the only Western medical assistance in Palestine.

McGowan knew that there would be difficulties and so it proved. He communicated with the Society, sharing the difficulties and tensions created by the hospital, the result of which divided the Jewish community.[163] Kelvin Crombie writes that, after the death of a Jewish patient, the Chief Rabbi issued an ultimatum that Dr. McGowan should exclude all present and future Jewish patients and staff from the hospital. Following the disagreement over the burial of a Jewish patient, the Jews published a "cherem," or excommunication, for anyone using the hospital. The Jews immediately left the hospital, but two weeks later began to return. This human oscillation of patient arrival and return continued because the needs of the people were immense.[164] The medical situation in Jerusalem was about to change, however.

A Jewish hospital began its work the following year. The Rothschild family and Sir Moses Montefiore contributed funds to bring this about, acts which gratified the missionaries that human need was being met.[165] The issue for the LJS and the hospital became one of finding a working strategy that would achieve both their aims of evangelism and providing quality medical care. Although there was criticism of its methods, the LJS had a biblical justification for its medical work,[166] and one that was historical in relation to the wider concerns of Frey in 1808 for the physical needs of the Jews of East London. Nonetheless, the Jews, and others, remained suspicious of the motives of the medical work of the mission. From the position of the local inhabitants, their lot improved through the LJS initiative, because medical resources were made available where none had been before.

The strategic influence of Palmerston and Shaftesbury was significant in the development of the LJS. The Jewish historian, Alex Carmel, writes that the religious missionaries and politicians found favour with the English authorities: "The political context of Palestine in the 1830s facilitated the marriage of British religious sentiments and strategic interests."[167] Palmerston, especially, saw the political, military and economic advantages of the return of the Jews.[168] Having already given instructions for the expansion of the British Consulate to protect the Jews in 1839, Palmerston is seen by Carmel as having opened the consulate in Jerusalem for political motives. "He soon perceived that the Jewish factor was likely to serve British interests as well."[169] He describes the mixed motives: "The initiatives of Palmerston were inspired by a desire to help solve the Jewish problem, strengthen the Ottoman Empire economically and to provide England with a friendly community in Palestine."[170] Hence, in 1840, the British supported the Ottomans in overcoming the Egyptian forces. In 1841, the Anglo-Prussian Bishopric was established in Jerusalem with the LJS to the fore. Carmel, writing with the benefit of hindsight, describes the establishment of the religious/political bishopric and its post-1840 development that went ahead, despite the failure of its primary task to convert the Jews. "As for the Protestant mission to the Jews in Palestine, it had failed lamentably in spite of the enormous expenditure involved, and those missions directed to the Arabs had become the most active."[171]

Structural Faults And Achievements In The Enterprise

After the immense amount of work that went into the appointment of the Bishop, Alexander's contribution was a disappointment for many because of the lack of converts from the Jewish community. Alexander had to adjust to his role as Bishop, which was altogether different from his previous position as Professor of Hebrew Studies at King's College, London. As a converted Rabbi, the Jewish community would have looked on him with suspicion and disfavour. His task was to be more than the evangelist to the Jews and to engage in a series of relationships with his political, diplomatic and religious peers on an international stage. This would test the most able of people and Alexander had had a different professional background, more related to religion and academia. Unfortunately, he failed to create relationships with the representatives of the Orthodox communions, who had been present in the land for centuries, and whose culture and churchmanship were very different from his own as a Protestant evangelical.

For Bishop Alexander to have success in his work, he needed the resources of an informed, competent, experienced and supportive body. Despite its enthusiasm and encouragement, the LJS committee had little hands-on experience of the Middle East and the conditions that prevailed, both physically and in terms of relationships with the local population. Few are known to have ventured beyond Europe, or knew anything about the cultures and the ways of life of the people they intended to convert. They had little way of knowing if the person they appointed was either trained, or equipped, for the task they had in mind and the complexities of his position. He was appointed and the committee members would wait for the results with some serious expectation of success.

Alexander arrived in Jerusalem in January, 1842 and, despite high expectations, his bishopric was to last for only three years. One of Alexander's primary, formal relationships would have been with Hugh Rose, the British Consul

General in Beirut, who was his main intermediary with the Ottoman authorities. The delicate issue of the building of Christ Church in Jerusalem had reached an impasse, and was a matter of immediate concern. The mission had moved ahead with the building of its foundations, without formal, written approval by means of a "firman" or licence, as distinct from a series of word-of-mouth reports.[172] The status of the Bishop was paradoxical because, although possibly personally respected in some quarters, Alexander was not seen as head of a "millet." This legal word was used to describe a community that was free to organise itself, but its leader was accountable to the Turkish authorities for their behaviour. The Bishop had to familiarise himself with the situation for which he had neither the experience, nor the expertise. Meanwhile the Consul could not support the Bishop in building work without the required "firman," or licence.

The situation of the Bishop deteriorated during his first autumn in the post when he fell out with the Vice-Consul, the Russian Consulate, and the local Jewish community. One complicated situation arose when three fugitive Russian Jews received sanctuary from a member of Alexander's missionary staff, offering themselves as prospective converts.[173] The Russian Consul demanded that they should be placed under his jurisdiction for trial and, when asked by the British Vice-Consul, William Young, to comply, the Bishop refused. This led to alienation between the Bishop and the Consul and, although the Bishop eventually gave way, the disruption in the relationship became severe. Similarly, the Jewish leaders were angry at such high-handedness and once more issued a "cherem" to all Jews who had any kind of contact with the mission. Despite the best of intentions by the Bishop, he was showing insensitivity and lack of understanding toward the due processes of diplomacy and law, as well as international relationships and inter-religious harmony. The intended creative relationship between the Bishop, the Consulate, and the Jewish people was mortally wounded and never recovered.

When a suitable time had elapsed, the Consul General moved again in 1843 to deal with the unfinished business of Christ Church.[174] Hugh Rose saw the issue in terms of international prestige and, accordingly, the British Ambassador, Stratford Canning, again pressed the Ottoman Porte in Constantinople to grant the "firman." It took until September, 1845 before the Sultan agreed to it, but there were to be even further delays. Smith refers to its passage through the obstacles until 4 October, 1845,[175] when, after the death of Alexander in November, 1845, the local Governor of Jerusalem finally allowed its implementation. The Bishop was not alive to see the agreement, nor the completion and consecration of Christ Church, which took place on 21 January, 1849.

Despite the immense problems that Bishop Alexander confronted, or created himself, during his brief episcopacy, there was also a legacy of accomplishments, which Lewis has noted.[176] Within the work of the mission, he was able to flourish in a brief period of three years by establishing a number of small projects. He set up a "Hebrew College," intended for the education and training of future converts, as well as a "House of Industry" to house and gainfully employ other converts in various trades. As a means of filtering new converts for what might suit them most, he established the "Enquirers Home," which provided residential accommodation, during which time their abilities could be discovered and monitored. These were not innovations because they had been introduced in the time of Frey at Palestine Place in London. They were important projects for an evangelical organisation nonetheless. It recognised the familial and social limitations on new converts who might well be ostracised by the local Jewish community and would need practical assistance, as Frey had understood.

Probably his most lasting achievement was the drive he provided to advance the hospital with Doctor McGowan and the unfailing, if insensitive, support he gave to Nicolayson in the quest to build Christ Church. As it still stands and functions as a working church and LJS centre, it is a monument to the man, who was both flawed and faithful to LJS.

The Development Into The Arab Community

The death of Bishop Michael Solomon Alexander in 1845 meant a change in the joint British-Prussian bishopric. This brought to Jerusalem the Prussian, Samuel Gobat, whose primary interest included the needs of the Arabs as well as the Jews. His appointment came from the nomination of the King of Prussia, the blessing of the LJS and the Archbishop of Canterbury, and his consecration took place on 5 July, 1846.[177] In the same period, there was a change in the consular leadership, William Young being replaced by James Finn.

The appointments of Samuel Gobat as Bishop and James Finn as Consul brought about another watershed in the work of CMJ. Things were to change from the earlier appointments of the original Bishop, Alexander, and the Consul, Young. Crombie writes: "The activities of Finn and Gobat, both of whom were closely associated with Christ Church, drastically affected both the Jewish and Arab communities in Eretz Israel."[178] The new Bishop, although appointed by LJS, was also focused on the Arab community. Finn, the new Consul, was a member of the LJS committee and threw his weight behind the work of the Society when he arrived in 1846. Perry notes that, after the change of leading personnel, the work of the Society became less effective and the cause was: "... probably the growing detachment of the London Society from the bishopric which began after the appointment of the second Bishop." [179]

When Gobat was appointed Bishop in 1846, the LJS had certain expectations of him,[180] not least because he accepted the position of its vice-patron and it was assumed that he would support the Society. Lord Shaftesbury thought highly of Gobat but it is recorded by Hodder that he expressed some disappointment because: "The bishopric did not answer the expectation formed of it."[181] On 21 October, 1846, Gobat wrote about his intentions, which included references to the conversion of the Jews, extracts of which were printed by the Society.[182] Nicolayson writes at length, and with enthusiasm, about the Bishop's arrival in Jerusalem.[183] It came to be seen that his own personal brief was one that was not limited to Jews but more expansive and unrestricted. In the Bishop's Annual Letter of January, 1848, he commented that since 1839, 31 Jews had been baptised and 26 of their children. He wrote: "It is a small number indeed."[184] In contrast, the biographer, John Pollock, in comparing Gobat's Arab interests with Shaftesbury's Jewish fascination, describes Gobat as: "a nonentity ... of little consequence ... But 'Lord Shaftesbury's vision' is enshrined in Israeli history as having inspired the first steps towards the return of Jews to Palestine."[185]

Quite differently, Perry points to the development of Christian education work within the Arab Muslim community, which led to the entry of the Church Missionary Society, with which Gobat had once worked.[186] Gobat is seen to have successfully encouraged the network of wider educational establishments to include the Arab population which included members of the other Christian denominations, namely the Greek and Russian Orthodox constituencies. Having previously worked for the Church Missionary Society, on his retirement he entrusted the educational work among Arabs, including almost 50 schools, to that Society. In contrast to the work of LJS, the work among the Arabs resulted in educational and medical resources throughout the country.[187] Apart from Pollock, Gobat can be seen to be an early ecumenical leader well before his time, but those with a more restricted perspective did not willingly embrace his initiatives.

Conclusion – The Influence of the London Society for The Promotion Of Christianity Amongst the Jews

By the time of the untimely death of Bishop Alexander in 1845, three strategic foundations had been laid by the Society. One was the fact that through the bishopric, the Society was formally part of the structure of the Church of England. The second was that it had diplomatic recognition and support from the Consulate. Third, that it had ongoing, consistent, political support from Lord Shaftesbury and his evangelical associates for the foreseeable future. In addition, it had substantial public support. These combined resources were to have an impact when the Zionist movement began towards the end of the 19th century. This influence continued apace in the 20th century as political leaders, who were cognisant of the Biblical and ecclesiastical ramifications, were able to be supportive to the Jewish drives for their secure, independent statehood in Israel. The groundwork of the LJS had produced the kind of base which would facilitate the move towards the Balfour Declaration of 1917.

It was a long journey from the earliest steps, which can be seen to stem from the translation of the Bible, from the Latin Vulgate into English in 1382, so that the stories in the Bible were available to be read by ordinary people. Afterwards, the Authorised Version of the Bible became available in 1611. Over a very long period, a significant portion of the British public had thereby acquired knowledge about the Jews, as well as sympathy for them. This continued throughout the following centuries. The Society struggled to find its mission strategy and ways of fulfilling its sense of divine call. Personality clashes, coupled with financial misdemeanours, poor accounting, to say nothing of the religious urgings of others, have all been mentioned in this chapter so far. Leadership of quality and good management skills seemed to have been less important than theological rectitude. Thus, it was inevitable that the early years would be difficult until it had leadership of ability, vision and tenacity.

In this chapter, it is seen that the work of LJS had an influence on the British public by creating a perception of the people and land of Israel as possessing a divine inheritance in which Christians were involved with responsibility for achieving its fulfilment. Leading preachers like Bicheno, Simeon, Scott, the Rt. Rev. George Horne, the Bishop of Norwich, Fuller, as well as leading laymen and nobles, including the Duke of Kent, William Wilberforce and Lord Shaftesbury supported the society. This understanding was to have profound implications in preparing a substantial pro-Jewish mindset for many in the churches as well as those outside. There were a number of steps in that process, at first not apparent in the early years but, with hindsight, a progression can now be more easily perceived. Moving from Frey, in 1801, to the founding of the LSPCAJ in 1809, becoming an Anglican society in 1815, the move to Palestine thereafter, until the arrival of Nicolayson in Jerusalem in 1833, marked a number of significant steps. The next twelve years were to be marked by the political connections, in the form of the vice-consulate in 1838, followed soon after by the establishment of the Anglican Bishopric in 1841. In England and Palestine, the work was acknowledged, developed, and supported by the establishment. Much of Europe knew of its expansion and responded to it, while at home in the UK, the LJS was widely known and acknowledged. By 1845, it had gathered sufficient support in strategic places of influence, including finance, politics, diplomacy and the Church of England to create a position of power and prestige through its Bishopric and Consul.

Its primary task of evangelism and the conversion of Jews had not been so impressive. Although many people of note and influence, as well as dedication, had supported it, little had been achieved in terms of conversions. Its target group of Jews was hostile to Christians, organised against them and rigorously controlled. This was to lessen somewhat in 1825 in the time of William Lewis and again in 1838, when the medical missionaries tended the Jewish sick during an outbreak of plague. However, that lessening did not endure and the rabbis were largely aware of the ulterior, evangelical drives of the LJS. When the hospital was built, although Jews used the facilities and were treated by the medical staff, official rabbinic instructions were to come and be enforced.

It is seen that many of the achievements of CMJ are consonant with the objectives of Gush Emunim, which are seen as focused on the land and the Jews, in order to allow for the coming of the Messiah. The evangelical society was, unwittingly, a forerunner for its own religious ideological movement. It created a Christian support base, which assisted in publicising the Jewish predicament and gathering sympathy and support for their restoration to Israel. For Theodore

Herzl, there was a prepared, organised and powerful organisation to reinforce his efforts, long before he commenced his work for a Jewish state. Although he would have viewed them as heretical, Rabbi Abraham Kook would have been mindful of its achievements, from which he would benefit. Similarly, religious Zionists still appreciate the activities of the Christian Right, of which the Society, now CMJ, is perceived by some to be a part. It can be seen in this chapter that, without LJS, the work of Herzl, Kook and many others would have had to begin in barren land, rather than the fertile terrain created by the evangelicals in the previous century.

Jewish writers have paid tribute to the work of the LJS and acknowledge with appreciation, the influence it had in the long term for the development of Israel. Perry gives his view of the latter part of the nineteenth century as a time when the Society grew immensely, despite the few small numbers of Jewish converts. He writes:

> The meteoric rise of the London Society in its first decades was made possible by ... their belief that the return of the Jews to the land of Israel and their conversion to Christianity, followed by the millennium and the second coming of the Messiah was closer than ever ... [and with] sweeping popular support ... touched higher echelons of society [and] which became a leading factor in the process of transforming the land of Israel from a forsaken desert land ... into a regenerating, repopulated country by its end.[188]

The Society's aim to promote Christianity among the Jews was hardly achieved, according to Perry, but it did highlight and expand the development of interest in, and knowledge of, the Holy Land. He sees that its work contributed to development and progress in Israel. Indeed, in the final sentence of his book, he opines: "If nothing else, then for this alone, the land of Israel is greatly indebted to the London Society for Promoting Christianity Amongst the Jews." [189]

In similar vein, the diplomat, Michael Pragai, writes: "Long before the emergence of a Jewish movement for the Return – the Zionist movement at the end of the nineteenth century – Christian belief in and support of the Return was evident."[190] The appreciation by the English of the Biblical accounts had a connecting link with those who were working towards the Balfour Declaration of 1917 and thereafter. As she traces the influence of the Biblical tradition in the life of England, Barbara Tuchman discerns political and economic connections between Cromwell and the Jews in 1656, and between David Lloyd George and Chaim Weizmann in World War I.[191] Those connections meant that, through the Balfour Declaration in 1917, the Jews were able to return to what they saw as their ancient land, promised to Abraham.

The decision of the United Nations in 1947 to partition land that was not its own, in order to provide Jews with the State of Israel in their former Biblical land, can be seen to be part of that continuum. The conversion of the Jews to Christianity has been minimal. Despite that, the Society remains optimistic about the Second Advent of Jesus Christ, which it believes will accord with the coming of the Messiah. Although having no formal connection with Gush Emunim, the

CMJ leadership in 2008 then viewed the creation and expansion of settlements in the West Bank as a positive process. Nonetheless, there are different philosophies and theological positions, which separate them, despite also having similar interests and goals.[192] David Goldberg states: "The two millennia, and more, of Diaspora history that separate ancient from modern Israel are lightly skated over, like an unfortunate interlude between past and present ownership of the territory promised to Abraham."[193] It is possible that Gush Emunim could have a view of CMJ doing much of the preparatory work for the Messiah and, as such, is a version of "Messiah's Donkey," because it facilitates the coming of the Messiah.[194]

It was not to be known by either organisation that their work of returning the Jews would spawn perceived terrorism as they established occupation and control of the land.

In conversations with some of those connected to CMJ, there is satisfaction that their history played a pivotal part in the creation of a substantial political and ecclesiastical bloc which resulted in the Balfour Declaration. This was to lead to the establishment of the State of Israel and they look and work for its culmination by the Return of Jesus Christ and the coming Messiah. If they are correct, and unless there are serious, alternative interpretations, after this there will be the judgement of God and the slaughter of the majority of the population of the world! Can this really be held to be the case?

It is appropriate, therefore, that this chapter moves on in Chapter 4 to examine the Biblical Covenants, which underlay the ideological processes of Gush Emunim and Church's Ministry Among Jewish People.

Notes

[1] It began its mission as part of the London Missionary Society. LMS in 1801 and was known as the London Jews Society. LJS before becoming both The London Society for Promoting Christianity Among the Jews. LSPCAJ in 1809, and, sometimes, The London Society for the Promotion of Christianity Amongst the Jews. It was regularly referred to as LJS for many years and is more often used in this chapter, unless the context requires a more clear designation as LSPCAJ. After World War I, it became known as "Church's Mission to the Jews," and was further renamed "Church's Ministry Among Jewish People" CMJ.

[2] Idinopulos, T. A., *Weathered by Miracles* (Chicago: Ivan R. Dee, 1998), 58ff.

[3] Idinopolus, 64-66.

[4] Idinopulos, 69-70.

[5] Karmi G., *Married to Another Man* (London: Pluto, 2007), 105.

[6] The names, Abram and Abraham, were used by different sources, with separate emphases, for the same person.

[7] Goldberg D. J., *The Divided Self* (London: I. B. Tauris, 2006), 12. Goldberg was Chief Rabbi at the Liberal Jewish Synagogue in London.

[8] Christopher Hill 'Till the conversion of the Jews' in *Millenarianism and Messianism in English Literature and Thought 1650-1800,* Clark Library Lectures, ed. by Richard H. Popkin 1981-82 (Leiden – New York: E. J. Brill 1988), 12-36. Senate House 7th floor PCW-MIL.

[9] Perry Y. *British Mission to the Jews in Nineteenth Century Palestine* (London: Frank Cass, 2003), 2-3.

[10] Pragai Michael J., *Faith and Fulfilment* (London: Vallentine, Mitchell & Co. Ltd, 1985).

[11] Pragai, 4.

[12] Goldberg, 17.

[13] Stunt T., *From Awakening to Secession* (Edinburgh: T. & T. Clark 2000), 18.

[14] Stunt, 21.

[15] Stunt, 22.

[16] Bicheno James *The Signs of the Times in Three Parts* (London: 1799. Senate House, London), Eighteenth Century Collections On Line Gale Group.

[17] Bicheno, vi.

[18] Bicheno James, *The restoration of the Jews, the crisis of all nations, or an arrangement of scripture prophecies which relate to the restoration of the Jews* (London: Bye & Law 1800). Also in the British Library in "Tracts on Prophecy" printed on the spine but inside it is entitled, *The Illuminator or "Looking glass of the times,"* being a selection of wonderful predictions and prophecies, past, present and to come from the following distinguished persons...to which is added a recent prediction of a celebrated preacher" which refers to Bicheno (Published by London: J. Moxon, no year given).

[19] Bicheno, 2-10.

[20] Jewish Repository 1815, Report, 7ff, 48ff, 90ff, 128ff, 174ff, 216ff.

[21] Lewis D. M. *Lord Shaftesbury and the Rise of Christian Zionism.* Unpublished – presently contained in manuscript form by the Rev. Geoffrey Whitfield, prior to proposed publication by CUP. In 2009, it is intended to be published under an amended title, *The Origins of Christian Zionism: Lord Shaftesbury and Evangelical Support for a Jewish Homeland.*

[22] Charles Jerram *An Essay tending to show the grounds contained in Scripture expecting a future restoration of the Jews.* (Cambridge, 1796).

[23] Lewis, 43.

[24] Lewis, 44.

[25] Scott T., 'The Jews a blessing to the nations, and Christians bound to seek their conversion to the Saviour' in *Sermons 1804-1808* (Leeds: George Wilson. No date given). British Library. Inside, the general title is given as, "The Importance of Christian Ministry" and contains a number of sermons by different preachers. Scott, Sermon Number 10.

[26] Preached at St. Lawrence Jewry, King St., Cheapside, London, 13 June, but no year mentioned but publisher given as. London: F. Thorogood 1810. Date of sermon was probably between 1804 and 1808 and published with the others in 1810. The practice of the publisher seems to have been to collect a number of sermons from popular preachers and then to put them together–this explains why the sequence of page numbers is restricted to each sermon and does not carry through numerically from the beginning to the end of the book. Hence, Scott's sermon is given as number 10 but had its own page numbering from 1-39.

[27] Scott, 2-3.

[28] Scott, 18-21.

[29] R. Lovett. *The History of the London Missionary Society, 1795-1895, Volumes I & II* (London: Henry Frowde 1899). SOAS Special Collections.

[30] Lovett, Vol. I., 4. William Carey. "Enquiry into the obligation of Christians to use means for the conversion of the heathen."

[31] Lovett, 4.

³² London Missionary Society Annual Reports, 1799-1801, 78. SOAS Special Collections.

³³ CMJ Archives in London Missionary Society Collection, held in SOAS Special Collections. Box number CWM/LMS Europe Mission to the Jews, Box 1. One box only.

³⁴ Lovett, 196.

³⁵ Lovett, 96.

³⁶ R. Lovett. *The History of the London Missionary Society, 1795-1895, Volumes I & II* (London: Henry Frowde 1899. Vol. 1., 3-42).

³⁷ London Missionary Society Annual Reports 1805-1807, 69. SOAS Special Collections.

³⁸ London Missionary Society Annual Reports 1805-1807, 72.

³⁹ London Missionary Society Annual Reports 1805-1807, 75.

⁴⁰ Lovett, 97, soon to become the "Jewish Auxiliary Committee."

⁴¹ Lovett, 97.

⁴² Lovett, 97.

⁴³ CMJ Archives within LMS Archives. Folder 2. SOAS Special Collections.

⁴⁴ General Committee Minute Book 1808-1810. CMJ Archives, Bodleian Library. Shelf mark/call number Dep. CMJ c.5. Also contained in, *Report of the Committee to the Second Half Year Meeting of the London Society for the Promotion of Christianity Amongst the Jews.1810, 29.* CMJ Library, St. Albans.

⁴⁵ This information is also found in bound form in the CMJ Archives, Folder 5. SOAS Special Collections.

⁴⁶ General Committee Minute Book 1808-1810.CMJ Archives, Bodleian Library. Shelfmark/call number Dep. CMJ c.5.

⁴⁷ CMJ archives within LMS Archives. Folder 2. SOAS Special Collections.

⁴⁸ R. Lovett. *The History of the London Missionary Society, 1795-1895, Volumes I & II.* London: Henry Frowde 1899. Vol. 97. SOAS Special Collections.

⁴⁹ Lovett, 97-98. Also CMJ Archives within LMS Archives, SOAS Special Collections, Folder 4, 28 November, 1808.

⁵⁰ Lovett, 98.

⁵¹ Box marked "CMJ Mission to Jews London" within LMS Archives. Folder 2. SOAS Special Collections. NB. It needs to be noted that the papers are used by different people. It was discovered that, in between visits by the writer, papers that were originally in one folder were moved into other folders. The staff of the Archives was informed on 12 April, 2008.

⁵² CMJ Archives within LMS Archives. Folder 5. SOAS Special Collections. These are two small documents, one of four sheets and the other more expansive of the same material on six double-sided sheets, bound with cotton, between blue covers.

⁵³ CMJ Archives within LMS Archives. Folder 2. SOAS Special Collections.

⁵⁴ The London Jews Society, or the LJS, was an abbreviation of The London Society for the Promoting of Christianity Among the Jews (LSPCAJ), formed in 1809 as a separate society to the LMS. It was also known as the London Society for the Promotion of Christianity Amongst the Jews.

⁵⁵ *Report of the Committee to the First Half-Yearly Meeting of the London Society for the Promoting of Christianity Among the Jews 23 May, 1809-1814*, 1. CMJ Archives, St. Albans.

⁵⁶ *Report of the Committee to the Second Half-Yearly Meeting of the London Society for the Promotion of Christianity Amongst the Jews 27 December, 1809-1810*, 29ff. CMJ Archives, St. Albans.

[57] *Report of the Committee to the Second Half-Yearly meeting of the London Society for the Promotion of Christianity Amongst the Jews*, 29-30.
[58] *Report of the Committee to the Second Half-Yearly meeting of the London Society for the Promotion of Christianity Amongst the Jews*, 7.
[59] CMJ Archives within LMS Archives. Folder 3. SOAS Special Collections.
[60] CMJ Archives within LMS Archives. Folder 5. SOAS Special Collections.
[61] CMJ Archives within LMS Archives. Folder 5. SOAS Special Collections.
[62] *Second Half-Yearly Report for the London Society for the Promotion of Christianity Amongst the Jews LSPCAJ, 27 December, 1809-1810,,* 5. CMJ Archives, St. Albans.
[63] *LSPCAJ*, 6-7.
[64] *LSPCAJ*, 26.
[65] *Third Report to the Committee of the London Society for the Promotion of Christianity Amongst the Jews LSPCAJ, 6 June, 1811*. CMJ Archives, St. Albans.
[66] *Fourth Report of the Committee of 21 May, 1812*, 3-5. CMJ Archives, St. Albans.
[67] Gidney W. T. *The History of the London Society for the Promotion of Christianity Amongst the Jews from 1809 to 1908*. London: LSPCAJ, 1908., 416-417. This book is to be found in the SOAS Special Collections and CMJ Library, St. Albans.
[68] The Jewish Repository was the monthly communication regarding the Jews and the proceedings of the London Society. CMJ Archives, St. Albans
[69] Jewish Repository, Vol. II, 6 May, 1814, 210ff. CMJ Archives, St. Albans.
[70] Jewish Repository, 210.
[71] Jewish Repository, 211.
[72] Simeon C., *Horae Homileticae Volume No. 10.* London Holdsworth & Ball, 1832, 240.
[73] Pollard A. 'The Influence and Significance of Simeon's Work', in *Charles Simeon, 1759-1836,* eds. Arthur Pollard & Michael Hennells. London SPCK, 1964, 180-181, 184.
[74] Carus, W., ed., *Memoirs of the Life of the Rev. Charles Simeon*. London: Hatchard & Son 1847.
[75] Carus, 405 ff.
[76] Carus, 514.
[77] The Jewish Repository Vol. II, January 1814., 321. CMJ Archives St. Albans.
[78] The Jewish Repository Vol. II, 321-322.
[79] The Jewish Repository Vol. II, 368
[80] The Jewish Repository Vol. II, 474-480.
[81] Tibawi, A. L. *British Interests in Palestine 1800-1901*. London: OUP, 1962, 6.
[82] Gidney, 35ff.
[83] Gidney, W. T. *The History of the London Society for the Promotion of Christianity Amongst the Jews from 1809 to 1908*. London: LSPCAJ, 1908, 416-419. SOAS Special Collections and CMJ, St. Albans.
[84] *The General Committee Minutes of the London Society, February 1815-December 1816* CMJ Archives, the Bodleian Library Oxford. Shelfmark/call number Dep. CMJ c.7.
[85] Perry Endnotes, 44-45. Perry makes reference to Frey, who moved to America with reports about his misbehaviour in London before his departure. It is not the intention to follow these accusations in this thesis, as they are not relevant.
[86] London Society Annual Reports 1815-1819, *Seventh Report of the Committee of the London Society for the Promotion of Christianity Amongst the Jews*. Sir Thomas Baring MP is described as President.
[87] Gidney, 47. Smith H., *The Jerusalem Bishopric* (London: Wertheim, 1847), 136-137.

[88] Sizer S. *Christian Zionism* (London: IVP, 2004), 35.
[89] Carus W., ed., *Memoirs of the Life of the Rev. Charles Simeon* (London: Hatchard & Son 1847). 514.
[90] G. S. Faber, *The Sacred Calendar of Prophecy*, 3 Vols. 1828 (London: C. & J. Rivington 1828 British Library) Vol. I, 253ff.
[91] Faber, 265.
[92] Faber, 275.
[93] Faber, 480-484.
[94] Ezekiel 39. 9-16.
[95] Faber, 480.
[96] Tibawi A. L. *British Interests in Palestine 1800-1901* (London: OUP, 1962), 6-7.
[97] *The Jewish Repository and Monthly Communication respecting Jews and the London Society 1814*, 119. CMJ Archives, St. Albans.
[98] The Jewish Expositor Vol. II. 1817, 76-79. CMJ Archives St. Albans.
[99] Tibawi, 8-12.
[100] Perry Endnotes, 44-45, Nos. 11, 17 and 19.
[101] Perry Endnotes, 44, No. 11.
[102] Perry Endnotes, 45, Nos. 17, 19.
[103] Perry Endnotes, 45, Nos. 17, 19.
[104] Jewish Expositor 1821, 16-23. CMJ Archives, St. Albans.
[105] Perry, 17-19.
[106] Tibawi, 8.
[107] Lieber S., *Mystics and Missionaries* (Salt Lake City: University of Utah 1992), 177.
[108] Tibawi, 8-10.
[109] Gidney, 101-111.
[110] Gidney, 101-111.
[111] Lieber S., *Mystics and Missionaries* (Salt Lake City: University of Utah Press, 1992), 163-170.
[112] *Jewish Intelligence and Monthly Account of Proceedings of the London Society for the Promotion of Christianity Amongst the Jews*, Vol. XI, May 1845, 137. CMJ Archives St. Albans.
[113] Gidney, 212.
[114] Lewis D. *Lord Shaftesbury and the Rise of Christian Zionism.* Unpublished – contained in manuscript form by the Rev. Geoffrey Whitfield, 231.
[115] Gidney, 105.
[116] Lewis, 233.
[117] Gidney, 155-156.
[118] Gidney, 233-234.
[119] Gidney, 234-235.
[120] Gidney, 235-236.
[121] Tibawi, 12-13.
[122] Lewis, 237.
[123] Lewis describes Nicolayson as a German, 239, but Crombie, 20, Finlayson, 113 and Tibawi, 13 describe him as a Dane.
[124] Lewis, 238.
[125] Lieber S., *Mystics and Missionaries.* Salt Lake City: University of Utah 1992, 182. *Jewish Expositor,* 1829, 151-152.
[126] Tibawi, 13.
[127] *Jewish Intelligence and Monthly Account of Proceedings of the London Society for*

the Promotion of Christianity Amongst the Jews, Vol. IV, 1833, 150-160, 161-176, 177-188. CMJ Archives, St. Albans.

[128] Perry, 25.

[129] Finlayson G. B. A. M. *The Seventh Earl of Shaftesbury.* (Vancouver: Regent College Publishing, 2004), 113-114.

[130] Finlayson, 103 and 112.

[131] Hodder E., *The Life and Work of the Seventh Earl of Shaftesbury K. G.* (London: Cassell & Co. Ltd., 1886), Vol. I, 313. Senate House Library Special Collections.

[132] Hodder Vol. III, 477.

[133] Hodder Vol. I, 314.

[134] Tuchman B., *Bible and Sword* (New York: Ballantine, 1956), 175.

[135] *The Times* 17 (August, 1840).

[136] *The Times* 17 (August, 1840).

[137] Tuchman, 176-180.

[138] Tibawi A. L. British Interests in Palestine 1800-1901. London: OUP 1961.

[139] Tibawi, 45.

[140] Lewis D., 248.

[141] Tibawi, 33. Carmel A., 'The Activities of the European Powers in Palestine 1799-1914', in *Asian and African Studies,* Journal of the Israel Oriental Society, Vol. 19 No. 1 March. 1985, 43-92 (Published by The Institute of Middle Eastern Studies, University of Haifa), 57.

[142] Lieber S., *Mystics and Missionaries* (Salt Lake City: University of Utah Press, 1992), 395.

[143] Tibawi, 36.

[144] Tibawi, 37.

[145] *Jewish Intelligence and the Monthly Account of the Proceedings of the London Society for the Promotion of Christianity Amongst the Jews* Vol. III, 1835-1837, 132-133. CMJ Archives, St. Albans.

[146] Tibawi, 38-42.

[147] London Society's Annual Reports 1836-1839; 1838, vi. CMJ Archives, St. Albans.

[148] Tibawi, 41.

[149] Perry, 41. Nicolayson's papers, to which he refers, are currently held by CMJ in Christ Church, Jerusalem, including his journal of 28 December, 1838 - 11 February, 1839.

[150] Finlayson G. B. A. M. *The Seventh Earl of Shaftesbury.* (Vancouver: Regent College Publishing, 2004), 114-115.

[151] Smith H., *The Protestant Bishopric in Jerusalem: Its Origin and Progress.* (London: Bertheim, 1847), 41. Ref. British Library 4766.f.2.

[152] Finlayson, 115, 154.

[153] Smith, 127-130.

[154] Hodder Vol. I., 371.

[155] Also known as the Puseyites.

[156] *Jewish Intelligence and the Monthly Account of the Proceedings of the London Society for the Promotion of Christianity Amongst the Jews,* Vol. VII. November 1841, 382-385. CMJ Archives, St. Albans.

[157] *Jewish Intelligence and the Monthly Account of the Proceedings of the London Society for the Promotion of Christianity Amongst the Jews,* Vol. VII. December 1841, 391. CMJ Archives, St. Albans.

[158] Clements R. E., 'A Fruitful Venture: the Origin of Hebrew Studies at King's College, London', in *Biblical Traditions in Transmission: Essays in Honour of Michael A.*

Knibb, eds. J. M. Lieu & C. Hempel (Leiden: Brill, 2006), 61-79.

[159] Crombie K., *A Prophetic Property.* Unpublished paper, held in CMJ Archives, St. Albans and Christ Church, Jerusalem, 6.

[160] Lieber S., *Mystics and Missionaries* (Salt Lake City: University of Utah Press, 1992), 309-313.

[161] *Jewish Intelligence and the Monthly Account of the Proceedings of the London Society for the Promotion of Christianity Amongst the Jews,* Vol. III 1842, 162-165. CMJ Archives, St. Albans.

[162] Lewis, 326.

[163] *Jewish Intelligence and the Monthly Account of the Proceedings of the London Society for the Promotion of Christianity Amongst the Jews 1845,* Vol. XI, 90-92. CMJ Archives, St. Albans.

[164] Crombie K., *For the Love of Zion* (London: Hodder & Stoughton, 1991), 58-59.

[165] Tibawi, 77.

[166] "He sent them to preach the kingdom of God and to heal the sick." St. Luke 9. 2.

[167] Carmel A., 'The Activities of the European Powers in Palestine 1799-1914', in *Asian and African Studies,* Journal of the Israel Oriental Society, Vol. 19. No. 1, March. 1985, 43-92 (Published by The Institute of Middle Eastern Studies, University of Haifa), 56.

[168] Finlayson, 115.

[169] Carmel, 56.

[170] Carmel, 57.

[171] Carmel, 57.

[172] Tibawi, 60-61.

[173] Tibawi, 63-64.

[174] Tibawi, 72-74.

[175] Smith H. *The Protestant Bishopric in Jerusalem: Its Origin and Progress* (London: Bertheim, 1847), 150-152.

[176] Lewis, 327.

[177] Crombie, 70-72.

[178] Crombie, 70.

[179] Perry, 98.

[180] Perry Y., *British Mission to the Jews in Nineteenth Century Palestine* (London: Frank Cass, 2003), 93.

[181] Hodder Vol. II, 172.

[182] *Jewish Intelligence and the Monthly Account of the Proceedings of the London Society for the Promotion of Christianity Amongst the Jews 1847.* CMJ Archives, St. Albans.

[183] *Jewish Intelligence and the Monthly Account of the Proceedings of the London Society for the Promotion of Christianity Amongst the Jews 1847,* 95-100. CMJ Archives, St. Albans.

[184] *Jewish Intelligence and the Monthly Account of the Proceedings of the London Society for the Promotion of Christianity Amongst the Jews 1848,* 1-6. CMJ Archives, St. Albans.

[185] Pollock J., *Shaftesbury* (London: Hodder & Stoughton 1985), 55.

[186] Perry, 97-98.

[187] Carmel A. 'The Activities of the European Powers in Palestine 1799-1914', in *Asian and African Studies,* Journal of the Israel Oriental Society, Vol. 19 No. 1, March. 1985, 43-92 (Published by The Institute of Middle Eastern Studies, University of Haifa), 58.

[188] Perry, 205.
[189] Perry, 210.
[190] Pragai M. *Faith and Fulfilment (*London: Vallentine, Mitchell & Co. Ltd, 1985) , 4.
[191] Tuchman B., *Bible and Sword* (New York: First Ballantine Books Trade Edition 1984), 146.
[192] See www.destinyofbritain.org.uk. Documentary refers to Kelvin Crombie of CMJ, presenting the story of Britain's part in the Balfour Declaration of 1917, citing the Wesleys, Simeon, Spurgeon, Wilberforce, Palmerston and Shaftesbury as influencing the British government to support the restoration of the Jewish people to their Promised Land – scheduled for release on 11 December, 2007 to coincide with Allenby's entry into Jerusalem, 90 years earlier.
[193] Goldberg D. J. *The Divided Self* (London: I. B. Tauris 2006), 214.
[194] Zechariah 9. 9.

Chapter 4

Israel Past and Present–
The Land of Too Many Covenants

The Covenants

The embarrassment of the Covenant in the Bible is not so much that one exists but that there are so many of them, each with a different emphasis. Moreover, as they develop, they are seen to move from a Covenant which began with relationships, but only to end with the destruction of relationships, through violence, extermination and rigid control. The introduction to the Covenant with Abraham is far more one of grace, blessing and spiritual depth, but becomes gradually transformed into one of fear, legalism and conditionality.

Despite being different from secular sources, many Jewish political claims are based on perceptions of religious Zionism, which are firmly attached to the Covenant with Abraham. It is made clear in Chapter 1 that these claims stem from two passages in the book of Genesis. The first described the land between the major rivers of Egypt and Iraq and is known as larger, or Eretz Israel.

> On that day, the Lord made a Covenant with Abram and said, "To your descendants I give this land from the river of Egypt to the great river, the river Euphrates– the land of the Kenites, the Kenizzites, Kadmonites, Hittites, Perizzites, Rephaites, Amorites, Canaanites, Girgashites and Jebusites.[1]

The second did not specify the territory but the inheritance for the descendants of Abraham:

> No longer will your name be Abram; your name will be Abraham for I have made you a father of many nations. I will make you very fruitful; I will make nations of you and kings shall come from you, I will establish my covenant as an everlasting covenant between me and you and your descendants after you for the generations to come, to be your God and the God of your descendants after you. The whole land of Canaan where you are now an alien, I will give you as an everlasting possession to you and to your descendants after you, and I will be their God.[2]

It has been stated previously that these accounts are taken by many as the narrative of factual history, instead of mythical, religious stories with a spiritual message. The notion of myth does not necessarily stem from objective history, but emanates rather from stories of the past being incorporated into the present as matters of fact. Although they may not be seen to have historical veracity, as some might insist, they are not without significance because their meaning as a sacred narrative can hold integrity for many.

However, a hypothetical visitor from afar would be puzzled, even incredulous, that the costly and vicious warfare in the last hundred years has been partly founded on those two sets of verses from the book of Genesis. He might be informed that the land was given by God to the Jews for their exclusive possession by what is known as the Abrahamic Covenant. The visitor might wonder how the world could allow the destruction of life and liberty for so many, when it is based on such limited information, and how it could be considered to be trustworthy evidence.

Those who did these things, and those who recorded them, acted and wrote as though such behaviour was acceptable. In Chapter 2, we saw that this is believed to be the case by some in Israel in the 21st century, who hold that every word in the Torah is inspired and inerrant. Others can look back and be appalled at what appear to be atrocities, understanding such actions, but hardly approving of them. This is the dilemma for Israelis, within whose ranks there are those for whom such beliefs are still held and accepted. For others in Israel, as well as involved nations, there is a dilemma of how far the Covenant of Abraham can be implemented. For many settlers, including those in Gush Emunim, the Covenant has become a national ideology of conquest, control, expulsion, extermination, exclusivity and a Jewish "Democratic" state, heavily influenced by the Torah and Talmud.

For religious Jews, there is no doubt that Abraham is seen as the founding father of their race and the symbol of the beginning of Jewish existence, despite the variations in the different accounts of the Covenant. It is God who chooses Abraham and initiates the relationship with him and not the other way round.[3] Before the Covenant accounts, there is a series of promises of personal blessings on Abraham by God:

> I will make you into a great nation and I will bless you, I will make your name great, and you will be a blessing. I will bless those who bless you, and whoever curses you, I will curse; and all peoples on the earth will be blessed by you.[4]

This is followed by the promise of an heir,[5] and so the theme of divine-human relationship is developed. Following those accounts of the developing relationship, the first Covenant account begins and Abraham is promised extensive territory belonging to others, situated between the major river systems of Egypt and Iraq.[6] Later, there is the very different Covenant version, possibly from another of the sources compiled by the editor, or after some experience of subsequent developments.[7] In that version, Abraham is given a triple assurance of permanent territory for him and his posterity, and that God would be the God of his future generations.

Confusingly, there are four different descriptions of the actual land involved, described in four separate books of the Bible, each one being distinguishable from the others and which are listed by Professor William Davies showing the different descriptions of the extent of the land, stating: "It is clear that 'the land of Israel' was never defined with geographic precision: it is an idea as well as a territory. It seems always to have carried ideal overtones without geographical and political precision."[8] This may account for the fact that, at the time of writing, Israel has still to be precise, in relation to its neighbouring countries, about what it holds to be its exact international boundaries.

The connection of land and people is described by Davies as "the bedrock on which all Israel's subsequent history rests."[9] The promise of the land of Canaan by God to the seed of Abraham was irrevocable. If the people failed to be holy and thereby defiled the land, they would be disbarred by their own behaviour, but it would not be revoked by God for other generations of Jews. Whatever might become of the Jews, the land that was God's, and set apart as holy for him and his purposes, was irrefutable. Jewish connection with the race and with God is realised in the act of male circumcision which began with Abraham and is the mark of the Jew,[10] although the rite is not confined to that race only. This Covenant promise to Abraham was eventually to be put into coded form in the account of Moses and the Book of the Covenant.[11] This was to become the divine mission of the religious Zionists, especially after the Six Day War of 1967.

During the Diaspora years after AD 135, the focus of faithful Jews was the first five books of the Bible, called the Torah, which sustained them throughout the centuries until 1948 and thereafter. Jewish religion is relatively small in numbers, whether by birth or conversion, and in 2002 was minimally assessed[12] at approximately 13-14 million people scattered throughout the world. Some are seen to claim familial connections, although not necessarily maintaining any personal involvement. The majority of more than five million are in the USA, closely followed by Israel with more than three million, and with two million in Europe. The estimate is 0.2 per cent of the world's population. Those who see themselves as Orthodox religious Jews will hold to the belief in the literal truth of the Covenants despite the questionable meaning and authority which they bestow on them. Their conviction is that the land was God's to give and he gave it to the Jews and he would live there with them.[13] This belief was the undergirding principle through the centuries for the Jews, even throughout the Diaspora. Such people, including supporters of Gush Emunim, would never voluntarily give that land back to anyone, because it would represent disloyalty to the deity as they understood him. Their values are different from those European Jews who, according to Bruno Bettelheim in *The Informed Heart*, submitted to Nazi atrocities during the Shoah.[14] Religious Israeli settlers have fought, and will continue to fight, any threat rather than renounce their promised land for others to control. Moreover, threats from outside provide an automatic joining together of the different parties in their preparedness to hold to the land by force. In contrast, there are others who see that such ways are not for the future and see the reasonableness of accommodation with Arabs in Palestine for a just peace.

The Different Covenants

While the exact historical facts may never be discovered, the reality is that generations have seen the Biblical stories as giving insight into either spiritual enlightenment or ideological preoccupation. Meanwhile, the inexactitudes of both the original material and their interpretations mean that the field is always open to divergent views and applications. Sceptics would need to be cautious before dismissing the accounts altogether because they could miss the rich meanings within the stories. Professor Ronald Clements holds that, because the sources of the Covenant were so varied "Israel did not have a single unified doctrine of the Covenant,"[15] and neither did the Old Testament. When one looks closely at the different accounts of Covenants with God, it appears that some sources build it around Abraham, while others present it through Moses and still others focus more on David. The alternative views of the Mosaic and Davidic traditions, both lay claim to their origins within the Abrahamic stories by their focus on the Patriarchs, or the royal house of David. These are separate from the logic of the Eighth Century prophets who called for levels of ethics and morality as befits the people of God. Israel's present claims for possession of huge areas of land, drawn from perspectives of both history and religion, are now heavily criticised from within their own ranks.[16] The question can also be raised about how the ancient occupancy of land for two centuries after King David in 1011 BC, until its breakdown, can be reckoned to be valid for the contemporary situation, even if their accounts could be substantiated from admittedly disputed records. This can hardly be a universally accepted criterion for such claims particularly if, in the first place, they occupied the land by conquest, as did the ancient Israelites who displaced the previous occupants.

It was the ancient account of the promise of the land to the Jews by God which became the unifying factor for all the Covenant traditions, in the late nineteenth century and thereafter. This promise gave divine authority to contemplate a land, as well as to conquer and retain it against all odds. The view of Professor W. D. Davies is apposite:

> What is important is not the rediscovery of the origin of the promise to Abraham, but the recognition that that promise was so interpreted from age to age that it became a living power in the life of the people of Israel...The legend of the promise entered so deeply into the experience of the Jews that it acquired its own reality.[17]

It is now clear that there were a number of Covenants recorded in the Old Testament (known by Jews as the *Tanak*),[18] from separate sources, rather than by one writer. Hence, there is a need to specify the Abrahamic Covenant as the one which originated both the race and the promise of God, as distinct from those which came later in different forms to Moses,[19] Joshua[20] and David.[21] The first Covenant with Abraham is personal, spiritual and relational, where the emphasis is on a gracious God who takes the initiative in moving to a person and, from that relationship, promises territory as his gift. The gift is unconditional, although the precise boundaries are unclear. This chapter shows how the relational and spiritual relationship, first promised to Abraham, Isaac and Jacob,[22] became developed. Differently, the next Covenant with Moses is understood to be less to do with an unconditional relationship but summarised by laws of obedience, with conditions for the individual and the community.[23] It was thereby extended to be expansionist, violent, merciless and exclusive to the point of extermination of those who stood in the way of the Jewish forces.[24] The Covenant with Joshua became understood to be political and national, against a backcloth of battle, conquest and possession of land so that the Covenant continually involved violence and extermination.[25] Centuries later, under David, there was a further Covenant, which extended to both political and international interests. The Covenant with David was wide-ranging, linking back to the Patriarchs and focusing on the pivotal place of the earlier supreme act of faith by Abraham when, in Jerusalem, he apparently offered his son Isaac as a human sacrifice to God.[26] This progression is now discussed at greater length.

The Covenants With Abraham

The background to the Jewish focus on Abraham is not difficult to find, but a problem arises with the interpretation of the accounts as myths and not as historical, factual accounts. Myth is not to be seen here as literal fact of history but having meaning beyond the story, even though some see the word as a sacred narrative, rather than allowing for a richer interpretation beyond the obvious. There are a small number of fragments which give the two mythical accounts of the Covenant relationship made between God and Abraham.[27] [28] To recapitulate, it has already been shown that God makes Abraham a promise of land for his own use and the use of his seed forever. This became known as the Abrahamic Covenant and the Covenant land is specifically described in a second passage.[29] The passage is geographically descriptive and this wider territory is known as Eretz Israel. For many Jews, this is the land which is perceived to be the ultimate land of Israel.[30] There is a less-quoted passage in which Abraham is told by God: "As for me, this is my Covenant with you: You will be the father of many nations."[31] The Covenant made between God and Abraham was based on the relationship between Abraham as the man of faith *par excellence* and God as the Creator of all things.[32]

It is important to note that the relationship between God and Abraham extended to include certain traditional, geographical sites which were seen to be sacred to Jews thereafter and critically affect the Israel-Palestinian Conflict. The crucial importance of Jerusalem, focusing on Mount Moriah, is the place where Abraham was prepared to offer his son Isaac as a living sacrifice to God.[33] The pivotal nature of Hebron stems from it being the place where Abraham lived and where he and his wife are buried,[34] as well as Isaac, Jacob and Esau.[35] Hebron was undoubtedly important but was subsumed as Jerusalem came to the fore with its Citadel, Temple and Royal Court. These places have become centres of bitter conflict since 1967. The issue of the ownership and control of those sites which are considered holy is still unresolved. The settler movement holds fast to the notion that places with their religious significance are crucial to Israel's exclusive possession of the land. Nablus, known to Jews as Shechem, assumed significance after 1967 as it was the burial place of Joseph, as well as the place where Joshua made a Covenant with the people who vowed to serve and obey the Lord.[36] In similar ways, the town of Bethlehem is revered because it is the burial place of Rachel, the wife of the Patriarch Jacob.[37]

One of the primary factors in the Abrahamic Covenant is that of the personal promise by God to Abraham. This will be seen to be different in quality and content from that of the Mosaic Covenant which is directional, legal and conditional and is now explored.[38]

The Mosaic Covenant

The Abrahamic Covenant was within the original foundation of Jewish Law as written in the Torah and which became gradually developed from the time of Moses. After Abraham, the account of the structure of the Covenant as a relationship with the Jewish people was developed through the Ten Commandments which were received by Moses, from God on Mount Sinai *c*. thirteenth century BC.[39] The Covenant legal system of Commandments[40] was gradually extended and eventually became a binding system for Jews, through the written Law of the Torah and the rabbinic Oral Law of the Talmud.[41] There is no history of Abraham, apart from the Book of Genesis, or Moses apart from the Biblical accounts contained in the Books of Exodus, Numbers and Deuteronomy.

Moses did not simply receive a new Covenant from Abraham and pass it unchanged to Joshua, because it was one that became developed into a religious and legal ideology. The biblical background we have of Moses is a story of insecurity and survival from birth and through his infancy, eventually moving into slavery, with perpetual anxiety about his survival and that of his people.[42] He became both the leader of his people in Egypt and the bearer of another Covenant. After the Exodus of the Jews from Egypt, Moses conveyed God's Covenant to the people regarding their status and the land.[43] The Mosaic Covenant refers to Abraham and the promise of the land of Canaan,[44] and is followed by the confirmation of the Jews as a special, particular people, superior to the others who would be supreme as a kingdom of priests and a holy nation.[45] This was established in a ceremony on Mount Sinai[46] and the Covenant was accordingly confirmed by the writing down of the commandments.[47]

The development of the Abrahamic Covenant can be seen to have been developed so that the Jews had entered into a tribal system, or nationhood, with a uniting, organising, religious and legal basis for the people. However, it still did not possess a land of its own and this was to become the reality in the next stage in the development of the Abrahamic Covenant. The Mosaic Covenant was different insofar as it was more developed for a community, rather than that of Abraham which was one that was relational. It will be seen how, under Moses and his successor Joshua, it was to become ideological, violent and one of conquest, even to the point of extermination. Moses gave the structure of the Ten Commandments to the people which provided a religious and legal code for the organisation of the community.[48] He thereby transformed the Jewish escapees from Egypt into an organised people and tribal nation, with a code of laws and a uniting, common religion of obedience and faithfulness.[49]

The nature of the Covenant relationship between God and his people is seen to be guaranteed for the Jews by the relationship with Abraham and the Patriarchs.[50] The people are warned that God will not break his side of the Covenant which he began with Abraham and the land but, if his descendants are unfaithful, they would be severely punished. The focus on the exquisite nature of the land is described where, in the context of a range of rules about living in Canaan, Moses is instructed by God that the land should not be defiled in any way because God would be living there among his people.[51] The development, from the personal, spiritual and relational aspects of the Abrahamic Covenant, into one that encompassed the entire community, is seen to have taken place under Moses. This was to move further, into the realm of extermination of perceived enemies and those who were disloyal, in the time of Joshua, the successor of Moses. The Book of Joshua records that the execution of both Canaanite enemies and disobedient Jews was accepted and implemented by religious Jews. He had inherited from Moses a people prepared for struggle, conflict, possession of land and control through conquest, and including extermination.

The Covenant with Joshua

Following the death of Moses, Joshua is given the task by God to take the land as far as Lebanon and Iraq.[52] Although outside the Torah, and therefore less sacred than the Law of Moses, the biblical account of the early method of occupation is stated. The biblical account of the early method of occupation is given. At a victorious battle at Jericho, against an uncoordinated people and vulnerable defence, the God of Abraham had become a God of war, victory and occupation. The Bible records not only the victory, but the extermination of the occupants except for a family of collaborators in Jericho who were spared.[53] Furthermore, when they experienced defeat, because of disloyalty from within their own ranks, the family of Achan was considered to be responsible.[54] The account of their extermination without mercy, together with all their possessions, is detailed.[55] The policy of the extermination of opponents was also maintained.[56] The sequence reveals that what had commenced with Abraham as a spiritual and relational Covenant had been developed into an ideological religion which included conflict, killing, destruction, extermination, occupation and control. What was left for Jewish history was the precedent and building blocks of a warlike, ideological tradition, traced back to interpretations of the Covenant of Abraham and Moses and extended by Joshua.

Violence between Israel and other peoples is consistently recorded in the Old Testament, or *Tanak*. The writer, Rabbi Norman Solomon, describes the Jewish war against the Canaanites[57] as a war of extermination in order to avoid contamination from their perceived wickedness.[58] The principles of defence as obligatory are set down in the Book of Exodus.[59] Thus, defensive wars are mandatory, which means that Israel cannot be an aggressor, but it must act in its defence if it feels threatened. Hence the issues of "Defence" and "Security" have justified military conflict and been consistently used in relation to what it sees as the protection of its land under God.

The Davidic Covenant

From being a nomadic tribe during the time of Moses, the Jews were gradually to establish themselves by having permanent territory and became a force to be reckoned with in the region. This came to be centred on the hilly terrain of Judah, or Judea, where they were to establish a fortress and capital named Jerusalem. For Jews, the significance of Jerusalem is seen to begin when God blessed the faithfulness of Abraham in being prepared to sacrifice his son Isaac at the place named Mount Moriah.[60] The Book of Genesis goes on to record that he made further promises to Abraham about the enlargement of his people and their possession of the land.[61] This was not to come about until centuries later, in the time of King David, when Jerusalem was seen to be set apart as distinctive and unique. At the time the area was relatively limited and was not enlarged until later. It was largely situated on two small hills, later known as Mount Zion and Temple Mount. The biblical claims which assert the rights to the land from the time of Abraham are contested by the archaeologists, Finkelstein and Silberman. They found that Jerusalem was small and "perhaps not more than a typical hill country village."[62] David made it the capital of his Kingdom in 1011 BC because of another apparent encounter with God which revealed the benevolence of God to him and, in turn, David built an altar on the same Mount Moriah as Abraham.[63] The connection between David and Abraham on that precise position would have led to the centrality of Jerusalem as a place of religion, kingly power and Jewish solidarity as a united people.

The multi-level significance of this decision was validated and firmly established when David brought the Ark of the Covenant[64] to Jerusalem from Kiryiat Yearim in Abu Gosh, where it had been for forty years. The Ark, containing the Ten Commandments, with all the significance for the spirit of Jahweh, was placed a short distance from the citadel of Zion and on Mount Moriah itself. This was both the traditional place of the intended sacrifice of Isaac by Abraham, and David's intended new altar. This political move served to unite the tribes of Israel in the north and the south for over a hundred years. The promise by God of the land of the Jebusites[65] to Abraham was sealed.[66] The splendour of David before his people is declared by the Psalmist as he affirms the Covenant between God and the king.[67] By housing the Ark of the Covenant in his capital, David made what has been described as: "A master stroke of statesmanship for it tied the monarchy firmly to the ancient Yahweh tradition. Both monarchy and capital became themselves elements in Yahweh's religion."[68] Moreover, it linked David directly with Abraham and the Covenant. Thus the strategic, political and religious components became conjoined and this was further reinforced by the building of the Temple by King Solomon, David's son, to house the Ark of the Covenant in the area known as "the Holy of Holies," with an elaborate priesthood and ritual.

The kingdom, created by David in the 11th century BC, was not to last beyond two generations, but divided under Rehoboam. What had begun in mythology with Abraham had been fulfilled in history, albeit only temporarily. After Rehoboam, the country divided into two separate kingdoms, the larger in the north and the smaller in the south, which centred on Jerusalem. When the Israeli ambassador to Great Britain, Ron Prosor, wrote: "From time immemorial, Jerusalem has been the eternal capital of the Jewish people, and will always remain so,"[69] history does not entirely support his view. David conquered the city in 1011 BC when it was small in area and which, though not without significance, did not last long. It had been peopled by others before David, and was peopled by others after the demise of his family. Jerusalem in the twenty-first century bears no resemblance in size to the far smaller citadel of King David and it is difficult to support the larger view of the ambassador. Because David is held in great regard, the same can hardly be said for his son and grandson. It takes a great leap of imagination to justify the claim for the large and expanding present-day Jerusalem to be the eternal capital of the Jews, and always to remain so, on such a limited basis. Nonetheless, this is the sincere and passionately held view of a great many Jews, who view the city, primarily from a religious perspective rather than one that is political.

There were other, more significant, connections between Abraham and David in Hebron, quite apart from Jerusalem. Abraham settled there and built an altar to God[70] and Sarah, his wife, was buried there.[71] The biblical accounts record that it was also in Hebron that David was anointed King of Judah and reigned there before moving to Jerusalem.[72] It is possible that the writers and editors of the accounts made the connection between the separate traditions of the two, one who founded and the other who fulfilled the two Covenants. Despite the centuries-long gap, the age of Abraham and the Patriarchs became completed, both through the Davidic royal state and his rule over the nations as the servant of the Lord.[73] The State of Israel was thereby seen to have a divine origin, dating back to Abraham. During the time of David, there had been little reason to refer to

Abraham because the lineage of the house of David had commenced and his rule was evident. What God had promised to Abraham in terms of territory had been accomplished by David. The significance of the Abrahamic Covenant was implied and fulfilled by the existence of the Monarch, via Moses and Joshua.[74] Furthermore, God's gracious promise was irrevocable but conditional, depending on the faithfulness of the Jews who, if they broke the Covenant, could be cast aside, to be replaced by others who would be faithful. God, the land and the people were holy and were meant to conjoin in a union of holiness.

The belief in the Temple as the home of God and its symbolic influence on the religion and culture of the Jews cannot be overestimated, according to Karen Armstrong.[75] Jerusalem has been the religious focus for Jews ever since and is relevant to the current present conflict. Later, this was to become complicated through Islamic reverence for its place in the life of Muhammad the Prophet. The long-term outcome is that Jerusalem has become a metaphorical and literal battleground between those who see it as an exclusive possession for either Jews or Muslims, and those who see it as a place of holiness for all people to respect.[76] Professor Alan Richardson differed and held that implicit in the choice of the Jews as an elect nation was not for special privileges over against other nations, so much as for the purposes of God's will for mankind to be realised.[77]

The Kingdom of David was to last for little more than a century because, after the death of Solomon in 922 BC, the ten northern tribes broke from the new king, Rehoboam. The northern kingdom became known as Ephraim, with only the two tribes of Judah and Benjamin remaining as the southern kingdom. The northern kingdom was swept away in 721 BC by the Assyrian conquest but the southern kingdom, Judah, held out until the Babylonian conquests of 597 and 586 BC. The Jews were then exiled in Babylon for fifty years, after which Judah became ruled by Persia when the Jewish return to Jerusalem was permitted in 536 BC. After the return, Judah was a small area with a small population, at the mercy of larger powers with whom, thereafter, it had to seek alliances in order to survive. It was never the same again as successive empires of Greece and Rome continued to make Israel a subservient people, apart from the period under the Maccabean leadership from 164-63 BC.

The Exile Of 586 BC

While exiled in the land of Babylon, Jews felt they could not communicate with their God because they saw him as a territorial God who did not dwell in that land, but in Zion.[78] Nonetheless, on their release from Exile, many Jews remained in Babylon, despite the opportunity to return to the land of Abraham. This is even more the case regarding modern-day Jews, only a proportion of whom have taken the opportunity of returning to the land of Abraham. This has to raise difficulties for those Jews who hold to the essential nature of that special territory which is unlike any other because God lives there. In the post-Exilic period, after 536 BC, they returned to the land they believed God had originally given them and prepared for the building of the Second Temple as the dwelling place of God.[79] In this, they were led by their scribes and religious leaders, notably Ezra and Nehemiah. After the disasters of 597 and 586 BC they were demoralised but had managed to survive as an entity in Babylon. On their return, it was essential that their morale was restored and this was achieved by the religious leaders. Taking the ancient stories, myths and writings, they were edited into a whole, built around a series of principal stories, beginning with Creation and moving into specific relationships. These not only gave the Jews their history but a rationale for their special relationship with God as his carefully selected people with a divine eternal, relationship and destiny. They were thereby given a backcloth of being special and unique, which gave the Jews a different story to their experiences as a conquered, humiliated people and being of no consequence. The Jews reinforced their sense of worth and value by having the status where they held that there were no other gods in existence at all but only their own, Jahweh.

The Jewish concept of their uniqueness as a holy people, set apart with exclusive rights and an exclusive destiny bestowed by God, developed at the time of Nehemiah in 515 BC, after the return from Exile.[80] This uniqueness was emphasised internally by the obligation that marriage could only take place from within the sacred community of faith and not outside. Thus, exclusivity and segregation were put in place and then reinforced by another leader, Ezra, and his insistence on adhering to the Hebrew writings of the Torah. This may be seen to be another building block of Israel's emphasis on its unique and distinctive claims for special status for itself; one exclusive God and no others, one exclusive Covenant people of God and no others, one exclusive Covenant land and no other. They were to have an exclusive capital, Jerusalem, the City of Zion, which was the dwelling place of God and no other.

It was strategically important for the Jews to provide themselves with a history, showing themselves and the land in a special, distinctive light of holiness. The ancient stories in the Torah would have been inserted into the text by the post-Exilic editors, who worked with the benefit of hindsight. The patriarchal accounts were taken from their oral tradition and so positioned in the Pentateuch to present a sequence of Jewish history from unrecorded time. The argument for a literal record of events, rather than the symbolic meaning of the accounts, misses the point of the richness in the tradition, which is seen by liberal Jews to be far more significant. Those traditionalists who see the scriptures as inspired, God-breathed, inerrant history make their case for the Abrahamic Covenant and the logical consequence of the Jewish occupation and exclusive possession of the land. Successive generations of Jews and Arabs have paid the price for such views as they have been interpreted by the LSPCAJ and Gush Emunim.

One is left with a number of questions, of which there is one that stands out. However the Abrahamic Covenant is interpreted, what would it take for enlightened religious people in the 21st century to be prepared to forgo their perceived rights to exclusive possession of a territory, for the sake of humanity? Such is the question that is there for Jews and Muslims to resolve.

132   Israeli And Palestinian Terrorism: The 'Unintentional' Agents

The next, final, chapter looks at the structure of the relationship between Jews and Arabs in Israel and Palestine which remains disastrous and intransigent. The primary factors in the relationship remain as fear and ideology on the one hand and injustice and hatred on the other. How long it will take for all the parties concerned to become sufficiently aware of the futile nature of what they have constructed remains to be seen. Perhaps they do not know! Meanwhile, the work of Gush Emunim and the present Church's Ministry among Jewish People still continues.

Notes

[1] Genesis 15.18-21. Holy Bible, New International Version (London: Hodder & Stoughton, 1986).
[2] Genesis 17. 5-8.
[3] Genesis 15. 7.
[4] Genesis 12. 2-3.
[5] Genesis 15. 4.
[6] Genesis 15. 18-21.
[7] Genesis 17. 1-14.
[8] Davies W. D. *The Gospel and the Lan.* (Sheffield: Sheffield Academic Press, 1994), 16-17. Exodus 23. 31ff; Numbers 31. 1-10; Deuteronomy 11. 24; Joshua 1. 2-4.
[9] Davies W. D. *The Territorial Dimension of Judaism* (Minneapolis: First Fortress Press, 1991), 8.
[10] Genesis 17. 10-11.
[11] Exodus 20. 22-34. 28.
[12] Wikipaedia, *Jew,* 8 August, 2008.
[13] Exodus 29. 45-46. Numbers 35. 34.
[14] Bettelheim B., *The Informed Heart* (Harmondsworth: Peregrine Books, 1986).
[15] Clements R. E. *Abraham and David.* (London: Studies in Biblical Theology. Second series, SCM, 1967), 82-83.
[16] Neumann M., *The Case against Israel* (Petrolia, Calif.: CounterPunch and AK Press, 2005), 66-78.
[17] Davies W. D. *The Territorial Dimension of Judaism* (Minneapolis: First Fortress Press, 1991), 6.
[18] Jews use the word "Tanak." See Davies W. D., *The Territorial Dimension of Judaism* (Los Angeles: University of California Press, 1982), xiv.
[19] Exodus 20ff.
[20] Joshua 24. 25.
[21] II Samuel 23. 5; II Samuel 7.
[22] Deuteronomy 1. 8.
[23] Exodus 20 1-17.
[24] Deuteronomy 7. 1-11.
[25] Joshua 6. 21.
[26] Genesis 22.
[27] Genesis 17. 5-8 Holy Bible, *New International Version*: "Your name will be Abraham, for I have made you a father of many nations. I will make you very fruitful; I will make nations of you, and kings will come from you. I will establish my covenant as an everlasting covenant between me and you and your descendants after you for the gen-

erations to come, to be your God and the God of your descendants after you. The whole land of Canaan, where you are now an alien, I will give as an everlasting possession to you and your descendants after you; and I will be their God."

[28] There is another account where the first-born son of Abraham, named Ishmael, was born to his servant Hagar, and was blessed by God. Genesis 16. 15; 17. 20. Despite that blessing, the Abrahamic succession is recorded as passing through the second son, Isaac, who was born to his wife Sarah. Genesis 17. 19-21.

[29] Genesis 15. 18-21. "The Lord made a covenant with Abram and said 'To your descendants I give this land, from the river of Egypt, to the great river, the Euphrates - the land of the Kenites, Kenizzites, Kadmonites, Hittites, Perizzites, Rephaites, Amorites, Canaanites, Girgashites and Jebusites.' "

[30] The London office of Dr Jonathan Sacks, the Chief Rabbi of the United Hebrew Congregations of the Commonwealth, contains framed correspondence with Prime Minister Yitzhak Rabin and Dr Sacks concerning the territory, including maps. Seen by the author, 14 November, 2000.

[31] Genesis 17. 4.

[32] Sheridan S., 'Abraham from a Jewish Perspective', in *Abraham's Children: Jews, Christians and Muslims in Conversation,* ed. by Norman Solomon, Richard Harries and Tim Winter (London: T. & T. Clark, 2005), 10.

[33] Genesis 22.

[34] Genesis 25. 9-10.

[35] Genesis 35. 29.

[36] Joshua 24. 24-25, 32.

[37] Genesis 35. 19.

[38] Clements, 14.

[39] Deuteronomy 1. 1-46.

[40] Exodus 20. 22-23. 33; Leviticus 17-26.

[41] The Torah is the first five books of the Bible, the written Law, and the Talmud, the Oral Law, consists of the canon of rabbinic, religious law of the Mishna, and is also known as the Halacha.

[42] Exodus 2ff.

[43] Exodus 19. 5-6.

[44] Exodus 6. 1ff.

[45] Exodus 19. 5-6.

[46] Exodus 24. 1-18.

[47] Exodus 34. 27-28.

[48] Exodus 20.

[49] Exodus 6. 1-8.

[50] Leviticus 26. 42.

[51] Numbers 35. 34.

[52] Joshua 1. 1-9.

[53] Joshua 6. 22ff.

[54] Joshua 7. 1-12.

[55] Joshua 7. 19-26.

[56] Joshua 10-11.

[57] Deuteronomy 20. 1-20.

[58] Solomon N., 'The Ethics of War: Judaism' in *The Ethics of War* ed. by Richard Sorabji & David Rodin (Aldershot: Ashgate Publishing House, 2006), 108-137.

[59] Exodus 21.

[60] Genesis 22. 1-18.
[61] Genesis 22. 15-18.
[62] Finkelstein I. & Silberman N. A. *The Bible Unearthed, Archaeology's New Vision of Ancient Israel and the Origin of its Sacred Texts* (New York: Touchstone, 2002), 33.
[63] II Samuel 24. 18-25.
[64] The Ark of the Covenant was seen as the literal dwelling place of God.
[65] Genesis 15. 21.
[66] II Samuel 5. 6-9.
[67] Psalm 89. 28.
[68] James F., *Personalities of the Old Testament* (New York: Charles Scribner's Sons, 1938), 138.
[69] Ron Prosor, 'A gulf worth bridging' *The Guardian,* 9 December, 2008, 32.
[70] Genesis 13. 18.
[71] Genesis 23. 2.
[72] II Samuel 5. 1-5.
[73] Clements R. E. *Abraham and David*. London: Studies in Biblical Theology. Second series (SCM, 1967), 56-60.
[74] Clements, 63.
[75] Armstrong K. *Jerusalem: One City, Three Faiths* (New York: Ballantine, 1997), 51.
[76] "Jerusalem is not a piece of real estate, it is spiritual for both. Recognising, though not agreeing, brings respect, but land brings disputes. Jerusalem should be open and not sovereign." Rabbi Herschel Gluck, Director, Muslim-Jewish Forum. London, 18 July, 2005.
[77] Richardson A., 'Abraham' in *A Theological Wordbook of the Bible* ed. by Alan Richardson (London SCM Press, 1956), 12-13.
[78] Psalm 37.
[79] After its completion, it remained until destroyed by the Romans in AD 70.
[80] Armstrong, 99.

Chapter 5

The 21st Century–The Bridge Is Not Safe

In the Introduction, I used the metaphor of a "swamp" to describe the source of terrorism in Israel and Palestine, which needed to be transformed into a place of health and life. This concluding chapter uses a different metaphor, of a "bridge" and its structure, looking especially at the structural faults in the construction of the "bridge" between Israel and Palestine. Does a person need to know how to build a bridge before he can say: "The bridge is not safe"? I may not say how a bridge should be built, or how peace should be created between Jews and Arabs, but I can say and write what will not work! This chapter identifies some of the faults in the structure of that bridge. Inevitably it will cause offence to many. It was the prophet Isaiah who called people to remember to deal with their alienation by saying: "Come, let us reason together." Thus, where there are disagreements, they can be used either, to further bitterness, or to further discussion. So far, with hindsight, one can see that Resolutions, Accords and Agreements over the years have brought little but dissolution, discord and disagreement – and disaster. The bridge is still not safe for my friends, and it is in doubt whether one exists at all. The personnel of the "Unintentional Agents," Gush Emunim and CMJ, still function in Israel and Palestine, some using different titles for identification purposes. They contributed to the situation in the past and still contribute to its decline. We must move on but how and where is the future bridge-building to begin?

Both sides still have their stories of atrocities and these are regularly used to stall creative processes which might lead to peace and security with justice for all concerned. Two "incompatibles" focus on Israeli oppression of Palestinians and Palestinian violence against Israelis, both of which provide arguments for one side against the other. Finding ways to establish conflict prevention and co-existence for two viable, secure, neighbouring states, in harmony with each other, are urgent goals. There was a frequent cry by Israeli politicians that they did not have a Palestinian partner. What is more the case is that neither Israelis nor Palestinians have ever had a partner. If there had been a skilled, professional construction system in place, they could have produced a viable working structure a long time ago and without necessarily offending the vested interests of the United States of America and Europe.

There are many serious faults between the two peoples, not least the terrifying Palestinian suicide attacks, but also the Israeli occupation, land expropriation for settlement expansion, and impoverishment of the civilian population. As the stronger party, and the Occupying Power, Israel has the greater opportunity to end the impasse and bring about an authentic resolution. Because of the post-1947 history, there will be incredulity among future generations of Jews who will look back and be ashamed at the bullying and oppression of a weaker people by their own forebears. In the meantime, Michael Keating of Chatham House[1] poses the question: "How far can the presence of millions of disenfranchised, impoverished, angry and traumatised Palestinians, living in squalid conditions in a small, crowded geographical area and restricted in their movements, ever be a basis for Israeli security?"[2]

What has made the situation far more complex is that, in a Palestinian democratic election, Fatah was outvoted by Hamas, which became duly installed as the properly constituted government in Gaza. This has created a huge impasse within the Palestinian community, which has to be resolved. What is an even greater issue is the oft-repeated refusal by Hamas to recognise the State of Israel but instead threatens its existence. This intransigence remains a permanent obstacle and its election caused outrage in Israel. In this, Israel was supported by the United States which withdrew virtually all aid to Hamas, followed by the European Union. The embargo on aid in Gaza, caused massive internal distress to the civilian population, and was still in force at the start of 2009. For the overall situation to change "a more transparent analysis of Israel's strategies" is suggested by the economist, Mushtaq Kahn, who presents the problem quite squarely: "In the long run, resolution of the conflict requires a frank debate within Israel and between it and its friends about what, if anything, can be done to preserve Zionism, given the demographic reality of modern Israel-Palestine."[3] A further resolution of the conflict requires other "frank" debates and has to involve Hamas, separately, and Fatah and Hamas, collectively, so that they become part of the solution, and not part of the disease.

In order to concentrate on the present position I have drawn almost exclusively from recent writers and scholars from 2005 onwards. I have limited the subjects to those that seem pivotal in the attempts at bridge-building and that need to be constructed differently if the bridge is to be safe. There are three main issues, namely: internal, external and political structures, which inevitably impact on each other but which will now be considered in turn.

The Internal Structures

In confronting the internal structural faults within Israel and Palestine, the component list is considerable. This section will limit its focus to the occupation and its many supporting elements, the settlements, the security wall and international law, as well as the much-disputed constituent factor of apartheid. But first, the Palestinian factions, Fatah and Hamas have to be included.

Fatah and Hamas

There are factions in both of the major parties in Palestinian politics which have good reason to fear each other, while there are others who see the need to find ways to end the alienation of the years. It would be a diversion at this point to go down the road of examining the separate drives of Fatah and Hamas, but the problems that they represent in the larger picture should not be put aside. It can be noted that Hamas was supported by Israel at one period, as a way of reducing the influence of Fatah and Arafat. This has become a boomerang, inflicting itself on Israel, as well as Fatah, and that element in its origins is now largely forgotten. Just as there was a need to find an ideology in Northern Ireland that exceeded those of the separate groups, in order that they might create a working alliance, so this is the case in Palestine. As in Northern Ireland, they will need outside assistance to achieve this and Egypt, despite its questionable political record, is a prime mover and is involved in seeking to create a constructive dialogue between the two. To bring this about will be neither simple nor swift and will take a very long time, but it has to be noted as essential to the overall bridge-building enterprise. It is not intended, here, to be involved in any extensive discussion about the origins and structure of their own impasse, except to raise it as a principle. It would be negligent and partially-sighted to ignore the issue and the pressing need for its resolution in the West Bank and Gaza. In their present, divided state they represent an obstacle to meaningful discussions with Israel. Certainly, present policies which treat Hamas as a pariah organisation hold no hope for the future, just as similar ostracism of the IRA was unfruitful, and has to give way to a more inclusive strategy. (The situation of Hamas and Gaza is discussed in greater detail later in this chapter and is in a separate dimension to the basic principle of internal Palestinian divisions raised here).

The Occupation

As has been shown earlier, how to create and maintain a secure Jewish state in a land inhabited by another people was a primary question for the Jews in the late 19th and early 20th centuries. One self-evident solution was to follow the dubious European model of colonialism, under which the indigenous people were overpowered by a stronger, invading force, the land taken and the people used as labourers to serve their masters who set down permanent roots. This had happened successfully in Africa, America, Australia, New Zealand and Asia. Why not in the land held by the Ottoman Empire, especially because, although now seriously questioned, the accounts of Israel being the Promised Land for Jews were largely accepted by world-wide Christendom?

This colonial model turned out to be the case, following three fundamentals namely: alleged Jewish uniqueness, the privilege of Zionist settlers over the colonised and what Piterberg describes as the denial that the presence of the Arabs determined the manner of Jewish colonisation, i.e. militarism through theft of land and property, oppression, domination and control.[4] In this, aided by

Western powers, Israel imposed its own vision for the future, colonising Palestinian land and excluding or expelling its inhabitants.[5] Is this to be continued or changed? In blaming the West, Ghada Karmi argues: "It was the permissive attitude and the inaction of the international community that led ultimately to the current problems."[6] Israel's enterprise was never checked, but has grown steadily since 1948, having begun even before then.

The outcome is that, in Israel and Palestine, there is now a massive power imbalance. Even so, is it realistic at this point in time to believe that Palestinians will accept an occupation, or one where they are divided into small units, or even one with a truncated state of enclaves? The dangers of the impositions of the stronger party, which were tolerated in the nineteenth century, could no longer hold after 1919 and the Versailles Treaty which, containing so much imbalance, humiliation and unfairness, led to 1939 and World War II.[7] Israel's apparently rightful demand for the cessation of Palestinian hostilities may seem reasonable, as long as there is no reason for unrest. Now, one can ask about those reasons and begin to examine the Palestinian claims of injustice and the failure of human rights. Who believes that there will be peace any time in the foreseeable future as long as there is a two-class citizenship in asymmetric territory and one-sided wealth and opportunity?

The use of the word "occupation" is challenged, Israel preferring the use of the term, "disputed territories." Nonetheless, writing in 2005, before the election of Hamas, Michael Keating identifies a number of destructive factors, especially concerning the occupation and the expansion of settlements. He offers insights into the situation and predicts: "The cycle of violence, terrorism, Palestinian destitution and failed diplomacy will not be broken effectively unless there is political agreement that arrests and reverses the destructive dynamics on the ground."[8] The primary issue of the occupation is the Israeli Matrix of Control[9] through restriction of movement for Palestinians, checkpoints, military control, settlements and bureaucracy by Israel. This practice will always be experienced as a stranglehold on the people and their way of life. Any hope of advancement for the growing generation and the Palestinian state will take place when Israel changes the structure with new, creative policies.

The issue of international law, especially in relation to the occupation, will be taken up shortly. For the moment it needs to be made clear that the wording of the Fourth Geneva Convention applies directly to the issue of the occupation. It states: "The Occupying Power shall not deport or transfer parts of its own civilian population into the territory it occupies." [10] Israel, although a signatory to the Convention, refuses to accept the use of the words "occupy" or "occupation" as being valid. The outcome is the presence of hundreds of thousands of Jewish settlers on Palestinian land, with maximum government support and the protection of the IDF.

Settlements

The system of settlements on Palestinian land, Israeli-only roads and the Security Wall, or Barrier, which have fragmented the Palestinian population into semi-isolated blocs in the West Bank, is already documented in this book. Any viable Palestinian state would necessitate the removal of settlements and would take a very long time to achieve because: "The mass of legal and administrative arrangements underpinning the control of Israel and by settlers of Palestinian land will take decades, and immense political will, to overturn."[11]

Although their English version of the book was prepared before the Annapolis conference in November and December, 2007, Idith Zertal and Akiva Eldar detail how, despite the Lebanon War in the summer of 2006, the settlement building in the West Bank has continued apace. They write:

> The wall and the roadblocks are thwarting the movement of Palestinians in their lands and their ability to work. They are separating people from their fields, their relatives, and their neighbours and their children from their schools. Not only have the wall and the roadblocks made the Palestinians' lives less and less tolerable, but they are also collapsing the foundation on which Israel has based its policy since 1967 and undermining its legitimacy as well as its moral and security claims.... The network of infrastructures that link the settlements – the electricity grid, the water system, the formidable military forces that move around in the territory – are the elixir of life for the settlements, the secret of their power. Remove them from the equation and this [settlement] project collapses like a house of cards. If Israeli society ever finds the courage to separate itself from the territories it occupied in war, forty years ago, the country might finally restore its place in the region, and among the community of nations.[12]

The background story of the settlements is traced by Zertal and Eldar who see them as having the sense of a "sacred national-religious mission," the expansion of which would not have been possible without massive assistance from state institutions, legal assent and military support and protection.[13] They highlight the layers within the legal structures which enabled the violations of international law to be given legal legitimacy.[14] They register the collusion between the IDF and the settler movement, with the protection of the settlers, the supply of equipment for the settlements, and the passivity of the IDF when the settlers turned with violence on Palestinian farmers. In particular, when the military were called to dismantle a settlement, no matter how small, the soldiers could be forbidden to obey their orders by the *din moser* and *din rodef* rabbinic rulings by which the command structure could be rendered impotent for carrying out instructions. Although that particular ruling would only directly apply to religious Jews, Zertal and Eldar are able to sum up the overall situation by referring to "the phenomenal involvement of the State of Israel and all its institutions in the 'illegal activity' concerning the outposts and settlement in general, and the culture of deceit, concealment and evasion that has characterised this involvement."[15] This information was included in an extensive report, publicly submitted to Prime Minister Ariel

Sharon by the attorney Talia Sasson on 8 March, 2005, despite which, no action was taken to stop construction.[16]

The most significant of all the Israeli leaders identified by Zertal and Eldar is Ariel Sharon. They point to the dissonance between his words and his deeds. They reveal that, in 2004, the American Ambassador said: "Until now, Sharon has not kept his commitment."[17] "His explicit written commitment to President George W. Bush...to take down all of the outposts that had been established after March, 2001, was another of those countless times when he did not speak the truth."[18] They write that he continued to prevaricate at the 2003 Aqaba summit and again in December, 2003 at the Herzliya Conference. They further record that, in the spring of 2003, there was a celebration dinner in Jerusalem in honour of the former prime minister of Italy, Massimo d'Alema, who had had discussions with Sharon a few years earlier. The Italian statesman described his discussion over maps that Sharon had brought at the time, which addressed the future Palestinian state but: "It was a chopped-up bit of land in part of the occupied territories with no continuity between the various bits. Sharon declared: 'the only possibility for the Palestinians would be the establishment of Bantustans.'"[19]

International Law: The Security Wall and The International Court of Justice

In the Introduction to the English translation of their book, Zertal and Eldar, similarly to Professor Eyal Benvenisti[20] in his previous comment on the Occupation, refer to Article 49 of the Fourth Geneva Convention, to which Israel is a signatory, "The Occupying Power shall not deport or transfer parts of its own civilian population into the territory it occupies."[21] In so doing they describe Israel as an occupying state in contravention of international law. They distinguish between the State of Israel, consisting of the political, legal and civic entity, and the Land of Israel, or Eretz Israel, which they see as the embodiment of millenarian, religious, and national aspirations and myths. The political leadership of the State of Israel has the responsibility to honour its international obligations, but it is heavily influenced by the power of the military, ideological sector, as shown by both Professor David Kretzmer [22] and Uri Avnery.[23]

There are serious questions to be asked about international law and its effectiveness, particularly in regard to its relationship to international humanitarian law. The question has been posed by David Shearer and Anuschka Meyer of the United Nations, in relation to the International Court of Justice (ICJ) and its ruling that the Separation Barrier is illegal:

> Does the funding of new roads in the West Bank [by Israel] reinforce Israeli settlements deemed by law and the international community to be illegal? And should donors rebuild Palestinian houses, demolished by the Israeli Defence Forces (IDF) as part of their military operations, when international humanitarian law places that onus clearly on the Occupying Power? ... The concept of Israel meeting its

international obligations and paying for its occupation has yet to receive serious donor attention.[24]

In relation to the effects of the Barrier, they further highlight "the negative effects of a barrier which Israel has consistently been requested by the international community to remove."[25] The ICJ ruling of July, 2004, on the Separation Barrier in the West Bank included two important findings. One was the applicability of the Fourth Geneva Convention and the other was the responsibility of all the state parties to the Conventions being obliged to ensure Israel's respect for international law.[26] They describe Israel as the Occupying Power, under international law and, thereby:

> bears primary responsibility for assisting Palestinians in the current humanitarian crisis – not outside agencies or donors. The responsibilities of the occupier are laid down in the 1907 Hague Regulations and the 1949 Geneva Convention, to which Israel is a signatory. Under Article 43 of the Hague Regulations, Israel has a broad obligation to ensure the welfare of the population in the territories. Under the Fourth Geneva Convention, it is responsible for ensuring food, medical supplies and services for the population, as well as for maintaining institutions dedicated to the education and care of children.[27]

They go on to state: "Israel has traditionally disputed the applicability of the Geneva Convention to the occupied Palestinian territory, but an overwhelming body of international opinion has rejected this stance."[28] They also point out that the Israeli Supreme Court, after a delay of many years, now concedes that parts of the Convention should be observed. Moreover, outside assistance "does not relieve Israel of its ultimate responsibility to ensure. to the fullest extent possible that protected persons have access to food, medical supplies and medical services."[29] Nonetheless, it is not easily discerned whether any organisation has successfully sought to press that Israel should fulfil its responsibility, despite it being a signatory to the 1949 Conventions.

It seems astonishing to the onlooker that matters of urgent human need cannot be resolved by those charged with responsibility for effective resolution. That kind of failure in responsibility adds to an increasingly urgent need for creating a new structure for the bridge, if it is to be safe.

Racism and Apartheid

It is nothing new to associate separation devices with racism. In 1945 and 1946, I first encountered the divide between Catholics and Protestants in Ireland, both North and South. Fear and hatred, distrust and ostracism on both sides were the norm. The word "Apartheid" was not used but it was practised and evident in many areas. Similarly, between 1973 and 1977, I found similar divisions in the United States of America, both North and South. This time the issue was colour, and not religion, but the separation was accepted by both sides in many places, each disparaging the other. Intolerance, bigotry, ignorance and apartheid were both formal and informal. In both Ireland and America these issues now are past history, although the memories are still painful and deeply felt. The situation in Israel and Palestine has too many similar connections for one not to perceive signs of racism and its poisoned fruit of apartheid.

To introduce the notion of apartheid into any discussion of Israel's treatment of Palestinians in the Occupied Territories is to raise a storm, as ex-President Jimmy Carter discovered after the publication of his book in 2006.[30] In his own book, the Harvard lawyer, Professor Alan Dershowitz accuses him of "lying" and being "bigoted."[31] Dershowitz admits that, in the composition of his book, he used a number of "student research assistants" and his language is less than moderate, but unnecessarily inappropriate. He rightly calls for "balanced scholarship" and "reasoned discourse"[32] but seems to stray, himself, into the use of smears. In attacking the views of Carter, Professor John Dugard and others about their use of the word, "apartheid," Dershowitz draws attention to atrocities in other countries. He seems to argue that, because the measures used elsewhere are as bad, or worse, than Israel's, but not condemned, then Israel's actions should not be condemned.[33] Yet what satisfactory language is to be used to describe the situation? Although, he does not give his own definition to what others call "apartheid," he does seek to justify Israel's violent actions in terms of defence. Unfortunately, he seems to find it difficult to examine the cause and effect syndrome of violence, which others see as state and non- state terrorism, of which apartheid is a factor, and in this his arguments are weak.

Semantic differences were raised by some critics, but few, if any, questioned the objective realities of what Carter had raised, which concerned the system of legal racial separation and the acquisition of land. If the Israeli occupation, and the means it uses to sustain it, is neither racist nor apartheid, what definitions are to be used to describe them? It is Henry Siegman in the weekly US publication, *The Nation,* who brings out Carter's deep admiration for the Jewish people and that he calls for three conditions for peace.[34] They are Israel's security, the end to Palestinian violence and recognition by Israel of Palestine's right to statehood within the 1967 borders. These are not the characteristics of someone, "anti-semitic," as Carter had been labelled.

The issue of perceived apartheid in Israel has been frequently raised within Israel. Recently, in 2008, the liberation theology organisation in Jerusalem, Sabeel, raised the issue again in one of its publications, under the heading: 'The Apartheid Paradigm.'[35] The notion of apartheid in Israel is close to the reality for Palestinians as there are areas from which they are excluded, namely settlements and exclusive road systems. Two new words have been introduced into that Israeli context by the Director of Sabeel, the Rev. Naim Ateek, namely, Hafrada, used to describe separation by race, and Nishool, the word used for dispossession. Calling for the implementation of international law in Palestine, Ateek regards this form of racist apartheid that is practised by Israel as a crime.

This view is supported by Professor John Dugard, the Special Rapporteur to the United Nations on Human Rights in the Occupied Palestinian Territories. oPt.[36] He holds that, in international law, occupation is tolerated on an interim and temporary basis, under which the Occupying Power is obliged to protect the occupied people. Equally, as Professor Eyal Benvenisti pointed out to me in an interview, the occupied population is not meant to endanger the security of the Occupying Power.[37] Nonetheless, when occupation is blended with an apartheid system, it becomes like the system of colonialism, as described by Professor Gabriel Piterberg.[38] In this respect, Dugard sees settlements as a form of colonialism that the international community had condemned during the 1960s. He states the occupation that is apartheid has, in Israeli laws for Palestinians, become an exercise in racial discrimination. He holds that the occupation should be described as "an aggravated occupation, one which has elements of colonialism and elements of apartheid." [39] He calls for action by the International Court of Justice:

> to be asked for a further advisory opinion on the legal consequences of prolonged occupation, the consequences for the occupied people, the consequences for the occupying power and the consequences for third states…who have obligations in respect of the occupied people.[40]

In a discussion with Professor Anat Biletzki at Tel Aviv University,[41] she described for the author some of the privations which the Palestinians endured during the occupation. More recently, she expands her analysis against the background of the Israeli Declaration of Independence, which includes: "It will ensure complete equality of social and political rights to all its inhabitants, irrespective of religion, race or sex." Although the Occupied Territories are not formally part of the State of Israel, she points to the inequality, through the use of apartheid, which dominates the Palestinians in the West Bank. She gives as examples:

> 47 internal permanent checkpoints manned and womaned. *sic* by Israeli soldiers. There are 33 checkpoints between the West Bank and Israel. There are 73 gates in the wall. There are 200 flying checkpoints, you never know where they will be. There are 217 dirt piles at entrances to villages. There are 83 fences along the roadways. There are 93 locked gates at entrances to villages. There are 73 checkpoints in Hebron alone. These checkpoints are the icon of domination.[42]

References to the forbidden roads (700 kilometres) which are literally apartheid roads, segregated, and not for use by Palestinians, are amplified by Biletzki. She details the "separation barrier," a wall of 780 kilometres, largely built on Palestinian land:

> on its eastern side there are 69 settlements with around 60,000 Jews. On its western side there are still 21 villages with around 20,000 Palestinians. But there are another 200,000 Palestinians in enclosed villages and towns that are completely surrounded by the wall with one gate to go out. There are the approximately 25% of the 253,000 Palestinians in East Jerusalem [according to a January 2009 OCHA

report], who are on the wrong side of the wall. There are the million Palestinians in the old Green Line in Israel.... What kind of separation is this?[43]

The question is answered by Biletzki herself: "The realities on the ground are apartheid and apartheid is immoral." She holds that beneath the immoral elements of domination, inequality and separation lies the issue of racism which motivates the desire for separation – hence the separation barrier, wall, or fence. Although the question of racism and apartheid is highly charged, racism in the Israeli Jewish community is not new. It was present in the Histradut in the 1920s when Arabs were prevented from joining the trade union of the railway workers, at the instigation of Ben-Gurion.[44] It had not stopped in 2008. Internally, both sides have had, and still have, extremists who seek the end of the other, whether members of Hamas or Kach.

Such indeed appear to be the realities on the ground but it will be remembered that no state is immune from racism, or bellicosity. They are neither confined to Jewish policies towards Palestinians, nor to Palestinians, who are seen by some Jews as modern-day Amalekites. Hatred of Jews by certain leaders of countries in the Middle East is well documented, the most notorious of whom is President Mahmoud Ahmedinejad, with some of the Hizbollah leadership in close company. Racial superiority is often a defence against fears of inferiority which we project on to others, in order to protect ourselves and our damaged self-esteem. It would be a mark of superior statesmanship by Israel if its political and religious leaders joined in protest against policies and practice, by word and deed, against all forms of racism. It is here that Israel could take the lead, to be joined at speed by the rest of humanity.

The External Structures

The structures that involve outside interests in this section are of immense significance because they have been involved in the traumas since the Displaced Persons problems following the wars of 1948. Despite the human effort put in over the years and the countless millions of euros, pounds and dollars that have been poured into the region, the situation is worse now by far for both Israelis and Palestinians. For Palestinians, they are without their state, and look unlikely to have one that is viable, having been reduced in size, freedom and power. For Israelis, they are still insecure and fearful, despite their wealth, military strength and freedom. Apart from the massive annual financial and military aid from America to Israel, international aid goes almost exclusively to relieving the plight of Palestinians. Beyond the partial and limited meeting of immediate need, it does not bring about real change in the capacity of a people to function fully as an autonomous nation and to be part of the international community. The different types of external aid and the concept of proper accountability are shown to be deficient in terms of creating and developing a structure that bodes well for the future of both peoples.

Development, Humanitarian and Emergency Aid

Generally speaking, "Aid" is perceived to be a generic word rather than specific. However, donors at the international level are more prescriptive about the purpose for which their funds should be directed. The examination of the different uses of aid is well described by Keating and his colleagues.[45] There are crucial differences between Development Aid, Humanitarian Aid and Emergency Aid. In Palestine, most of the aid from donor organisations has been a combination of humanitarian and emergency relief in order to relieve suffering and to save lives. It has not been used for development projects.[46] The international community does provide immense amounts of both money and goods to assist the Palestinians, and it could be argued that it is Israel's obligation, as the controlling power, to meet the needs of the calamitous situation for which it is partly responsible and has the power to change. There are no statistics for the loss of Palestinian trade and income, caused by Israeli policies of closures, checkpoints, restriction of movement, prevention of transportation of goods, etc. The destruction of the airport in Gaza and the refusal to allow the construction of a seaport, combined with complete control over borders with Egypt, Jordan, Syria and Lebanon prevents the Strip's independent, commercial existence. Despite the obvious advantages that such structural expansion would bring to the Palestinian economy, there is neither development aid, nor donor pressure, for such an obvious task to be undertaken as a matter of urgency.

The gap between humanitarian aid and societal construction is blurred because it deals with symptoms and not the causes. It deals with the disease instead of focusing on its causes, particularly poverty and injustice. Quite rightly, in certain conditions elsewhere, donors create emergency medical services and clinics, with appropriate staff to deal with the presenting problems. Proper analysis and adequate resources need to be put in place to deal with the underlying structural causes, for example inadequate drainage, sewage disposal, sanitation, in addition to shelter, food and water. Without such infrastructure, those who cannot leave can become institutionalised and pauperised. The principles of analysis and resources can be extended to cover any human situation, if there is the will so to do, with emphasis being placed by the donors on those who are involved in both the presenting problems and the structural causes, especially Israel and Palestine.

The vacuum in effective aid is recognised by many, including Halper who refers to conflict between humanitarianism and political work. Although donor assistance is well-intended, the afflicted are not empowered and enabled to join together in political resistance, thereby shielding Israel from the suffering it causes, for example, in making families homeless. Halper views the unintended consequence of humanitarian aid as the subsidising of an occupation that Israel could otherwise not afford to maintain. As it is, humanitarian aid sustains and makes oppression tolerable and does nothing to promote empowerment or development. He writes: "Development assistance may be appropriate if political processes are indeed leading to self-determination, but it may be premature, even harmful to its intended beneficiaries, if no political horizon exists."[47]

When humanitarian aid replaces development aid, it reduces the crucially important strategy which should replace the destroyed infrastructure, as was the case in Germany after the cessation of hostilities in 1945 and thereafter. Instead, there appears to be little political, international intervention on behalf of Palestinian manufacturers, farmers and fishermen who, in a number of ways, are prevented from attending to the production of food and the distribution of harvests. These hostile interventions by settlers, often with the protection of the IDF, are regularly monitored and recorded by Rabbis for Human Rights (RHR) and B'tselem[48] who report on malign, violent activities by settlers and the IDF.

How far is it true that Israel deliberately refuses to meet its obligations, yet profits by what the State inflicts or permits to be inflicted? In 2005, the international lawyers, Shearer and Meyer posed the problem as follows:

> Contrary to most perceptions, aid is not necessarily positive or benign. Pouring an immense amount of aid into a conflict, without either the structure of a peace agreement or a solid analysis of its impact, is comparable to speeding along a road at night without headlights. Blindly continuing aid without seriously examining donors' responsibilities, the obligations of the occupier and its general impact could undermine the ground for future peace agreements.... It is time for donors to examine how $1 billion a year might be used more effectively – with imposed conditions – as a lever for peace rather than being suckered. *sic* into simply buying the sticking plasters.[49]

The issue is still a matter of priorities and human will. This was plain for the eye to see in 2005 in Bethlehem and Beit Jala, when the infrastructure, which had been put in place for the Millennium in 2000, was destroyed. [50] Keating stated in 2005:

> The issue now is whether there is a practical basis and political will to square Israel's security requirements with the imperative of meeting humanitarian needs and reviving the Palestinian economy... It [Sharon's enthusiasm] has been dampened by constant reminders that the immediate cause of Palestinian impoverishment and the humanitarian crisis is Israel's policy of closure.[51]

It needs to be stated clearly that Israeli leaders, then and now, have little, if any, confidence in the capacity of the Palestinians to guarantee the security of Israel from extremists within the Palestinian community. Despite this issue, Keating continues with his query: "Israel justifies its actions, whether on closure, settlements or the barrier on the grounds of security ... The question is ... whether Israeli security measures are being extended and used ... by Israeli leaders as 'cover' for a far broader political agenda."[52]

Accountability and Responsibility

The issue of aid became increasingly complex after Oslo. Israel was given more and more financial aid without any strings attached and the IDF grew and the settlements expanded. President Bill Clinton was primarily concerned for Israel's security which he made his priority.[53] The annual financial package for Israel was to grow to become in excess of $3 billion. The Palestinians were also given aid without proper accountability while the economy declined. The issues of corruption and mismanagement were widely known, as well as funds being distributed without either monitoring or reckoning. Proper accounting procedures, so that they are in the public domain, have not been disclosed by either Israel or Palestine.

Following the failures of Oslo, there were what first appeared to be meaningful meetings at Camp David in July, 2000. In the end, there were differing versions forthcoming and scapegoats sought and found. Public attention was first drawn to the apparent failures of Yasser Arafat and Barak's "generous offer" but over time, other perspectives were given greater consideration. Zertal and Eldar reveal that the settler movement mounted opposition meetings with some 200,000 protesting in Rabin Square, Tel Aviv on 17 July, 2000, while settlements were still being built.[54] Further Israeli-Palestinian meetings with President Clinton were planned for Taba in January, 2001 but came to nothing, despite more constructive moves being put forward. It was too late although, by then, it was realised that the fault had been not so much because of Arafat as much as Barak and Clinton. [55] Karmi writes: "Israel was not prepared to withdraw to the pre-1967 borders, would not remove the settlements, would not relinquish East Jerusalem and rejected the Palestinian right of return."[56] The Second Intifada was to follow.

There was temporary hope that the Road Map of 2003 might be creative and productive if the custodians had exercised their responsibilities with due diligence and mutual, determined commitment. Three assumptions were: Palestinian security reform, a freeze on Israeli settlement expansion, and diplomatic instruments at the disposal of the custodians of the Road Map would be used if and when they were required.[57] This has not happened. The two recipient parties have not been held accountable for the promises they made to the international community and for the aid they received from international donors. There has been no visible sign of successful moves by the Quartet of the United Nations, the European Union, the United States of America and Russia to bring about any health to the asymmetric relationship of Israel and Palestine.

The issue of responsibility for ensuring that aid is properly managed and accountable has yet to happen. Nor is its international largesse dependent on wider issues of peace, security and confidence building, on a basis of even-handedness. Israel should not have a veto on Palestinian expenditure on an airport and seaport, any more than the Palestinians should be able to veto Israeli expenditure. Neither side need have *carte blanche* for their distribution of millions of dollars in aid, but could be made subject to approval, monitoring and payment by results, provided that the donors had the will. As the aid is provided without conditions, the recipients are free to pursue their goals, whether honourable and idealistic, or ideological, security-based and questionable.

It is likely that things will not remain the same. The financial power of the USA may be strong but other countries are coming into the world frame, not least China and India, while Russia still has power of influence. The Islamic nations still have the capacity for greater involvement and persuasion. However, the aid issue has become increasingly suspect. Huge sums of money have been given by the USA and other nations and the outcome has been a more military Israel and a shattered, fragmented, disempowered Palestine. As a result, there is no symmetry so that the two peoples can meet as partners; one is dominant and the other is resentful and weak, dependent on foreign aid which produces no stimulation of the economy. Meanwhile, the status quo continues, with the USA bankrolling the expansion by Israel of its land control and military machine. The world meanwhile also becomes increasingly unsafe.

The system has been described by the Harvard lecturer and barrister, Claude Bruderlein as: "... dysfunctionality in the aid process."[58] Focusing on the reduced circumstances of the Palestinians in particular, he is another who holds that, despite massive funding, the international community has not helped to improve their human security within their restricted land base. The financial aid from voluntary and statutory agencies has not been seen to be sufficiently accountable, monitored and strategically used, beyond meeting immediate humanitarian needs.

The creation of investment structures was raised in separate meetings in 1995, with two organisations, Sabeel and World Vision, which worked on the ground from their bases in Jerusalem.[59] The idea was to explore how to create job opportunities for Palestinians. Although seen as an essential ingredient to the peace process, it was never carried through by those larger organisations which had the finance and infrastructure so to do. Nor was adequate pressure brought to bear on Israel to bring about change. Unless this alters, on a massive scale, financial aid will continue to fail to address the fundamental problems of employment, with freedom of movement to work and for the sale and export of produce.

The Ad Hoc Liaison Committee (AHLC) for development assistance in Palestine met in Oslo during December, 2004 and discussed the notion of a "conditional donor financing strategy" and argued that:

> large, additional sums of assistance ... should be made conditional on the performance of both parties ... [The underlying causes of the crisis include] ... the system of closure and Israeli restrictions on the movement of Palestinian goods and people ... [therefore] international actors can, and must, play a decisive role in ending the conflict. [60]

This means a more responsible way of distribution and accountability for the aid and pressure by government on those who subvert or obstruct the process. Otherwise, donors: " ... will remain complicit in a dynamic ... that cannot bring sustainable peace to Palestinians and Israelis."[61]

Political Structures

The major issue of human dignity is part of the desired structure for any civilised nationhood and, all too easily, it can be forfeited by factors such as Guantanamo Bay or Abu Ghraib in Iraq. Whether suicide bombing, or occupation and displacement of a people in defiance of international law, onlookers perceive levels of human behaviour in Israel and Palestine which are beyond the pale. It is not only that they bring affliction to others but, of themselves, they demean those who perform such acts of cruelty and violence. In their quest for security and statehood, the means regularly employed are opened here for analysis as they affect the culture and standing of the activists. This applies to both Hamas and the security apparatus of the State of Israel

Israeli Security and Palestinian Statehood

Apart from some threatened, remote, native tribes in South America, few from outside the Jewish community can empathise with the fear of utter annihilation because they have not been exposed to the same terror. It is the primary issue of the Shoah which, understandably, is still a determining factor for life in Israel. When that crucial factor is understood and appreciated, there is likely to be less misunderstanding about apparent failures in international negotiations which fail to bring security for Jews who still remember the camps in which so many died. The notion of exploitation of fears of a future Shoah may well be the case by some who use the fear as an opportunity to exploit a situation in terms of land appropriation or for disproportionate retaliation against an aggressor. Nonetheless, that does not do away with the objective reality of their history of pogroms and persecution through the ages. In terms of the Six Day War of 1967, the issue of preventive strikes against an Egyptian threat to its existence is perceived to be understandable. Similarly, the settlement expansion can be seen to be not only religious zealotry, but national security. Not only the religious, but the secular are reluctant to go close to compromising the safety of the Jews in Israel. When threats are made to its existence by Iran, Hizbollah or Hamas, the fears of the Jews for their extermination are reignited. Although it has not brought peace in sixty years, any notion of an end to the occupation disappears from sight and reason.

The reduction of the size of Palestine since 1947 and the restrictions on the potency of Palestinians since 1967, provoke serious, multiple anxieties in the Arab population. One would have expected an empathy for them from the Jews who had their own experience of deprivation. In fact, that expectation was unrealistic in the face of acute Jewish fears for themselves, especially when they are aware of the demographic imbalance that is rapidly growing. The impasse that has been created by Israel's policy of occupation, subjugation and control cannot last forever. Change will surely happen eventually, but on what basis and in what time frame? The Matrix of Control, with its system of settlements, checkpoints, exclusive roads and the gradually extending Security Barrier or Wall, coupled with the segmenting of Palestinian communities from each other, reveal a sham society for, supposedly, civilised communities. Mushtaq Khan asks the international community "to reconsider some of its own assumptions about the strategic goals of both parties, and the price that is to be paid, if Israel's underlying strategic goal [of security through Palestinian Bantustans] is not to be questioned."[62]

United Nations Resolution 242, dated 22 November, 1967 was designed to facilitate the return to the pre-war borders of 1967. The Security Council Resolution included:

(i) Withdrawal of Israeli armed forces from territories occupied in the recent conflict;

(ii) Termination of all claims or states of belligerency and respect for and acknowledgment of the sovereignty, territorial integrity and political independence of every State in the area and their right to live in peace within secure and recognised boundaries free from threats or acts of force;

(iii) Affirms further the necessity:
For achieving a just settlement of the refugee problem.

That it has still not come about is because of the determination of the Israeli government, aided and abetted by the religious settlers, to be proactive in defence and expansion by retaining the land. Any future Palestinian state that was to become viable and strong was hardly to be considered essential by a security-first government. They were all too aware of the Arab threat to its existence from within the West Bank and from the bordering Arab nations. Hamas still resists the 1947 Partition by the United Nations and inflames the situation with its threats to destroy Israel. Ever since the Partition, there have been regular Israeli concessions to the principle of a Palestinian state but avoidance and vacillation on its details. In the background is always the looming threat of what would happen if there was a fully independent Palestinian state with external borders and a successful, functioning economy. In addition, within Israel is the demand by many in the religious minority that the population of the land should be entirely Jewish, although such a move would mean that it could not be a democracy. Regardless of Israel's disengagement from Gaza, there is daily evidence of restricting the survival and growth of a Palestinian entity. In its policies, Israel is permitted to exercise a suzerainty without effective intervention by the international community. It is a long way from becoming a democratic state.

Meanwhile, Israel manages an untenable, extremely long-term situation, at immense cost in terms of finance and respect on an international scale, and which does not bode well for the future. Its own internal dilemmas confuse and thereby prevent any resolution. It refuses to permit the development of a two-state solution, as long as it sees such a development not providing the security it seeks. Its restrictive policies result in increasing suspicion about, and animosity towards, its motives and actions. Some see that Israel intends to manage this situation by creating Palestinian enclaves or Bantustans of Palestinian communities, none of which would be viable. Despite bringing poverty and despair to Palestinians, a worse scenario for Israel is to make itself vulnerable if it allowed for a sovereign, contiguous and viable state with international borders, including a seaport and an airport. Those who advocate a single Jewish-Arab state are not perceived to be grounded in the difficulties of an ethnic-demographic equality, which would involve equal rights across the board. This is unthinkable for those who seek for a Jewish state. Meanwhile, Israel makes agreements and undertakings, accompanied by caveats concerning security, but pursues its policies of settlement building and control of Palestinians.

The international community stands back and tolerates these double-standards, especially the United States which has fortified successive Israeli governments with financial aid, military support, diplomatic protection and political reinforcement in the UN Security Council. The European Union and Russia, while not so generous, nonetheless appear largely uncritical of Israel's actions and policies, so that Israel continues with its "security" measures, at great cost to Palestinians and the Universal Declaration of Human Rights. It is not a matter of finding Israel as either villain or victim of the scenario. It is rather one of honest appreciation and confrontation of Israel's limited and paranoid destructive strategy for security. As such, it makes a policy of militarism more important than bridge building. Meanwhile, Palestinians look at the international community in the United Nations with despair, where there should be hope.

The relation between the cabinet leadership of Israel and the legal-security structure of the country is one that is vital for Israel. Over all else, the cabinet has one supreme priority, that of "Security," and that includes a strategic involvement in the economy of Israel through the military-industrial complex. Because of that priority, the security hierarchy, which includes the IDF, Shin Bet and Mossad, are represented by the Chief of Staff at all cabinet meetings. The power, influence and control that can be exerted by the military establishment is evident, where security is the ultimate, crucial factor. As a lawyer of some substance, Dershowitz has made much of Israel's enlightened legal system. He holds that Israel: "in actuality leads the world in human rights jurisprudence and whose Supreme Court is trusted even by Israel's harshest critics."[63] This is not the case and he omits the fact that its decisions are always subject to issues deemed to be matters of "Security." In contrast to Dershowitz, Professor of Law, David Kretzmer,[64] holds that the strategy of security is acknowledged as paramount and the advice of the security chiefs in the decision making of any cabinet meeting takes precedence. The intertwining of the military with settlers has also been seen as symbiotic, where many settlers are from within the military structures. Because of the military-security culture within Israel, the notion of breaking free from its dominant influence awaits change that is unlikely to come about in the immediate future. Meanwhile, any relaxation of the stranglehold on Palestinians cannot be foreseen.

Gaza and Hamas

When it comes to referring to Gaza, one cannot but be reminded of the shame of Germany, which still exists in relation to its treatment of Jews in ghettoes, perhaps most appallingly in Warsaw. Of all the nations to be sensitive to the treatment of civilians in restricted areas, one would have expected that Israel would be the most responsible of nations. Sadly, the treatment of Palestinians by Israel evokes too many connections with the oppression of one people by another. Was nothing learned during the Shoah about levels of human behaviour? Quite understandably, Israelis are frightened by the stance of the Hamas leadership when it appears to be antagonistic and threatening to Israel. Moreover, in many respects, Israeli fears of Hamas in Gaza cannot be separated from fears of what might happen if Hamas was elected in the West Bank. If rockets can be fired into Israel from Gaza, they could be fired from the West Bank into Tel Aviv and Ben-Gurion International Airport. Even during the Hamas cease-fire in the latter half of 2008, Hamas did not prevent the firing of rockets into southern Israel by other groups.

Equally, it is understandable that Hamas feels under massive pressure from Israel and its American and European supporters. The ongoing impasse helps no one but results in animosity and intransigence. There is no space created by those involved to construct opportunities for the proper examination of the fears and injustices of both Jews and Arabs. This has to include space for examining resentment over previous international agreements, such as the Oslo Accords of 1993, which appear one-sided and disadvantageous for Palestinians and, seemingly, without mutual justice. Although existing agreements are considered sacrosanct under normal circumstances, the present situation is not normal. Therefore, is it too much to expect that the participants might be sufficiently strong to re-examine, and even reconsider agreements, such as the Oslo Accords? For Hamas in Gaza and Jews in Israel is this a bridge too far? As long as the gulf exists, both sides bring out the worst in each other and the civilian populations live under the threat of state and non-state terrorism. As in Northern Ireland, both sides have to be strong enough to move beyond their intransigence and to find common ground.

One of the paramount obstacles is the demand by Israel and the West that Hamas should recognise Israel's right to exist. This recognition is a one-sided demand and has yet to become part of a mutual recognition so that Israel equally recognises the right of Palestine to exist as a defined, viable State. This has never been agreed, beyond a general, imprecise set of words, which carry no weight or significance while lands are occupied, movement of people and goods restricted, and without international borders of land and sea.

In relation to the disengagement from Gaza in 2005, Michael Keating predicted:

> if it is not linked to a political agreement that ends occupation and the expansion of settlements in the West Bank, and is not accompanied by a lifting of restrictions

on the Palestinian economy, it is unlikely to achieve peace – let alone the realization of a viable Palestinian state.[65]

With hindsight, it can be seen that this was a prophetic statement. At the time, there was no Hamas government in Gaza but its election in 2006 was followed by a virtual blockade of a people who had made a democratic choice in the elections. The success of Hamas was a choice which appalled those in Israel and the United States who then constructed a clampdown on the people. There was no longer a bridge, or a structure, or any kind of blueprint. What continued was a case where no side was innocent, but seriously culpable, and with no effective interlocutor.

The disengagement from Gaza in 2005 had been preceded by the destruction of Jewish property by the owners. Furthermore, because of the blockade by Israel against Gaza, the access to Egypt is restricted and access to Israel is limited to a trickle. The pathetic, but alarming, rocket attacks on Israel by Palestinian resistance are met with disproportionate, retaliatory violence against the civilian population by the IDF. No one can defend the use of armaments against Jewish civilians in Sderot and Ashkelon, even if they are considered to be invaders. Equally, the failure to allow for new structures in terms of a seaport and airport, accompanied by restrictions of the movement of Gaza fishermen, all add to the destruction of Palestinian life. The failure of Israel and the international community to recognise the elected government of Hamas is a punitive, reactive and destructive process, rather than one that is enlightened, humanitarian and exhibits a willingness to find common concerns. It was argued by Uri Avnery, "Israel does not recognise the Hamas government in Gaza but holds it responsible for the attacks from there. Israel does not recognise the Hamas government in Gaza but demands that it guarantee the cease-fire there."[66] A strategy of sidelining the militants and encouraging the non-militants has yet to appear. Neither Israel, nor militant Hamas, show any sign of strategies that would encourage constructive moves for a creative future for both Gazans and Israelis. Yossi Alpher, formerly of the Jaffee Centre for Strategic Studies writes: "Israel should wish, for purely pragmatic reasons of self-interest, to ensure a reasonable level of Palestinian prosperity and economic growth as a means of enhancing regional stability."[67] Hopefully, that prosperity is not feared, but welcomed, by Israel.

The move from Gaza by Sharon did not herald a new dawn, even before the election of Hamas. After the settlements were stripped by the owners, there was no strategic plan put forward to create hope for the people. Israel turned it into a prison, partly because of the security threat from home-made rockets fired by extremists, to say nothing of Hamas. This has provided an opportunity to oppress the Gaza people even more, so that any aid for development is prevented and even humanitarian aid has been reduced. Basic public services of water, sewage systems, electricity, medical supplies have all been restricted through the Israeli blockade. The evacuation of Gaza by Israel has been followed by oppression, rather than support for it to become a viable part of a future Palestinian state. The situation prevails because the international community appears unwilling to countenance Hamas but is prepared to support Israel.

At the time of the disengagement, two sides of Israeli society were in conflict. One side saw it as a fresh start for Israeli-Palestinian relations and the other side saw it as a cunning strategy by Ariel Sharon to be relieved of an irksome problem in order to gain an even stronger position in the West Bank. This was to come to pass. Gaza was not released from: " ... Israel's military grip or from the price of the occupation ... nor did it bring quiet and security to the communities on the south-western border of Israel, or even to its other borders. It gave rise only to more hatred, more destruction and more hopelessness."[68] Meanwhile, the construction of the "separation wall" continued in the West Bank, along with a combination of several hundred roadblocks of varying size, either huge or small or mobile, that stifled the movement of Palestinians in the course of their daily undertakings.

The Gaza disengagement was intended to end the occupation there, but it seems possible to have been a move to deepen the occupation of the West Bank, bringing even greater control over the Palestinians. Zertal and Eldar hold: "Israel left behind a scorched earth, devastated services, and people with neither a present nor a future.[69] The settlements were left in a state of ruin and the population have been harassed, killed, bombed, shelled, and deprived of proper community services of health, water, power, sanitation and the means of production and distribution. The oft quoted statement of Sharon's adviser, Dov Weisglass, summarised the intention for Gaza. "The disengagement plan is ... the bottle of formaldehyde within which you place the president's [George W. Bush] formula so that it will be preserved for a very lengthy period ... there will not be a political process with the Palestinians." [70]

The election of Hamas in 2006 came about, partly and significantly, through the failure of Fatah to improve the life of Palestinians and its own corruption. Hamas was elected and was very different, rejecting Israel's right to exist, refusing to abandon violence and refusing to abide by previous agreements which were unequal. Led by the USA and Israel, the Quartet joined with them against Hamas because it was seen as a terrorist organisation which wanted to be rid of Israel. Yet it was democratically elected and needed open hands, not clenched fists. Nonetheless, the Quartet set down a financial and political blockade with the ultimatum for Hamas to recognise Israel and all previous agreements, and denounce violence. All non-negotiable!

This meant that the stalled peace process had become the fault of the Palestinians and not Israel, despite the latter having prevaricated since 1967. Karmi writes that by Israel's leaders continuing to declare that there was no "Palestinian partner," a number of restrictive practices were put in place to limit gas and fuel supplies and halt the monthly transfer of Palestinian tax and customs receipts which Israel collected for the Palestine Authority. Western aid of $1 billion each year, which paid the salaries of 160,000 government employees, was cut off and basic services were closed, impoverishing the families and halting basic services.⁷¹ It was a "pistol to the head" strategy, called "conditions," but EU states joined in. The outcome was not the expected submission, but impoverishment and burning resentment. There was, in 2006, and continued in 2008, a humanitarian crisis as 78 percent of Gazans are below the poverty line. Gaza fishermen are unable to fish for a larger catch because they are not allowed to sail beyond the beach and harbour area. In June, 2006 the ICRC announced a "major humanitarian emergency" unless aid was forthcoming.

In 2007, Karmi had raised the perennial question for the Jews which was how to establish a secure Jewish state when they did not have a land of their own. This subject has already been raised in this book. Piterberg shows that their solution was resolved by occupying territory where their ancestors had once lived, centuries earlier, according to their mythical tradition.⁷² Karmi holds that Israel, aided by Western powers: "was allowed to impose its own vision for the future, colonising Palestinian land and excluding or expelling its inhabitants ... It was their permissive attitude and the inaction of the international community that led ultimately to the current problems."⁷³ Israel's enterprise was never checked, but had grown steadily after 1947, and even before then. Its absolute power over Gaza is unmatched and is used brutally, with a very feeble response by a few militants. The outcome is poverty, hatred and a desire for revenge by Arabs. Israel's hegemony means that it has licence to do what it wants – for now – but in the long term one wonders. Both sides have visionaries and both sides have ungovernable forces who will not hesitate to use savagery. How long will enlightened Jews stay in that kind of society? How long will oppression and hegemonic force of Israel be tolerated, both from within and outside?

Despite the claim that "Israel ... goes to extraordinary lengths to avoid killing innocent people,"⁷⁴ there is a growing list of civilian deaths and injuries by Israeli forces. It is understandable if Israel responds to provocative acts of Palestinian violence, but it is the nature of the response that is of importance. It was B'tselem, the Israeli Centre for Human Rights in the Occupied Territories, which reported that, on 5 October, 2008, two Gaza fishermen in a row boat were fired on without warning by an Israeli navy vessel in the zone permitted for fishing by the army.⁷⁵ One of the fishermen, Muhammad Musleh, was severely injured in the leg and, at the time of the publication, was being treated in al-Muqassed Hospital in Jerusalem. B'tselem reported in the same item of news that it knew of numerous cases in the last two years, of soldiers shooting and abusing fishermen on the Gaza shoreline. Things could change if and when there is the will to create projects in which both can share and work together.

Even the banking system in Gaza is controlled by Israel. It was reported by Rabbis for Human Rights on 7 December, 2008, released on December 12 that, as part of its overall closure policy, Israel was preventing the transfer of cash to banks in Gaza. This primarily harmed the 77,000 employees of the Palestinian authority, and the family members they support, because they were not receiving their salaries for November. The report points out that, just as it is strictly forbidden by international law to fire rockets at Israeli citizens in southern Israel, so it is forbidden to punish 1.5 million civilians in Gaza in response, depriving them of the means necessary to support themselves. The report concludes: "It is not clear what the Government of Israel wishes to achieve by destroying the economic and humanitarian foundations of Palestinian society."

When the President of Israel, Shimon Peres, visited London and was interviewed on the Today Programme of BBC Radio 4 on 18 November, 2008, he referred to the Gaza situation. In it, he included the statement that the Israeli troops had completely withdrawn, despite the fact that there were still rockets being fired into Israel. This can be seen as only a partial truth. Peres described it as terrorism, whereas others would describe it as resistance. On 29 January, 2009, Dr Henry Siegman wrote, "In other words, when Jews target and kill innocent civilians to advance their national, struggle, they are patriots. When their adversaries do so, they are terrorists."[76] Peres had omitted two important facts: one was that Israeli land and sea forces consistently conducted attacks against Gaza, which resulted in loss of civilian lives and damage to property; the other was the regular prevention of essential supplies to sustain the Gazan import and export economy, as well as the medical and health services. In addition, he failed to mention the embargo at the border crossing so that fuel supplies could not be delivered to enable the power station to function. It would have been more statesmanlike to speak of using the considerable resources of Israel to engage more in conflict prevention and conflict resolution, rather than by the aggravation of the conflict. Was nothing to be learned from Northern Ireland, for example, where eventually, atrocities were not followed by atrocities, but by creating ways for meeting and finding common ground? The stronger party always has the major responsibility for creating opportunities for peace, because, unlike the weaker party, it has the power and the resources. For the weaker party, the Palestinians, they can submit or resist, but they cannot win. Israel has that power, and those resources, to enable the land to bloom for both peoples by creating initiatives for peace, justice and security in which Jew and Arab can strive together.

Having worked successfully on joint projects for years, Daniel Barenboim writes:

> I have come to believe that morality and strategy are not exclusive to each other, but rather go hand in hand in this conflict. If the two narratives [Jew and Arab] are legitimate, their destinies inseparable, and there is no military solution, then the acceptance of the narrative of the other must inevitably lead to the logical conclusion that what is good for the one is, in the long term, good for the other ... Israel undoubtedly has a right to exist. The Palestinian people undoubtedly have a right to a sovereign, legitimate state. Israel needs security. The Palestinians need equality and dignity. Only they can provide that to each other... Israel's security can, in the long term, come only through its acceptance by the Palestinians and other neighbours. At the moment, the Palestinians' equality and dignity can be provided only by Israel ... Isolation of parties will make them part of the problem; inclusion will make them part of the solution.[77]

There will, very likely, be "afterwords" and "postscripts" on the Israeli – Palestinian situation for another half-century! Here is mine in 2009.

Notes

[1] Royal Institute of International Affairs.

[2] Keating M., 'Introduction' in *Aid, Diplomacy and Facts on the Ground,* eds., Michael Keating, Anne Le More & Robert Lowe. London: Royal Institute of International Affairs 2005, 11.

[3] Kahn M. H., "'Security First' and its Implications for a Viable Palestinian State" in *Aid, Diplomacy and Facts on the Ground* eds., Michael Keating, Anne Le More & Robert Lowe. London: Royal Institute of International Affairs 2005, 73.

[4] Piterberg G. *The Returns of Zionism.* London: Verso, 2008, 62 ff.

[5] Karmi G., *Married to Another Man.* London: Pluto, 2007, 260.

[6] Karmi, 260.

[7] Interview with Professor of Political Theology, Dr. Haddon Wilmer, Leeds University.

[8] Keating M., 'Introduction' in *Aid, Diplomacy and Facts on the Ground* eds., Michael Keating, Anne Le More & Robert Lowe. London: Royal Institute of International Affairs 2005, 1-2.

[9] Halper J. *Obstacles to Peace.* Bethlehem: PalMap of GSE, 2004, 12-20.

[10] Benvenisti E., *The International Law of Occupation* (Princeton, N J: Princeton University Press 1993), 108ff.

[11] Keating. 3.

[12] Zertal & Eldar, *Lords of the Land* . (New York: Nation Books, 2008), xiv-xvi.

[13] Zertal & Eldar, xviiff.

[14] Zertal & Eldar, 333ff.

[15] Zertal & Eldar, 440.

[16] Zertal & Eldar, 440-441.

[17] Zertal & Eldar, 439.

[18] Zertal & Eldar, 438.

[19] Zertal & Eldar, 423.

[20] Benvenisti E., *The International Law of Occupation* (Princeton, NJ: Princeton University Press 1993), 108ff.

[21] Zertal & Eldar, x. and 455 n.2.

[22] Kretzmer D. *The Occupation of Justice (*Albany: SUNY, 2002).

[23] Avnery U., article Olmert's Successor.doc uri-avnery@list.avnery-news.co.il 15 September, 2008.

[24] Shearer D., & Meyer A., 'The Dilemma of Aid Under Occupation' in *Aid, Diplomacy and Facts on the Ground* eds., Michael Keating, Anne Le More & Robert Lowe (London: Royal Institute of International Affairs 2005), 166.

[25] Shearer & Meyer, 172.

[26] International Court of Justice, *Legal Consequences of the Construction of a Wall in the Occupied Palestinian Territory, Advisory Opinion,* 9 July, 2004, paras. 101 and 159.

[27] Shearer & Meyer, 169-170, re Fourth Geneva Convention, Articles 50, 55, 56.

[28] Shearer & Meyer, 170.

[29] Shearer & Meyer, 170.

[30] Carter J., *Palestine Peace Not Apartheid* (New York, Simon & Schuster, 2006).

[31] Dershowitz A., *The Case against Israel's Enemies* (Hoboken, N. J., John Wiley and Sons, 2008), 22.
[32] Dershowitz, 226.
[33] Dershowitz, 34.
[34] Henry Siegman, 'Hurricane Carter', *The Nation,* 22 January, 2007.
[35] Naim Ateek, 'The Apartheid Paradigm', *Cornerstone.* 48. Spring 2008, 1-4. *Cornerstone* is the quarterly publication by Sabeel Ecumenical Liberation Theology Center Jerusalem.
[36] John Dugard, 'Occupation, Apartheid and Colonialism in International Law', *Cornerstone.* 48. Spring 2008, 11-13.
[37] Eyal Benvenisti, interview with author, Tel Aviv University, 9 November, 2004.
[38] Piterberg G., *The Returns of Zionism.* London: Verso, 2008, 62-68.
[39] John Dugard, 'Occupation, Apartheid and Colonialism in International Law', *Cornerstone.* 48. Spring 2008, 11-13.
[40] Dugard, 13.
[41] Anat Biletzki, interview with author, TAU, 13 April, 2005, currently, 2008, at M.I.T., Boston, Mass.
[42] Anat Biletzki, 'Domination, Inequality and Apartheid', *Cornerstone.* 48. Spring 2008, 14-16.
[43] Biletzki, 14.
[44] Piterberg G., *The Returns of Zionism* (London: Verso, 2008), 71-73.
[45] *Aid, Diplomacy and Facts on the Ground*, eds., Michael Keating, Anne Le More & Robert Lowe, (London: Royal Institute of International Affairs 2005).
[46] Alpher Y., 'Israel's Aid Responsibilities towards the Palestinian Population' in *Aid, Diplomacy and Facts on the Ground* eds., Michael Keating, Anne Le More & Robert Lowe (London: Royal Institute of International Affairs 2005), 155.
[47] Halper J, "'Victims of War are not like Victims of Earthquake': the Conflict Between Humanitarianism and Political Work,'" in *Aid, Diplomacy and Facts on the Ground* eds., Michael Keating, Anne Le More & Robert Lowe (London: Royal Institute of International Affairs 2005), 192.
[48] See the websites of Rabbis for Human Rights and B'tselem for more detailed information.
[49] Shearer D., & Meyer A., 'The Dilemma of Aid Under Occupation' in *Aid, Diplomacy and Facts on the Ground* eds., Michael Keating, Anne Le More & Robert Lowe (London: Royal Institute of International Affairs 2005), 176.
[50] As witnessed by the author in Bethlehem and Beit Jala in April, 2005.
[51] Keating M., 'Introduction' in *Aid, Diplomacy and Facts on the Ground*, eds., Michael Keating, Anne Le More & Robert Lowe (London: Royal Institute of International Affairs 2005), 9.
[52] Keating M., 'Introduction' in *Aid, Diplomacy and Facts on the Ground*, eds., Michael Keating, Anne Le More & Robert Lowe (London: Royal Institute of International Affairs 2005), 10-11.
[53] Clinton W. J., My Life. London: Hutchinson 2004, 353-354.
[54] Zertal I., & Eldar A., *Lords of the Land* . New York: Nation Books, 2007, 176-178.
[55] Avnery U., 'Avnery on elections' in *Uri-Avnery@list.avnery-news.co.il* 1 November, 2008.
[56] Karmi G., *Married to Another Man* (London: Pluto, 2007), 151.

[57] Roberts N., 'Hard Lessons from Oslo: Foreign Aid and the Mistakes of the 1990s' in *Aid, Diplomacy and Facts on the Ground*, eds., Michael Keating, Anne Le More & Robert Lowe (London: Royal Institute of International Affairs 2005), 26.

[58] Bruderlein C., 'Human Security Challenges in the Occupied Palestinian Territory' in *Aid, Diplomacy and Facts on the Ground*, eds., Michael Keating, Anne Le More & Robert Lowe (London: Royal Institute of International Affairs 2005), 89.

[59] Sabeel is the Ecumenical Liberation Theology Centre in Jerusalem. World Vision is an international Christian relief, development and advocacy organisation, dedicated to overcome poverty. The author was present at both meetings.

[60] Keating M., 'Introduction' in *Aid, Diplomacy and Facts on the Ground*, eds., Michael Keating, Anne Le More & Robert Lowe (London: Royal Institute of International Affairs 2005), 12-13.

[61] Keating M., 'Introduction' in *Aid, Diplomacy and Facts on the Ground*, 12-13.

[62] Kahn M., " 'Security First' and its Implications for a Viable Palestinian State" in *Aid, Diplomacy and Facts on the Ground*, eds., Michael Keating, Anne Le More & Robert Lowe (London: Royal Institute of International Affairs 2005), 73.

[63] Dershowitz A., *The Case Against Israel's Enemies* (Hoboken N. J.: John Wiley & Sons, 2008), 27.

[64] Kretzmer D., *The Occupation of Justice* (Albany: SUNY, 2002), 194-198.

[65] Keating 1-3.

[66] Uri Avneri, 'Hamas', uri-avnery@list.avnery-news.co.il; 29 January 2009.

[67] Alpher, 161.

[68] Zertal & Eldar, xii.

[69] Zertal & Eldar, 450.

[70] Zertal & Eldar, 447, taken from Ari Shavit, "The Big Freeze," *Ha'aretz Magazine*, October 15, 2004.

[71] Karmi G., *Married to Another Man*, 105.

[72] Piterberg G., *The Returns of Zionism*. London: Verso, 2007, 62-68.

[73] Karmi G., 260-261.

[74] Dershowitz, 95.

[75] 'On the Agenda', in *B'tselem Update 30 October, 2008*. www.btselem.org

[76] Henry Siegman, 'Gaza: the Lies of War', *London Review of Books,* London Review of Books.

[77] Barenboim D. *Everything is Connected* (London: Weidenfeld & Nicolson, 2008), 183.

Afterword and Postscript

Annapolis, December, 2007

The previous statement by Daniel Barenboim appears more measured and statesmanlike than many. Failed structures can be seen in previous attempts at bridge-building, notably Oslo in 1993, The Road Map in 2003 and Annapolis in 2007. All have proved to be inadequate and faulty structures and they have not produced safety, in spite of great hopes and good intentions at Annapolis during November and December, 2007. When it commenced, the International Crisis Group (ICG) referred to its intentions but gave no details.[1] President George W. Bush had invited 40 countries to take part but there was a sombre background as they met. The ICG pointed to the weak ruling parties in Israel and Palestine, as well as the internal divisions between Hamas and Fatah. In addition, the major focus for America was away from Israel and Palestine and much more on the wars in Iraq and Afghanistan. At the end of December, after the conference had concluded, settlements were still being expanded and built in Jerusalem by Israel. After six months, the Annapolis Peace Initiative Monitoring Group produced an interim report in May, 2008, entitled, "Bringing Peace Together." It covered a great deal of ground and made a large number of observations, but showed serious shortcomings in the plan which was to achieve positive results by December, 2008. What was known in December, 2007 was that, despite the agreements, settlement building had not ceased but continued, the occupation remained, the Security Wall was still being constructed, restrictions on movement for Palestinians remained in force, Gaza was still a disaster area and Hamas and Fatah were still far apart. Since Annapolis, by the autumn of 2008, and with December looming, nothing significant had changed and settlements continued to be planned and built. Perhaps the issue was not so much whether the structure of the bridge was adequate but whether there was a bridge at all. But there was time for things to change – and there were some encouraging glimpses, perceived by some in this, "Afterword."

Towards The Future – Hope:
A Different Component In The Structure

In September, 2008, there were three small but significant events which not only demonstrate proactive initiatives but could cause a series of ripples that might turn into a wave of hope for both Jews and Arabs. These were followed by a fourth at the end of the month, which could be another damp squib, or turn from a ripple into a wave. The first, of tragedy and hope, could be seen to be the case on 9 September, 2008, when Dr Eyad el-Sarraj[2] wrote: "An Open Letter to Americans of Conscience," particularly the Jewish people. He asked for the support of Jews in terms of money and protest to help end the siege of Gaza. As he describes the clinical symptoms of the population of adults and children, he quotes ex-president Jimmy Carter who describes the siege of Gaza as: "an atrocity, a crime and an abomination." el-Sarraj describes the situation in Gaza as a huge prison for more than one million people, the majority of whom are children "being deliberately deprived of urgent medical care and medicines, of electricity and fuel to run hospitals and sewage systems, of potable water and supplies of food, clothing and raw materials." American Jews can now give a new lead for others to follow.

Secondly, in the same month, there was evidence of antagonism over an event in Gaza, about which there could have been sorrow and regret, accompanied by an honest, open exchange to see what happened and what can be learned. I refer to the incident in November, 2006, when eighteen members of a Palestinian family were killed by Israeli artillery in Beit Hanoun, Gaza. The United Nations Human Rights Council in Geneva sent the Nobel Prize winner, Archbishop Desmond Tutu, to investigate what happened and to ascertain the facts. Neither the Archbishop, nor his team, was granted a visa by Israel until May, 2008, eighteen months after the event. After the visit, and interviewing the family and senior Hamas personnel, the team from the UN were not permitted to travel to Israel to explore the Israeli version of events. The report had to conclude that, in the absence of the Israeli account, there was the possibility that the shelling of Beit Hanoun was a war crime. The Archbishop also said that the firing of rockets by Palestinian militants should stop and be investigated. "Those firing rockets on Israeli civilians are no less accountable than the Israeli military for their actions .... It is not too late for an independent, impartial and transparent investigation of the shelling to be held." *The Guardian* article noted that Israel's ambassador to the UN in Geneva rejected the report and the mission as, "regrettable." That attitude is unhelpful, when both sides would benefit from knowing what happened and what to do about it that could prevent any repetition. Similarly unhelpful was the American veto to a Security Council Resolution on 11 November, 2006, which condemned the operation, when the USA could have encouraged an open investigation by a respected external body. What is there to hide that would not benefit from openness which might move the process forward, instead of reinforcing the hardening of positions?[3] It might yet happen.

The third event is described by Halper, in "The End of an Odyssey." He writes of The Free Gaza Movement-Human Rights fleet of two boats from Cyprus to Gaza in August, 2008. Not only did it arrive safely, but it:

> forced the Israeli government to make a policy declaration that it is not occupying Gaza and therefore will not prevent the free movement of Palestinians in and out.

(at least by sea). Any attempt to backtrack by preventing ships in the future from entering or leaving Gaza with goods or passengers, may be interpreted as an assertion of control and therefore of occupation, opening Israel to accountability for war crimes before international law, something Israel tries to avoid at all costs. Gone is the obfuscation that has allowed Israel to maintain its control of the Occupied Territories without assuming any responsibility from now on. Israel is either an Occupying Power accountable for its actions and policies, or Palestinians have every right to enjoy their human right of travelling freely in and out of their country.[4]

At the end of the month, there was a fourth event, a quotation by the caretaker prime minister of Israel, Ehud Olmert, originally expressed in an interview given to the Israeli newspaper, Yedioth Ahronot.[5] In it he stated that, in order to have peace, Israel would have to withdraw from almost all of the territory captured in the 1967 war, including parts of East Jerusalem. His statements were seen to be a sensational disclosure from one who had been at the forefront of Israeli politics for many years, until his resignation from the post of prime minister in September, 2008. Parts of the interview were reported in *The Guardian*,[6] in which he developed his belief that, in order to achieve peace with the Palestinians, there would have to be a number of special solutions. It was also reported at greater length by Uri Avnery,[7] who referred to his change of mind, in which Olmert stressed the essential need to create peace with the Palestinians. In relation to Jerusalem, he said: "Anyone who wants to keep all the territory of the city will have to put 270 thousand Arabs behind fences within sovereign Israel. That won't work." He went on to raise the issue of the territory and the borders, saying "the aim is to try and fix for the first time a precise border between us and the Palestinians, a border that all the world [will recognise]."[8]

Of course, there were three immediate responses to the interview: first, that these were the words of a politician under threat of being found guilty of corruption; second, that he would not have been able to carry through those ideas had he raised them when prime minister; and the third, the furious reaction of those Zionists who are determined to ensure Israeli domination of the entire West Bank including Jerusalem. Nonetheless, Avnery saw it as "an unequivocal and final divorce from, 'All of Eretz Israel' and gives unequivocal support to the partition of the country...[and] he has fixed an Israeli position from which there can be no turning back in any future negotiations."[9]

The month of November that year brought more signs to the fore. On 4 November, 2008, America elected a new President, Barack Obama, an African American, and many hoped that he would bring a fresh energy and commitment to resolving the political impasse in Israel and Palestine. Although it cannot be denied that President George W. Bush made a number of promises to resolve the problems, the outcome had not only been negligible but, rather, even worse since his inauguration eight years earlier.

In a notice, written by Uri Avnery and published in Ha'aretz on 14 November, 2008, Gush Shalom drew a distinction between words and actions. It noted that the Hamas Prime Minister, Ismail Haniyeh, had announced his readiness to accept the State of Israel within the 1967 borders and the Israeli Prime Minister, Ehud Olmert, had declared that Israel must return to the 1967 borders. The notice then stated that: .".. on the ground, our government is carrying out weekly incursions into the Gaza strip, causing death and escalation."[10] Over the same period, the United Nations was prevented by Israel from delivering aid to Gaza, despite it being contrary to the Geneva Convention which insists on humanitarian aid being made available to civilians. After 4 November, Israel sealed its borders, thereby blocking deliveries of food, medicine and other supplies. In particular, the supply of industrial oil, that is essential for the only power station in Gaza, was prevented from passing through the border crossing by Israel. This led to power cuts of sixteen hours each day and the Israeli explanation was that their action was a response to rockets being fired from Gaza into Israeli communities. Both sets of behaviour are abhorrent and call for a political settlement which resolves the problem, and not the destructive interaction that exacerbates it.

On 26 November, 2008, *The Guardian* printed, the "Arab Peace Initiative." This had already been published in the major daily newspapers for their readers in Israel on 20 November and was praised by President Shimon Peres of Israel when he was in London at the time. The Initiative stated that it had been: "Adopted by the 14th Arab Summit in Beirut – Lebanon March, 2002." Its subheading stated, "57 Arab and Muslim Countries will establish Full Diplomatic and Normal Relations with Israel in Return for Comprehensive Peace Agreement and Ending the Occupation." In return, it asked for Israel to allow the establishment of a Palestinian state, with its capital in East Jerusalem and an Israeli withdrawal to the borders which existed before the 1967 War. Jews throughout the world know that Israel has a partner for peace. The *Financial Times* of 27 November, 2008 reported on the Initiative being supported by a group of over 500 former senior Israeli security officers.

All the above paragraphs will soon become history, but time will tell whether or not they have been stepping stones towards peace, or relics of good intentions. Whenever it is, terrorism has, one day, to end. Israelis and Palestinians have choices to make which will be neither simple, nor easy, but will determine the quality of life for future generations. Those choices call for great courage and an infinite capacity to handle setbacks in ways that are creative and not punitive. Eventually they will happen and will be established on the basis of either wisdom, hope and integrity, or fear, militarism and ideology.

Perhaps there is the beginning of hope when one considers the closing words of Alan Dershowitz in his book. He writes a final, but disappointingly inadequate, sentence:

> I call on all people of goodwill, everyone who truly wants a peaceful resolution to the Middle East conflict, to stop demonizing Israel, to end the double standard that has been imposed on Israel, to cease the name calling, to terminate the bigoted calls for boycotts and investments against the Jewish state, and to stop encouraging terrorism, and instead to propose constructive, realistic steps that can be taken

toward a compromise peace and produces a secure Israel and an economically viable, peaceful, and democratic Palestinian state – that finally allows the beleaguered people of this war-torn part of the world to enjoy the blessings of peace, *salaam* and *shalom*.. [sic][11]

While sounding excellent in many ways, Dershowitz will have already recognised by now that the ends he calls for are equally appropriate for those who attack Palestine and they must not be excluded. As yet, he is silent about the principles of borders, boundaries of land, sea and air. Moreover, while correctly calling for peace and security, the word "justice" is missing and cannot be omitted. When these are done the future could, indeed, begin to have hope. At the time of writing, time may tell!

A Postscript, 2009

And, indeed, it did tell. Although not the focus of this book, the calamity changed for the worse. Two days after Christmas Day, 2008, on 27 December, the Israeli Air Force, largely financed by the USA, attacked an already depleted Gaza with waves of bombers which killed hundreds of Palestinians and injured many hundreds more. In defiance, militants in Gaza retaliated every day with scores of their puny, but still terrifying, home-made rockets on Israeli civilian targets. Israel shelled and bombed, even United Nations areas, asserting that Hamas fighters were using civilian houses as shields. From the number of Palestinian civilian casualties, there must have been a vast number of such Hamas concealments although, so far, there has been little evidence given to substantiate that accusation. Both sides accused the other of breaking the ceasefire. Israel persistently argued that it had no choice but to defend itself, while Henry Siegman held that Israel's claims were lies because it was Israel which violated the truce by tightening its throttlehold on Gaza, when it should have been easing it as part of the truce.[12]

A number of facts were provided by Rabbis for Human Rights on January 30, 2009, as they were given to understand them.[13] They included, "1,314 people were accounted for as dead in Gaza as of19th January, 2009, of whom 412 were children and 110 were women. They numbered the wounded at 5,300, including 1,855 children and 795 women. Furthermore, 4,000 houses were destroyed and 17,000 damaged. They also reported that, "Despite promises to facilitate humanitarian aid, Israel is preventing repair of the electrical, water and sewage systems in Gaza." They further report that Israel only permits a limited amount of industrial diesel (64%) of the total needed to operate the power station, while the transfer of spare parts to repair the electrical water and sewage systems is totally obstructed Thus, the supplies of power and electricity to the population are extremely limited. What they had not included in their report was the massive destruction of farmland, crops and orchards! On the other side, it was shown on television how the tunnel systems were being repaired and used, allegedly by Hamas, for the re-supply of materials and included weaponry, although this was not shown, but only reported. The daily firing of rockets, from Gaza into Israel, has continued every day. Not all of these were home-made but some, apparently, had markings to indicate that they were manufactured in China.

Journalists reported on atrocities by both sides. Hamas was reported by Rory McCarthy to have conducted a murder campaign against Palestinians who were seen as collaborators. The Palestinian Centre for Human Right referred to the tightening of restrictions by Hamas on civil society groups.[14] Amira Hass had an article published on the *Ha'aretz* website, which accused Israeli forces of wearing Hamas uniforms during the ground invasion of Gaza, but which was then removed by the censor.[15] The *Guardian* newspaper reported evidence, provided by Amnesty International, that Hamas and Israel had violated international humanitarian law by launching attacks on civilians, and called for an independent investigation.[16] The report called on the Obama administration in the USA to suspend military aid to Israel, which included the large-scale supply of American arms and ordnance used in the conflict.

With both sides continuing their bellicosity, Shakespeare might have said: "A plague on both their houses!" Only there are more than two houses – there are the USA and Iran – and maybe more. Whether for good or bad we shall see. 2009, and all history, awaits hereafter.

Elsewhere, in the world of global warming and climate change, an alarming and fascinating change is taking place. Some small, low-lying islands in the Far East are faced with the prospect of non-existence due to the rise in water levels. The population will have to find a new land on which to live and, doubtless, the United Nations will be involved in their re-settlement. Having been directly involved in 1947 with the partition of land and the re-settlement of Jews in the Middle East, one can ask what lessons have been learned and what kind of model has been thereby provided? Will they follow the model of Israel and, if so, are there safeguards they would put in place and be prepared to implement? Quo vadis?

Notes

[1] International Crisis Group www.crisisgroup.org/home/index.

[2] Dr Eyad el-Sarraj. Founder and President of the Gaza Community Mental Health Program. See info@jewishvoiceforpeace.org 15 September, 2008.

[3] For full article, see Rory McCarthy, 'Tutu: Israeli shelling in Gaza may be war crime,' *The Guardian,* 16 September, 2008, p. 24.

[4] Halper J., 'End of an Odyssey.' in *Rabbis for Human Rights Report*, 4 September, 2008, 5-9.

[5] *Yedioth Ahronot,* 29 September, 2008.

[6] Rory McCarthy, 'Olmert: Israel has to return occupied lands to achieve peace,' *The Guardian,* 30 September, 2008, 26.

[7] Uri Avnery, 'Summing up.' *Uri-Avnery@list.avnery-news.co.il.* 4 October, 2008, 1-5.

[8] Avnery, 5.

[9] Avnery, 5.

[10] Uri Avnery, 'Talk and Action', Ha'aretz, 14 November, 2008.
[11] Dershowitz A., *The Case Against Israel's Enemies* (Hoboken N. J.: John Wiley & Sons, 2008), 228.
[12] Henry Siegman, 'Gaza: the Lies of the War', *London Review of Books* 29, January, 2009.
[13] Rabbis for Human Rights, 'Don't say we did not know' in *Social Economic Debate*, 30 January, 2009. info@rhr.israel.net.
[14] Rory McCarthy, 'Hamas murder campaign in Gaza exposed', *The Guardian*, 14 February, 2009, 31
[15] AMW reveals IDF censorship of Ha'aretz [18 February, 2009] info@arabmediawatch.com.
[16] Rory McCarthy, 'Suspend military aid to Israel, Amnesty urges Obama after detailing US weapons used in Gaza', *The Guardian,* 23 February, 2009, 19.

Bibliography

Aaronsohn, R., 'The Beginnings of Jewish Settlement and Zionism to World War I', in *Shared Histories* eds., Paul Scham, Walid Salem & Benjamin Pogrund. Walnut Creek, CA: Left Coast Press, 2005.

Abdel Haleem M. A. S. *Quran*. New York: OUP, 2005.

Abraham, A., 'The Spirituality of Christian Pilgrimage', in *Jerusalem: What Makes for Peace!* eds., Naim Ateek, Cedar Duaybis & Marla Schrader. London: Melisende, 1997, 107-110.

Abu el-Assal R., 'The Birth and Experience of the Christian Church: The Protestant/Anglican Identity in the Middle East', in *Christians in the Holy Land*, eds., Michael Prior & William Taylor. London: World of Islam Festival Trust, 1994, 131-140.

Abu Sitta S., 'The Implementation of the Right of Return', in *The New Intifada*, ed. by Roane Carey. London: Verso, 2001, 299-320.

Abunimah, A. & H. Ibish, 'The US Media and the New Intifada', in *The New Intifada*, ed. by Roane Carey. London: Verso, 2001, 233-258.

Achcar G., with M. Warschawski. *The 33-Day War*. London: Saqi, 2007.

Adam, H., & K. Moodley. *Seeking Mandela: Peacemaking Between Israelis and Palestinians*. London: UCL Press, 2005.

Adas, Janet, 'Norman Finkelstein discusses "Prospect for Peace" at Rutgers', *Washington Report on Middle East Affairs*, January/February. 2007 - Vol. xxvi, No. 1, 48.

Agha, H., & R. Malley. Camp David: The Tragedy of Errors. *New York Review of Books*. August, 9, 2001, 59-65.

Aghazarian, A., 'The Significance of Jerusalem to Christians', in *Christians in the Holy Land*, eds., Michael Prior & William Taylor. London: World of Islam Festival Trust, 1994, 99-108.

Akram, Susan & Michael Lynk, 'The Wall and the Law', *The European Journal of International Law Vol. 16, No. 5 © EJIL 2005*, 61-106.

Alexander, Y. *International Terrorism*. USA: Greenwood Press, 1976.

Al-Jubeh, N., 'The Effects of Politics on Archaeology', in *Jerusalem: What Makes for Peace!* eds., Naim Ateek, Cedar Duaybis & Marla Schrader. London: Melisende, 1997, 176-181.

Almond, G. A., 'Political Science: The History of the Discipline' in *New Handbook of Political Science* eds., Robert E. Goodin & Hans-Dieter Klingemann. Oxford: OUP, 1998, 50-96.

Alpher, Y., 'Israel's Aid Responsibilities towards the Palestinian Population' in *Aid, Diplomacy and Facts on the Ground* eds., Michael Keating, Anne Le More & Robert Lowe. London: Royal Institute of International Affairs 2005.

Al-Sarraf, F., 'Christianity in Gaza' in *Christians in the Holy Land*, eds., Michael Prior & William Taylor. London: World of Islam Festival Trust, 1994, 57-64.

Andoni, G., 'A Comparative Study of Intifada 1987 and Intifada 2000', in *The New Intifada,* ed. by Roane Carey. London: Verso, 2001, 209-220.

Andoni, L., 'Searching for Answers: Gaza's Suicide Bombers'. *Journal of Palestinian Studies,* 24/4. 1997, 33-45.

Aran, G., 'Jewish Zionist Fundamentalism: The Bloc of the Faithful in Israel. Gush Emunim' in *Fundamentalisms Observed* eds. Martin E. Marty & R. Scott Appleby. Chicago: University of Chicago Press, 1994, 265-344.

Armstrong, K. *A History of God.* New York: Ballantine, 1993.

_____. *In The Beginning.* London: Harper & Collins, 1986.

_____. *Islam.* London: Weidenfeld & Nicolson, 2000.

_____. 'Jerusalem in History', in *Jerusalem Today,* ed., by Ghada Karmi. Reading, Berks. Garnet, 1996, 111-118.

_____. *Jerusalem: One City, Three Faiths.* New York: Ballantine, 1997.

Aronoff, Myron J., 'The Institutionalisation and Co-optation of a Charismatic, Messianic, Religious-Political Revitalisation Movement' in *The Impact of Gush Emunim* ed. by David Newman. London: Croom Helm, 1985, 46-69.

Aronson, G., 'Israeli Settlements in and around Jerusalem', in *Jerusalem Today,* ed. by Ghada Karmi. Reading, Berks. Garnet, 1996, 75-82.

Aruri, N., 'The Right of Return and its Detractors', in *Speaking the Truth about Zionism and Israel,* ed. by Michael Prior. London: Melisende, 2004, 207-232.

Ashrawi, H. *This Side of Peace.* New York: Simon & Schuster, 1995.

Aslan, R. *No god but God.* London: Arrow Books, 2005.

Ateek, N., 'A Palestinian Theology of Jerusalem', in *Jerusalem: What Makes for Peace!* eds., Naim Ateek, Cedar Duaybis & Marla Schrader. London: Melisende, 1997, 94-106.

Ateek, N., Duaybis C., Schrader M., eds., *Jerusalem: What Makes for Peace!* London: Melisende, 1997.

Ateek, N., 'Introduction' in *Challenging Christian Zionism* ed. by Naim Ateek, Cedar Duabyis & Maurine Tobin. London: Melisende 2005, 5-6.

_____. *Justice and only Justice.* New York: Orbis, 1991.

_____. 'Suicide Bombers'. Sabeel: *Cornerstone,* Issue 25. Summer 2002.

Avnery, U., 'The Ownership of Jerusalem: An Israeli View', in *Jerusalem Today,* ed. by Ghada Karmi. Reading, Berks. Garnet, 1996, 53-58.

_____. *Truth against Truth.* Tel Aviv: Gush Shalom, 2005.

_____. *Israel's Vicious Circle.* London: Pluto, 2008.

Avnery, U., Webmail, January, 11, 2003, in Adam H., & Moodley K., *Seeking Mandela: Peacemaking Between Israelis and Palestinians.* London: UCL Press, 2005, 175-6.

Bach, G. R. & P. Wyden. *The Intimate Enemy.* New York: William Morrow & Co., 1969.

Badawi, Z., 'Jerusalem and Islam', in *Jerusalem Today,* ed. by Ghada Karmi. Reading, Berks. Garnet, 1996, 137-144.

Baramki, G., 'The Spiritual Significance and Experience of the Christian Church: The Orthodox Perspective', in *Christians in the Holy Land*, eds., Michael Prior & William Taylor. London: World of Islam Festival Trust, 1994, 141-142.

Barenboim, D. *Everything is Connected,* ed. by Elena Cheah. London: Weidenfeld & Nicolson, 2008.

Barghouti, O., 'Palestine's Tell-Tale Heart', in *The New Intifada,* ed. by Roane Carey. London: Verso, 2001, 165-180.

Barham, N. and the students of Talitha Kumi Lutheran School, 'The Agony of Beit Jala', in *The New Intifada,* ed. by Roane Carey. London: Verso, 2001, 125-138.

Barker, W. *A Fountain Opened: A Short History of Church's Ministry among the Jews, 1809-1982.* London: Olive Press, 1983.

Barlow, E., 'Waking the Sleeping Giant', in *Speaking the Truth about Zionism and Israel,* ed. by Michael Prior. London: Melisende, 2004, 233-254.

Barrows-Friedman, Nora, 'Israel's Economic Stranglehold a Silent Killer', *Antiwar.com,* February 1, 2007. A project of the Randolph Bourne Institute.

Barry, F. R. *The Relevance of Christianity.* London: SCM, 1931.

Bates, S. *God's Own Country.* London: Hodder & Stoughton, 2007.

Baylis, J. & Steve Smith, eds., *The Globalisation of World Politics,* Third Edition. Oxford: OUP, 2005.

Be'er, H., 'Gush Emunim-Canaanites who wear phylacteries,' in *Gush Emunim: History, Sociology and Theology.* Private paper, 8, by Michel Feige, sent to Geoffrey Whitfield December 13, 2007.

Bell, C. *Peace Agreements and Human Rights.* Oxford: OUP, 2000.

Bell, D., 'Ideology', in the *Fontana Dictionary of Modern Thought,* eds., Alan Bullock & Oliver Stallybrass. London: Fontana, 1977, 298-299.

Bennett, W. H. *Genesis Exodus.* London: The Caxton Publishing Company, 1926.

Benvenisti, E. *The International Law of Occupation* Second Edition. Oxford: Princeton University Press, 2004.

Bettelheim, B. *The Informed Heart.* Harmondsworth: Peregrine Books, 1986.

Bicheno, James, *The Signs of the Times* contained in Senate House. London, in 18th Century Collections On line, Gale Group.

_____. *The Restoration of the Jews.* London: Bye and Law, 1800 contained in Senate House. London, in 18th Century Collections On line, Gale Group.

Bindman, G., B. Bowring, Y. Waljee, "Human Rights in Palestine – What has happened since Oslo?" *International Human Rights Commission of the Law*

Society of England and Wales and the Bar Human Rights Committee of England and Wales from 7 to 14 June, 1998.
Bion, W. *Experiences in Groups.* London: Tavistock, 1961.
Bishara, M. *Palestine/Israel: Peace or Apartheid.* London: Zed Books, 2002.
_____. 'The Palestinians of Israel', in *The New Intifada,* ed. by Roane Carey. London: Verso, 2001, 139-157.
Blum, Y., 'The Legality of State Responses to Acts of Terrorism', in *Terrorism: How the West Can Win,* ed. by Binyamin Netanyahu. London: Weidenfeld & Nicolson, 1986, 133-138.
Bokser, B. Z. *The Essential Writings of Abraham Isaac Kook* ed. by Ben Zion Bokser. New York: Amity House, 1988.
Booth, K. & T. Dunne. *Worlds in Collision.* Basingstoke, Hants.: Palgrave, Macmillan, 2002.
Bowen, J. *Six Days.* London: Simon & Schuster, 2003.
Bowring, B., 'International Relations and the Legal Regulation of Conflict'. London Metropolitan University, 28 November, 2005.
Brayer, L., 'The Separation of Jerusalem from the West Bank and Gaza', in *Jerusalem: What Makes for Peace!* eds., Naim Ateek, Cedar Duaybis & Marla Schrader. London: Melisende, 1997, 141-153.
Brenner, L. *Zionism in the Age of the Dictators.* Westport, Connecticut: Laurence Hill & Co., 1983.
Brown, Wesley H. & Peter F. Penne, eds. *Christian Perspectives on the Israeli-Palestinian Conflicts..* Neufeld Verlag Schwarzenfeld, Germany: 2008.
Bruderlein, C., 'Human Security Challenges in the Occupied Palestinian Territory' in *Aid, Diplomacy and Facts on the Ground.* Editors, Michael Keating, Anne Le More & Robert Lowe. London: Royal Institute of International Affairs 2005.
Buber, M., 'Zionism and Zionism' in *A Land of Two Peoples: Martin Buber on Jews and Arabs* ed. by Paul Mendes-Flohr. New York: OUP, 1983, 220.
_____. *On Zion: The History of an Idea.* London: Horovitz Publishing, 1973.
Bundy, R., 'Legal Approaches to the Question of Jerusalem', in *Jerusalem Today,* ed. by Ghada Karmi. Reading, Berks. Garnet, 1996, 45-52.
Burke, J. *Al-Qaeda.* London: Penguin, 2004.
Burleigh, M. *Blood and Rage.* London: Harper Press, 2008.
Byers, M. *War Law.* London: Atlantic Books, 2005.
Carey R., ed. *The New Intifada.* London: Verso, 2001.
Carter, J. *Palestine Peace Not Apartheid.* New York, Simon & Schuster, 2006.
Carus, W., *Memoirs of the Life of the Rev. Charles Simeon M.A.,* ed. by the Rev. William Carus. London: Hatchard & Son, 1847. Volumes I & II.
Casanova, J. *Public Religions in the Modern World.* Chicago: University of Chicago Press, 1994.
Cassese, A. *International Criminal Law.* Oxford: OUP, 2003.
_____. *International Law,* 2nd ed. Oxford: OUP, 2005.
_____. *Terrorism, Politics and Law.* Cambridge: Polity, 1989.

Cavanaugh, K. A., 'Selective Justice: The Case of Israel and the Occupied Territories.' *Fordham International Law Journal.* Vol. 26, April 2003, 934-960: Part 4.

Ceronetti, G., "Considerazione sul valore del termine 'kamikaze'." *La Stampa*, November, 16, 2003.

Chacour, E., with D. Hazard. *Blood Brothers.* New York: Chosen, 1984.

Chacour, E., with M. E. Jensen. *We Belong to the Land.* San Francisco: Harper, 1990.

Chandler, D. *From Kosovo to Kabul.* London: Pluto, 2002.

Chomsky, N. *Fateful Triangle.* London: Pluto, 1999.

_____, 'Introduction', in *The New Intifada* ed. by Roane Carey. London: Verso, 2001, 5-23.

Clark, V. *Allies for Armageddon.* London: Yale University Press, 2007.

Clements, R. E. *Abraham and David.* London: SCM, 1967.

_____. 'A Fruitful Venture: the Origins of Hebrew Studies at King's College, London,' in *Biblical traditions in transmission: essays in honour of Michael A. Knibb,* ed. by J. M. Lieu & C. Hempel. JSJSup111; Leiden: Brill, 2006.

Clinton, W. J. *My Life.* London: Hutchinson, 2004.

Cobham, J. O., 'Covenant', in *A Theological Word Book of the Bible,* ed. by Alan Richardson. London: SCM, 1956, 54-56.

Cohen, E., 'Israel as a Post-Zionist Society' in *The Shaping of Israeli Identity: Myth, Memory and Trauma* eds. Robert Wistrich & David Ohana. London: Frank Cass & Company, 2005, 213-214.

Conway, John S., 'The Rise and Fall of the Protestant Missions to the Jews', *Humanitas.* Vol. 7, No. 1. Oct. 2005, 61-79.

Cooley, J. K. *An Alliance Against Babylon.* London: Pluto, 2005.

_____. *Unholy Wars 3rd ed.* London: Pluto, 2002.

Cragg, K., *A Certain Sympathy of Scriptures: Biblical and Quranic.* Brighton: Sussex Academic Press, 2004.

_____. *Am I not your Lord?* London: Melisende, 2002.

_____, 'Beginning at Jerusalem: the Church's Story – Then and Now', in *Christians in the Holy Land*, eds., Michael Prior & William Taylor. London: World of Islam Festival Trust, 1994, 153-160.

_____. *Defending the Faith.* London: New Millennium, 1997.

_____. *Faith at Suicide.* Brighton: Sussex Academic Press, 2005.

_____. *Muhammad and the Christian.* London: DLT, 1984.

_____. *Palestine The Prize and Price of Zion.* London: Cassell, 1997.

_____. *Semitism: The Whence and the Whither.* Brighton: Sussex Academic Press, 2005.

_____. *The Excellences of Jerusalem.* London: Altajir World of Islam Trust, 1998.

_____, 'The Place of the Name: A Christian Perspective', in *Jerusalem Today,* ed. by Ghada Karmi. Reading, Berks. Garnet, 1996, 145-172.

_____. *The Tragic in Islam.* London: Melisende, 2004.

_____. *This Year in Jerusalem*. London: Darton, Longman & Todd, 1982.
Crenshaw M. and Pimlott J., eds. *International Encyclopaedia of Terrorism*. Chicago: Fitzroy Dearborn, 1997.
Creswell, J. W. *Research Design: Qualitative, Quantitative and Mixed Methods Approaches*. London: Sage, 2003.
Crombie, K. *For the Love of Zion*. London: Hodder & Stoughton, 1991.
_____. *ANZACS, Empire and Israel's Restoration 1798-1948*. Washington: Vocational Education and Training Publications, 1998.
_____. *A Jewish Bishop in Jerusalem*. Jerusalem: Nicolayson Ltd., 2006.
Crooke, A., *Resistance: The Essence of the Islamist Revolution*. London: Pluto, 2009.
Dabbagh, N. T. *Suicide in Palestine*. London: Hurst & Co. 2005.
Dahan-Kalev, H., 'You're So Pretty – You Don't Look Moroccan' in *The Challenge of Post-Zionism* ed. by Ephraim Nimni. London: Zed Press 2003, 168-181.
Dalrymple, W. *From the Holy Mountain*. London: Flamingo, 1997.
David, R. *Arabs and Israel for Beginners*. Danbury Ct., Writers and Readers, 2001.
Davidson, R. The Old Testament. London: Hodder, 1964.
Davies, W. D. *The Gospel and the Land*. Sheffield: Sheffield University Press, 1994. Originally published by University of California Press, 1974.
_____. *The Territorial Dimension of Judaism*. Minneapolis: First Fortress Press Edition 1991. Originally published, Berkeley: University of California Press, 1982.
Davis, U. *Apartheid Israel*. London: Zed Books, 2003.
Dershowitz, A. *The Case for Israel*. Hoboken, New Jersey: John Wiley & Sons Inc., 2003.
Dinstein, Y. *The Conduct of Hostilities under the Law of International Armed Conflict*. Cambridge: CUP, 2004.
Domke, D. *God Willing?* London: Pluto, 2004.
Driver, S. R. *Deuteronomy*. Edinburgh: T. & T. Clark, 1895.
Drory, Z. *Israel's Reprisal Policy 1953-1956*. Abingdon: Frank Cass, 2005.
Dugard, J., 'Enforcement of Human Rights in the West Bank and the Gaza Strip', in *International Law and the Administration of the Occupied Territories,* ed. by Emma Playfair. New York: OUP, 1992, 461-462.
Dumper, M., 'Demographic and Border Issues Affecting the Future of Jerusalem', in *Jerusalem Today* ed. by Ghada Karmi. Reading, Berks. Garnet, 1996, 83-96.
Eagleton, T. *Holy Terror*. Oxford: OUP, 2005.
Eisen, P., 'Speaking the Truth to Jews', in *Speaking the Truth about Zionism and Israel,* ed. by Michael Prior. London: Melisende, 2004, 190-206.
Ellis, M. E. *Israel and Palestine: Out of the Ashes*. London: Pluto, 2002.
Elster, J., 'Motivations and Beliefs in Suicide Missions', in *Making Sense of Suicide Missions,* ed. by Diego Gambetta. Oxford: OUP, 2005, 233-258.

Encyclopaedia Judaica. Vol. 10. Jerusalem: Keter Publishing House, 1971.
Erhlich, A., 'Zionism, Anti-Zionism and Post-Zionism', in *The Challenge of Post-Zionism* ed. by Ephraim Nimni. London: Zed Books, 2003, 63-97.
Erlich, P. R., & J. Liu. *Some Roots of Terrorism, Population and Environment,* Nov. 2002, Vol. 24, No. 2, 183-192.
Eskidjian, S., 'The Holy City as an Image of a New Creation', in *Jerusalem: What Makes for Peace!* eds., Naim Ateek, Cedar Duaybis & Marla Schrader. London: Melisende, 1997, 230-232.
Esposito, J. L., 'Christian-Muslim Relations in Historic Perspective', in *Jerusalem: What Makes for Peace!* eds., Naim Ateek, Cedar Duaybis & Marla Schrader. London: Melisende, 1997, 31-37.
Faber, G. S. The Sacred Calendar of Prophecy 3 Vols. 1828 British Library.
Falk, R., 'Testing Patriotism and Citizenship in the Global Terror War', in *Worlds in Collision,* eds., Ken Booth & Tim Dunne. Basingstoke: Palgrave Macmillan, 2002, 335-336.

_____. 'The Overall Terrorist Challenge in International Political Life', in *Terrorism and National Liberation,* ed. by Hans Koechler. Frankfurt: Lang, 1988, 15-22.
Fasheh, M., 'The Message of Jerusalem Today', in *Jerusalem: What Makes for Peace!* eds., Naim Ateek, Cedar Duaybis & Marla Schrader. London: Melisende, 1997, 167-175.
Feige, M. *Gush Emunim: History, Sociology and Theology.* Private paper, December, 2007.

_____. *Space, Place and Memory in Gush Emunim Ideology.* Private paper, December, 2007.
Feiler, B. *Abraham.* London: Judy Piatkus. Publishers Ltd. 2002.
Feldman, N., 'War and Reason in Maimonides & Avrroes' in *The Ethics of War* eds., Richard Sorabji & David Rodin. Aldershot: Ashgate Publishing House, 2006, 92-107.
Finkelstein, I., & Silberman N. A. *The Bible Unearthed, Archaeology's New Vision of Ancient Israel and the Origin of its Sacred Texts.* New York: Touchstone, 2002.
Finkelstein, I. *The Archaeology of the Israelite Settlement.* Jerusalem: Israel Exploration Society, 1988.
Finkelstein, N. G., 'The Rise and Fall of Palestine: A Personal Account of the Intifada Years'. Minneapolis: University of Minnesota Press, 1996, 47 in *Bad News from Israel* eds., Greg Philo & Mike Berry. London: Pluto, 2004, 65.

_____. *Image and Reality of the Israel-Palestine Conflict.* London: Verso, 2001.
Finlayson, G.B.A.M. *The Seventh Earl of Shaftesbury 1801-1885.* Vancouver: Regent College Publishing, 2004. First published in 1981 by Eyre Methuen Ltd., 1981.
Fisch, H. *The Zionist Revolution.* London: Weidenfeld & Nicolson, 1978.

_____, 'The Zionism of Zion'. in Hebrew. Tel-Aviv: Zmora Bitan 1982, in *Bad News from Israel* eds., Greg Philo & Mike Berry. London: Pluto, 2004, 36-37.

Fisher, D. S. *The Birth of the Earth.* New York: Columbia UP, 1987.
Fisher, R., & W. Ury. *Getting to Yes.* London: Random, 1999.
Fisk, R., 'This is a place of filth and blood', in *The New Intifada,* ed. by Roane Carey. London: Verso, 2001, 293-298.
Foucault, M., *Discipline & Punish: The Birth of the Prison,* Trans. by Alan Sheridan. New York: Vintage, 1979.
Fouda,Y. & N. Fielding. *Masterminds of Terror.* Edinburgh: Mainstream, 2003.
Frankl, V. E. *Man's Search for Meaning.* New York: Washington Square Press, 1985 edn.
Frayling, N. *Pardon and Peace.* London: SPCK, 1996.
Freedman, L., C. Hill, A. Roberts, & R. J. Vincent. *Terrorism and International Order.* London: Routledge, 1986.
Friedman, David, 'The Political Reality of Living in Israel, with a Suggested Path towards Reconciliation' in *Christian Perspectives on the Israeli-Palestinian Conflict* eds. Wesley H. Brown & Peter F. Penner. Neufeld Verlag Schwarzenfeld, Germany: 2008, 69-70.
Friedman, R. I. *Zealots for Zion.* New Brunswick, New Jersey: Rutgers University Press, 1994.
Galtung, J., 'On the Causes of Terrorism and their Removal', in *Terrorism and National Liberation,* ed. by Hans Koechler. Frankfurt: Lang, 1988, 51-66.
Gambetta, D., 'Can We Make Sense of Suicide Missions?' in *Making Sense of Suicide Missions,* ed. Diego Gambetta. Oxford: OUP, 2005, 259-299.
Gazit, S. *Trapped Fools: Thirty Years of Israeli Policies in the Territories.* London: Frank Cass, 2003.
Geraisy, S. F., 'Socio-Demographic Characteristics: Reality, Problems and Aspirations within Israel', in *Christians in the Holy Land*, eds., Michael Prior & William Taylor. London: World of Islam Festival Trust, 1994, 45-56.
_____. 'Who are the Christians in Galilee?', in *Jerusalem: What Makes for Peace!* eds., Naim Ateek, Cedar Duaybis & Marla Schrader. London: Melisende, 1997, 213-216.
Ghanem, A., 'Zionism, Post-Zionism and Anti-Zionism in Israel', in *The Challenge of Post-Zionism* ed. by Ephraim Nimni. London: Zed Books, 2003, 98-116.
Gidney, W. T. *Jews and their Evangelisation.* London: Student Volunteer Missionary Union, 1899.
_____. *The History of the London Society for Promoting Christianity Amongst the Jews from 1809 to 1908.* London: LSPCAJ, 1908.
Gilley, S. W., 'George Stanley Faber: No Popery and Prophecy' in *New Heaven and New Earth. Prophecy and the Millennium. Essays in Honour of Anthony Gelston,* eds. P. J. Harland and R. Hayward. Leiden: E. J. Brill, 1999, 287-304.
Goldberg, D. J., 'Jerusalem and Judaism', in *Jerusalem Today* ed. by Ghada Karmi. Reading, Berks. Garnet, 1996, 133-136.
_____. *The Divided Self.* London: I. B. Tauris, 2006.

Goldhagen, Daniel, 'German Lessons', *Guardian,* April, 29, 1999.
Goodin, Robert E. & Hans-Dieter Klingemann, eds. *New Handbook of Political Science.* Oxford: OUP, 1998.
Gorenberg, G. *The Accidental Empire.* New York: Henry Holt & Co., 2006.
_____. *The End of Days.* New York: OUP, 2002.
Grant, L. *The People on the Street.* London: Virago, 2006.
Grossman, D. *Death as a Way of Life.* London: Bloomsbury, 2003.
_____. *See Under: Love.* London: Vintage, 1999.
Guelke, A. *The Age of Terrorism and the International Political System.* London: Tauris, 1995.
Hadawi, S. *Bitter Harvest.* New York: New World Publications, 1967.
Hadi, Mahdi Abdul, 'The Ownership of Jerusalem: A Palestinian View', in *Jerusalem Today,* ed. by Ghada Karmi. Reading, Berks. Garnet, 1996, 67-74.
Hagopian, H., 'The Armenians of Jerusalem and the Armenian Quarter', in *Christians in the Holy Land*, eds., Michael Prior & William Taylor. London: World of Islam Festival Trust, 1994, 115-126.
_____, 'The Mosaic of Jerusalem', in *Jerusalem: What Makes for Peace!* eds., Naim Ateek, Cedar Duaybis & Marla Schrader. London: Melisende, 1997, 233-235.
Halabi, U., 'Applicability of Israeli Law over East Jerusalem: Concept and Dimensions', in *Jerusalem: What Makes for Peace!* eds., Naim Ateek, Cedar Duaybis & Marla Schrader. London: Melisende, 1997, 200-208.
Halper, J. *Obstacles to Peace - A reframing of the Palestinian-Israeli conflict.* Jerusalem: ICAHD, 2004 Second Edition.
Halper, S., & Clarke J. *America Alone.* Cambridge: CUP, 2004.
Hamzeh, M., 'Notes from Dheisheh', in *The New Intifada,* ed. by Roane Carey. London: Verso, 2001, 221-232.
Han, H., ed. *Terrorism and Political Violence.* New York: Oceana, 1993.
Hanania, A. D., 'Churches of the Holy Land. Obligations and Expectations: A View from the Holy Land', in *Christians in the Holy Land*, eds., Michael Prior & William Taylor. London: World of Islam Festival Trust, 1994, 203-216.
Hareven, S., 'Sociological model against reality' in *In the Diaspora. Bitfutzot HaGola* 1977, 79/80: 104-108. in *Gush Emunim: History, Sociology and Theology,* Private paper, 8, by Michel Feige, sent to Geoffrey Whitfield, 13 December, 2007.
Harries, R., 'Application of Just War Criteria in the Period 1959-89' in *The Ethics of War* eds., Richard Sorabji & David Rodin. Aldershot: Ashgate Publishing House, 2006, 222-234.
Hassan, N., 'An Arsenal of Believers: Talking to the Human Bombs' *New Yorker*, November, 22, 2001.
Heilman, S. C. & M. Friedman, 'Religious Fundamentalism and Religious Jews: The Case of the Haredim' in *Fundamentalisms Observed,* eds. Martin E.

Marty & R. Scott Appleby. Chicago: University of Chicago Press, 1994, 197-264.

Herman, E. & N. Chomsky. *Manufacturing Dissent.* London: Vintage, 1994.

Herman, E. & G. O'Sullivan. *The Terrorism Industry.* New York: Pantheon, 1989.

Herman, T. & E. Yuchtman-Yaar, 'Oslo–A Dream or a Vision? Peace Index Findings'. The Tami Steinmetz Center for Peace Research, Tel Aviv University, 2005.

Herzl, T. *Der Judenstaat* trans. in Herzberg A., *The Zionist Idea.* New York: The Jewish Publication Secretariat, 1997.

Herzl, T. *The Jewish State.* London: Henry Pordes, 1993 Seventh Edition.

Herzog, H., 'Post-Zionist Discourse in Alternative Voices: A Feminist Perspective' in *The Challenge of Post-Zionism* ed. by Ephraim Nimni. London: Zed Books, 2003, 153-167.

Herzog, Yaacov, 'Israel in the Middle East: An Introduction' in *Jerusalem Papers on Peace Problems* ed., by Meir Vereté. The Leonard Davis Institute for International Relations: The Hebrew University of Jerusalem, 1975.

Hever, S. *The Economy of the Occupation, Part 3, Divide and Conquer.* Jerusalem, Alternative Information Centre, September 2005.

Hever, S. *The Economy of the Occupation Part 1. Foreign Aid to Palestine/Israel, Second Edition.* Jerusalem: Alternative Information Centre, February 2006.

Heywood, A. *Key Concepts in Politics.* Basingstoke: Palgrave Macmillan, 2000.

Higgins, R., & M. Flory, eds. *Terrorism and International Law.* London: Routledge, 1997.

Hill. C., 'Till the conversion of the Jews' in *Millenarianism and Messianism in English Literature and Thought 1650-1800.* Clark Library Lectures ed. by Richard H. Popkin 1981-82. Leiden – New York: E. J. Brill 1988, 12-36. Senate House 7th floor PCW-MIL.

Hintilian, K., 'Pathways to Christian Unity I', in *Jerusalem: What Makes for Peace!* eds., Naim Ateek, Cedar Duaybis & Marla Schrader. London: Melisende, 1997, 23-27.

Hirst, D. *The Gun and the Olive Branch.* New York: Thunders Mouth Press/Nations Books, 2003.

Hodder, E. *The Life and Work of the Seventh Earl of Shaftesbury K.G.* 3 Volumes. London: Cassell & Co. Ltd., 1886.

Hoffman, B. *Inside Terrorism.* London: Indigo. 1999.

Honderich, T. *After the Terror.* Edinburgh: Edinburgh University Press, 2002.

_____. *Humanity, Terrorism, Terrorist War.* London: Continuum International Publishing Group, 2006.

Horan, M. *Jesus and the Trojan War.* Exeter: Imprint Academic, 2007.

Human Rights and Social Justice Research Institute. Proceedings of the International Conference held at London Metropolitan University, 21 May, 2005, "Suspect Communities: The Real 'War on Terror' in Europe."

Hummel R., 'The House of Christian Heritage', in *Jerusalem: What Makes for Peace!* eds., Naim Ateek, Cedar Duaybis & Marla Schrader. London: Melisende, 1997, 195-199.
Hunter, James D., 'Fundamentalism' in *Jewish Fundamentalism in Comparative Perspective,* ed., Laurence A. Silberstein. New York: New York University Press, 1993, 32.
Huntington, S. P. *The Clash of Civilisations and the Remaking of World Order.* New York: Simon & Schuster Inc. 1996.
Huxley, A. "Ends and Means." Chatto & Windus in *A Year of Grace* ed. by Victor Gollanz. London: Penguin, 1955, 13.
Idinopolous T. A. *Weathered by Miracles.* Chicago: Ivan R. Dee 1998.
International Court of Justice, *Legal Consequences of the Construction of a Wall in the Occupied Palestinian Territory, Advisory Opinion,* 9 July, 2004.
Isaac, J. *A Geopolitical Atlas of Palestine.* Bethlehem: ARIJ, 2004.
_____. *An Atlas of Palestine - The West Bank and Gaza.* Jerusalem: ARIJ, 2000.
Isaac, J. & L. Hosh, 'Political Conflict and Environmental Degradation in Jerusalem', in *Jerusalem: What Makes for Peace!* eds., Naim Ateek, Cedar Duaybis & Marla Schrader. London: Melisende, 1997, 182-194.
Isaac, J. *The Status of the Environment in the West Bank.* Jerusalem: ARIJ, 1997.
Isaac, J. & W. Sabbah. *Water Resources and Irrigated Agriculture in the West Bank.* Jerusalem: ARIJ, 1998.
Israel Information Centre, *Facts About Israel.* Jerusalem: IOC, 2004.
James, F. *Personalities of the Old Testament.* New York: Charles Scribner's Sons, 1939.
Jenkins, B. *International Terrorism: A New Mode of Conflict.* Los Angeles: Crescent Publications, 1975.
Jews for Justice in the Middle East, The Origin of the Palestine Israel Conflict. *Berkeley: California, PO Box 14561, CA 94712,* April, 5, 2002.
Joint Parliamentary Middle East Councils Commission of Enquiry–Palestinian Refugees, *"Right of Return."* London: Labour Middle East Council, 2001. First Edition.
Joint Parliamentary Middle East Councils Commission of Enquiry–Palestinian Refugees, *"Right of Return."* London: Labour Middle East Council, 2004. Third Edition.
Juergensmeyer, M. *Terror in the Mind of God.* Berkeley, California: University of California Press, 2001.
Kahn, M., "Security First' and its Implications for a Viable Palestinian State" in *Aid, Diplomacy and Facts on the Ground* eds., Michael Keating, Anne Le More & Robert Lowe. London: Royal Institute of International Affairs 2005.
Kaleck, Wolfgang, 'On the concept of terrorism and on terrorism lists'. Paper presented at International Conference at London Metropolitan University, May, 21, 2005, "Suspect Communities: The Real 'War on Terror' in Europe," 23-26.

Kapitan, T., 'Terrorism in the Arab-Israeli Conflict', in *Terrorism: The Philosophical Issues*, ed. by I. Primoratz. Palgrave. 2004, 175-191.

Karmi, G., ed. *Jerusalem Today: What Future for the Peace Process?*. Reading, Berks. Ithaca, 1996.

_____. *Married to Another Man*. London Pluto, 2007.

Kattan, J., 'A Study of Muslim and Christian Students' Attitudes towards each other at Bethlehem University' in *Christians in the Holy Land*, eds., Michael Prior & William Taylor. London: World of Islam Festival Trust, 1994, 89-98.

Keating, M., 'Introduction' in *Aid, Diplomacy and Facts on the Ground* eds., Michael Keating, Anne Le More & Robert Lowe. London: Royal Institute of International Affairs, 2005.

Keating, Michael, Ann Le More, Robert Lowe. *Aid, Diplomacy and Facts on the Ground*. London: Royal Institute of International Affairs, 2005.

Keenan, B. *An Evil Cradling*. London: Hutchinson, 1992.

Kelsay, J., 'Arguments Concerning Resistance in Contemporary Islam' in *The Ethics of War*, eds., Richard Sorabji & David Rodin. Aldershot: Ashgate Publishing House, 2006, 61-91.

Kennedy, A. R. S. *The Book of Samuel*. Edinburgh: T. C. & E. C. Jack, 1926.

Khalidi, R., 'Palestinian Resistance to Zionism before World War I', in *Blaming the Victims*, eds. Edward Said & Peter Hitchens. London: Verso, 2001, 211-213.

Khoury, G., 'A Vision for Christian-Muslim Relations', in *Jerusalem: What Makes for Peace!* eds., Naim Ateek, Cedar Duaybis & Marla Schrader. London: Melisende, 1997, 38-44.

Kimmerling, B. & J. Migdal. *The Palestinian People: A History*. Cambridge, Mass.: Harvard University Press, 2003.

Kimmerling, B. *Politicide*. London: Verso, 2006.

_____. *Zionism & Territory: the Socio-Territorial Dimension of Zionist Politics*. Berkeley: University of California Press, 1983.

King, C. S. *My Life with Martin Luther King, Jnr.*, London: Hodder & Stoughton, 1970.

King, Jr., M. L. *The Autobiography of Martin Luther King, Jnr*. London: Abacus, 2000.

_____. *The Strength to Love*. New York: Harper & Row, 1963.

Kiras, J., 'Terrorism and Globalisation' in *The Globalisation of World Politics*, ed., Baylis J. & Smith S. Oxford: OUP, 2004. Third Edition, 479-492.

Kirschenbaum, A., 'Fundamentalism: A Jewish Traditional Perspective' in *Jewish Fundamentalism in Comparative Perspective* ed. by L. A. Silberstein. New York: Routledge, 1993, 184-188.

Knelman, Fred. H., 'Who are the terrorists?' in *Waging Peace,* October 2001, no page number. http://www.wagingpeace.org/articles/2001/10/00_knelman_who.htm.

Koechler, H. ed. *Terrorism and National Liberation*. Frankfurt: Lang, 1988.

Kretzmer, D. *The Occupation of Justice*. Albany: SUNY, 2002.

Kuttab, J., 'Avenues Open for Defence of Human Rights in the Israeli-Occupied Territories', in *International Law and the Administration of Occupied Territories,* ed. by Emma Playfair. New York: OUP, 1992, 504.

La Guardia, A. *Holy Land, Unholy War.* London: John Murray, 2002.

Lahham, M., 'The Continuity of the Christian Presence in Jerusalem', in *Jerusalem: What Makes for Peace!* eds. Naim Ateek, Cedar Duaybis & Marla Schrader. London: Melisende, 1997, 17-22.

_____., 'The Spiritual Meaning and Experience of the Roman Catholic Church in Jerusalem.' in *Christians in the Holy Land*, eds., Michael Prior & William Taylor. London: World of Islam Festival Trust, 1994, 109-114.

Laqueur, W. & R. Rubin, eds. *The Israel-Arab Reader* 6th revised and updated edition. London: Penguin, 2001.

Laqueur, W. *Confrontation: The Middle-East War and World Politics.* London: Abacus, 1974.

Lewis, D. M. *The Origins of Christian Zionism: Lord Shaftesbury and Evangelical Support for a Jewish Homeland.* Cambridge: CUP, 2009.

Lieber, S. *Mystics and Missionaries.* Salt Lake City: University of Utah Press 1992.

Linden, G. *Church Leadership in a Political Crisis.* Uppsala: Missio, 1994.

Livingston, M. *International Terrorism in the Contemporary World.* USA: Greenwood Press, 1978.

Livingstone, N.,*The War against Terrorism.* Lexington Mass.: Lexington, 1982.

Llewellyn, T., 'The Stolen City', in *Jerusalem Today,* ed. by Ghada Karmi. Reading, Berks. Garnet, 1996, 97-110.

Loewenstein, J., 'Banishment: the Palestinian Refugees of Lebanon', in *The New Intifada,* ed. by Roane Carey. London: Verso, 2001, 269-286.

_____., 'How Gaza Offends Us All', *Washington Report on Middle East Affairs,* January/February 2007 – Vol. xxvi, No. 1, 14-15.

Longley, C. *Chosen People.* London: Hodder & Stoughton, 2002.

Lovett, R. *The History of the London Missionary Society Vols. I & II.* London: Henry Frowde, 1899.

Lustick, Ian S., 'Jewish Fundamentalism and the Israeli-Palestinian Impasse', in *Jewish Fundamentalism in Comparative Perspective* ed. by L. A. Silberstein. New York: Routledge, 1993.

_____. *For the Land and the Lord.* New York: Council on Foreign Relations Press, 1988 and 1994 editions.

Lutz, J. M. & B. J. *Global Terrorism.* London: Routledge, 2004.

McCaul, A. *New Testament Evidence to prove that the Jews are to be Restored to the Land of Israel. Sixth Edition.* London: London Society's House, 1878.

_____. *Rabbi David Kimchi's Commentary upon the Prophecies of Zechariah.*

_____. *The Old Paths.* London: London Society's House, 1846.

_____. *The Old Paths, or the Talmud tested by Scripture.* London: London Jews Society, 1868.

McGowan, D., 'Why we remember Deir Yassin', in *Speaking the Truth about Zionism and Israel,* ed. by Michael Prior. London: Melisende, 2004, 89-103.

McMahon, J., 'Preventive War and the Killing of the Innocent' in *The Ethics of War,* eds. Richard Sorabji & David Rodin. Aldershot: Ashgate Publishing House, 2006, 169-190.

_____, 'Pro-Israel PACS Not Invincible in US. Mid-Term Elections; Complications Ensue' *Washington Report on Middle East Affairs,* January/February 2007 – Vol. xxvi, No. 1.

McPherson, D., 'Politics and Multi-Faith in the Holy Land: A Challenge for Christians', in *Speaking the Truth about Zionism and Israel,* ed. by Michael Prior. London: Melisende, 2004, 148-164.

McTernan, O. *Violence in God's Name.* London: DLT, 2003.

Magonet, J. *The Subversive Bible.* London: SCM, 1997.

Mahoney, A., 'Church, State and the Christian Communities and the Holy Places of Palestine', in *Christians in the Holy Land,* eds. Michael Prior and William Taylor. London: World of Islam Festival Trust, 1995, 26-27.

Mansour, C., 'Jerusalem: International Law and Proposed Solutions', in *Jerusalem: What Makes for Peace!* eds., Naim Ateek, Cedar Duaybis & Marla Schrader. London: Melisende, 1997, 209-212.

Mansour, J., 'The Perspective of a Lay Christian from Galilee on the City of Jerusalem', in *Jerusalem: What Makes for Peace!* eds., Naim Ateek, Cedar Duaybis & Marla Schrader. London: Melisende, 1997, 226-229.

Ma'oz, M., 'The UN Partition Resolution of 1947: Why wasn't it implemented?' in *Shared Histories* eds., Paul Scham, Walid Salem & Benjamin Pogrund. Walnut Creek, California: Left Coast Press, Inc. 2005, 177-181.

Margalit, A, Settling Scores: *New York Review of Books. 20 September, 2001,* 20-25.

_____. The Suicide Bombers: *New York Review of Books. 16 January, 2003,* 36-39.

Marty, M. E. & R. S. Appleby, eds. *Fundamentalisms Observed.* Chicago: University of Chicago, 1994.

Marty, M. E., 'The Future of World Fundamentalisms'*, Proceedings of the American Philosophical Society,* Vol. 142, No. 3. September 1998.

Maruzzo, B., 'The Importance of Jerusalem to the Christians of Galilee', in *Jerusalem: What Makes for Peace!* eds., Naim Ateek, Cedar Duaybis & Marla Schrader. London: Melisende, 1997, 221-225.

Masalha, N. *Expulsion of the Palestinians: The Concept of 'Transfer' in Zionist Political Thought, 1882-1948.* Washington DC: Institute for Palestine Studies, 1992.

_____. *The Politics of Denial: Israel and the Palestinian Refugee Problem.* London and Sterling VA: Pluto, 2003.

Matar, I., 'The Changing Face of Jerusalem', in *Jerusalem: What Makes for Peace!* eds., Naim Ateek, Cedar Duaybis & Marla Schrader. London: Melisende, 1997, 154-166.

May, T. *Social Research. Issues, Methods and Process.* Buckingham: OUP, 2001.
Mayhew, C., & Adams A. *Publish It Not.* Oxford: Signal Books Ltd., 2006.
Mearsheimer, J., & Walt S., 'The Israel Lobby and US Foreign Policy' in *London Review of Books.* Vol. 28. No 6. March, 23, 2006.
_____. *The Israel Lobby and US Foreign Policy.* New York: Farrar, Strauss and Giroux, 2007.
Merkley, P. C. *The Politics of Christian Zionism 1891-1948.* London: Frank Cass, 1998.
Miano, P., 'Mainstream Christian Zionism' in *Speaking the Truth about Zionism and Israel,* ed. by Michael Prior. London: Melisende, 2004, 126-147.
Midrash, *Bava Batra* 16b.
Miles, M. B. & A. M. Hubermann. *Qualitative Data Analysis.* Thousand Oaks, California: Sage, 1994.
Miller, A. *The Truth Will Set You Free.* Oxford: The Perseus Press, 2001.
Moltmann, J. *The Crucified God.* London, SCM, 1974.
Montell, J., 'Removing Some, Expanding Others', *Cornerstone, Issue 38,* Fall. 2005, 10-11.
Morris, B., 'Israel's Secret Wars: A History of Israel's Intelligence Services', in *Bad News from Israel* eds., Greg Philo & Mike Berry. London: Pluto, 2004, 61.
_____. *The Birth of the Palestinian Refugee Problem Revisited.* Cambridge: CUP, 2004.
Morrison, D. *The Gush.* Jerusalem: Gefen Publishing House, 2004.
Moustakas C. E. *Phenomenological Research Methods.* Thousand Oaks, California: Sage, 1994.
Mu'allem, I., 'Factors Affecting the Palestinian Christian Presence in Israel', in *Jerusalem: What Makes for Peace!* eds., Naim Ateek, Cedar Duaybis & Marla Schrader. London: Melisende, 1997, 217-220.
Mubarak, Awad, 'Their theology, Our nightmare' in *Christian Perspectives on the Israeli-Palestinian Conflict* eds. Wesley H. Brown & Peter F. Penner. Neufeld Verlag Schwarzenfeld, Germany: 2008.
Muller, Mark, 'Terrorism Lists'. Introductory paper presented at International Conference at London Metropolitan University, May, 21, 2005, "Suspect Communities: The Real 'War on Terror' in Europe," 19-22.
Munayer, S. J., 'Relations between Religions in Historic Palestine and the Future Prospects: Christians and Jews', in *Christians in the Holy Land,* eds., Michael Prior & William Taylor. London: World of Islam Festival Trust, 1994, 143-152.
Murray, N., 'Rebuilding our Activism', in *The New Intifada,* ed. by Roane Carey. London: Verso, 2001, 333-344.
Nabulsi, K., 'Conceptions of Justice in War' in *The Ethics of War,* eds., Richard Sorabji & David Rodin. Aldershot: Ashgate Publishing House, 2006, 44-60.
Nasr, K. B. *Arab and Israeli Terrorism.* North Carolina: McFarland & Co., 1997.

Nazir, Ali M., 'Christians in the Holy Land', in *Christians in the Holy Land*, eds., Michael Prior & William Taylor. London: World of Islam Festival Trust, 1994, 161-168.

Netanyahu, B., 'A Durable Peace: Israel and its Place Among the Nations'. New York: Warner Books, 2000 in *Bad News from Israel* eds., Greg Philo & Mike Berry. London: Pluto, 2004, 61.

_____. *Terrorism: How the West Can Win*. London: Weidenfeld & Nicolson, 1986.

Neumann, M. *The Case Against Israel*. Petrolia, California: Counterpunch & AK Press, 2005.

Newman, D., ed. *The Impact of Gush Emunim*. London: Croom Helm, 1985.

_____. *Jewish Settlement in the West Bank and the Role of Gush Emunim* in Occasional Papers, Series, No. 16. eds., John Dewdney & Heather Bleaney. Durham: Centre for Middle Eastern and Islamic Studies, University of Durham, 1982.

_____. *Population, Settlement and Conflict*. Cambridge: CUP, 1991.

Nimni, E., ed. *The Challenge of Post-Zionism*. London: Zed Books, 2003.

_____., 'From *Galut* to *T'futsoth*: Post-Zionism and the Dislocation of the Jewish Diasporas' in *The Challenge of Post-Zionism* ed. by Ephraim Nimni. London: Zed Books, 2003, 117-152.

Norman, R., 'War, Humanitarian Intervention and Human Rights' in *The Ethics of War* eds., Richard Sorabji & David Rodin. Aldershot: Ashgate Publishing House, 2006, 191-207.

Odeh, Adnan Abu, 'The Ownership of Jerusalem: A Jordanian View', in *Jerusalem Today*, ed. by Ghada Karmi. Reading, Berks. Garnet, 1996, 59-66.

Oliver, A. M. & Steinberg P. F. *The Road to Martyrs' Square*. New York: OUP, 2004.

O'Mahoney, A., 'Church, State and the Christian Communities and the Holy Places of Palestine, in *Christians in the Holy Land*, eds., Michael Prior & William Taylor. London: World of Islam Festival Trust, 1994, 11-30.

Omer, Y. *International Documents Relating to Terrorism*. Cavendish, 1995.

O'Neill, D., & D. Wagner. *Peace or Armageddon*. London: Marshall Pickering, 1993.

Pacheco, A., 'Flouting Convention: the Oslo Agreements', in *The New Intifada*, ed. by Roane Carey. London: Verso, 2001, 181-208.

Pappé, I., "Critique and Agenda: Post-Zionist Scholars in Israel." *History & Memory* 7, 1. Spring/Summer 1995, 66-90.

Pappé, I., 'The Square Circle: The Struggle for Survival of Traditional Zionism', in *The Challenge of Post-Zionism* ed. by Ephraim Nimni. London: Zed Books, 2003, 42-62.

_____, 'State of Denial: The *Nakbah* in Israeli History and Today', in *Speaking the Truth about Zionism and Israel*, eds., Michael Prior. London: Melisende, 2004, 71-78.

Parfitt, T. *The Jews in Palestine 1800-1882*. The Royal Historical Society: The Boydell Press, 1987.

Patriarchs and Heads of the Christian Communities in Jerusalem: Memorandum of 14 November, 1994, 'Significance of Jerusalem for Christians', in *Jerusalem: What Makes for Peace!* eds., Naim Ateek, Cedar Duaybis & Marla Schrader. London: Melisende, 1997, 236-241.

Perdue, W., 'The Selling of International Terrorism: the Reagan Administration, Israel and the American Media', in *Terrorism and National Liberation* ed. by Hans Koechler. Frankfurt: Lang, 1988, 217-236.

Perry, Y. *British Mission to Jews in Nineteenth - Century Palestine*. London: Frank Cass, 2003.

Philo, G. & M. Berry. *Bad News from Israel.* London: Pluto, 2004.

Piterberg, G. *The Returns of Zionism.* London: Verso, 2008.

Playfair, E., ed. *International Law and the Administration of Occupied Territories*. New York: OUP, 1992.

Pollard, A., & M. Hennell, eds. *Charles Simeon, 1759-1836*. London: SPCK, 1964.

Pollock, J. *Shaftesbury.* London: Hodder & Stoughton, 1985.

Porat, H. 'Eye in eye they shall see the return of the Lord to Zion' *Ptachim* 32: 3-12. Trans. from Hebrew in Michael Feige, *Space, Place and Memory in Gush Emunim Ideology,* 4, sent to Geoffrey Whitfield by Michael Feige, December, 13, 2007.

Pragai, M. J. *Faith and Fulfilment.* London: Vallentine, Mitchell and Company Ltd., 1985.

Primoratz, I., 'What is Terrorism?' *Journal of Applied Philosophy* 7. 1990, 131.

Prior, M. & W. Taylor, eds. *Christians in the Holy Land*. London: World of Islam Festival Trust, 1994.

Prior, M., 'A Perspective on Pilgrimage to the Holy Land', in *Jerusalem: What Makes for Peace!* eds., Naim Ateek, Cedar Duaybis & Marla Schrader. London: Melisende, 1997, 114-131.

_____, 'Pilgrimage to the Holy Land, Yesterday and Today', in *Christians in the Holy Land*, eds., Michael Prior & William Taylor. London: World of Islam Festival Trust, 1994, 169-202.

_____, ed. *Speaking the Truth about Zionism and Israel*. London: Melisende, 2004.

_____. *Zionism and the State of Israel*. London: Routledge, 1999.

Ptashnik, Ben-Zion, "The Other Side: A response to Rivage-Seul's 'Report from Palestine.'" http://www.globaljusticecenter.org/articles/ptashnik.htm

Quigley, J., 'Jerusalem in International Law', in *Jerusalem Today,* ed. by Ghada Karmi. Reading, Berks.: Garnet, 1996, 25-44.

_____. *Palestine and Israel*. Durham, USA: Duke University Press, 1990.

Rabbani, M., 'A Smorgasbord of Failure: Oslo and the Al-Aqsa Intifada', in *The New Intifada,* ed. by Roane Carey. London: Verso, 2001, 69-90.

Raheb, M., 'The Spiritual Significance and Experience of the Churches: the Lutheran Perspective', in *Christians in the Holy Land*, eds., Michael Prior & William Taylor. London: World of Islam Festival Trust, 1994, 127-130.

Ram, U., 'From Nation State – to Nation', in *The Challenge of Post-Zionism,* ed. by Ephraim Nimni. London: Zed Books, 2003, 20-41.

Rankin, O. S., 'God', in *A Theological Wordbook of the Bible* ed. by Alan Richardson. London: SCM Press, 1956.

Reese, C., 'Check your Beliefs', *Washington Report on Middle East Affairs*. Vol. 9. Issue 4. May/June 2006, 14-15.

Reeve, S. *One Day in September*. London: Faber, 2000.

Reinhart, T. *Israel/Palestine*. New York: Seven Stories, 2002.

———. *The Road Map to Nowhere*. London: Verso, 2006.

Rekhess, Elie, 'The Palestinian Resurgence of Islamic Fundamentalism' in *Jewish Fundamentalism in Comparative Perspective,* ed. by Laurence A. Silberstein. New York: New York University Press, 1993, 96.

Report of an ecumenical visit to the Middle East, March 2001, "*Who is my Neighbour?.*" London: Churches Together in Britain and Ireland, 2001.

Report by a Working Group of the Church of England's House of Bishops, September 2005*: Countering terrorism: Power, violence and democracy post 9/11.*

Reuter, C. *My Life is a Weapon: A Modern History of Suicide Bombing*. Princeton: Princeton University Press, 2004.

Richardson, A., ed. *A Theological Wordbook of the Bible*. London: SCM Press, 1956.

Ricolfi, L. 'Palestinians: 1981-2003', in *Making Sense of Suicide Missions,* ed. by Diego Gambetta. Oxford: OUP, 2005, 77-129.

Rivage-Seul, Mike, 'Report from Palestine', '*Center for Global Justice'*, 16 July, 2006. http://www.globaljusticecenter.org/articles/betterworld_palestine.htm.

Roberts, Adam and Richard Guelff, eds. *Documents on the Laws of War* 3rd ed., Oxford: OUP, 2000.

Robinson, G. E., 'The Peace of the Powerful', in *The New Intifada,* ed. by Roane Carey. London: Verso, 2001, 111-124.

Robinson, H. Wheeler, *Deuteronomy and Joshua*. Edinburgh: T. C. Jack & E. C. Jack, 1926.

Robinson, H. Wheeler *The Religious Ideas of the Old Testament*. London: Duckworth & Co. 1913.

Rodin, D. Terrorism without Intention, *Ethics* 114. July 2004, 752-771.

———. *War and Self Defense*. Oxford: OUP, 2004.

Rodin D. 'The Ethics of Asymmetric War' in *The Ethics of War* eds., Richard Sourabji & David Rodin. Aldershot, Hants. Ashgate, 2006, 153-168.

Rose, Jacqueline. *The Question of Zion*. Oxford: Princeton, 2005.

Rose, John. *The Myths of Zionism*. London: Pluto, 2004.

Ross, D. *The Missing Peace*. New York: Farrar, Strauss & Giroux, 2004.

Rowley, Gwyn, 'The Land of Israel: a Reconstructionist Approach' in *The Impact of Gush Emunim* ed. by David Newman. London: Croom Helm, 1985, 125-136.
Roy, S., 'Decline and Disfigurement: The Palestinian Economy after Oslo', in *The New Intifada,* ed. by Roane Carey. London: Verso, 2001, 91-110.
Rubin, B. *The Politics of Terrorism.* Washington DC: Bowman & Littlefield, 1989.
Rubinstein, W. R. 'The Secret of Leopold Amery' in *Historical Research. Vol. 73, no. 181. June 2000,* 175-196. Published by Blackwell Publishers Ltd., 108 Cowley Rd., Oxford OX4 1JF, UK and 350 Main St., Malden, MA 02148, USA.
Rudestam, K. E. & Newton R. R. *Surviving Your Dissertation. A Comprehensive Guide to Content and Process.* London: Sage, 2001.
Ruether, H. & R. R. Ruether, 'Zionism, Christianity and the Israel-Palestinian Conflict', in *Speaking the Truth about Zionism and Israel,* ed. by Michael Prior. London: Melisende, 2004, 51-70.
Rummel, R. J. *Death by Government.* New Brunswick, New Jersey: Transaction, 1997.
Rusk, D. *As I Saw It.* New York: Penguin, 1991.
Ruthven, M. *A Fury for God.* London: Granta, 2002.
_____. *Fundamentalism.* Oxford: OUP, 2004.
Ruthven, M. *Islam: A Very Short Introduction.* Oxford: OUP, 1997.
Saa'd, David, 'How shall we Interpret Scripture about the Land and Eschatology? Jewish and Arab Perspectives' in *Christian Perspectives on the Israeli-Palestinian Conflict* eds. Wesley H. Brown & Peter F. Penner. Neufeld Verlag Schwarzenfeld, Germany: 2008.
Sabella, B., 'Profile of the Christian Communities: Challenges and Hopes', in *Jerusalem: What Makes for Peace!* eds., Naim Ateek, Cedar Duaybis & Marla Sabella B., 'Socio-Economic Characteristics and the Challenges to Palestinian Christians in the Holy Land', in *Christians in the Holy Land*, eds., Michael Prior & William Taylor. London: World of Islam Festival Trust, 1994, 31-44.
Said, E. W. 'America's Last Taboo', in *The New Intifada,* ed. by Roane Carey. London: Verso, 2001, 259-268.
Said, E. W. & Hitchens C. *Blaming the Victims.* London: Verso, 2001.
Said, E. W. *From Oslo to Iraq and the Roadmap.* London: Bloomsbury, 2004.
_____, 'Keynote Essay', in *Jerusalem Today,* ed. by Ghada Karmi. Reading, Berks.: Ithaca, 1996, 11-12.
_____, 'New History, Old Ideas', in *The Challenge of Post-Zionism* ed. by Ephraim Nimni. London: Zed Books, 2003, 199-202. Also included in *Al Ahram Weekly no. 378, 21-27 May, 1998.*
_____, 'Palestinians Under Siege', in *The New Intifada,* ed. by Roane Carey. London: Verso, 2001, 27-44.
_____. *Peace and its Discontents.* London: Vintage, 1995.

_____. *The Politics of Dispossession*. London: Vintage, 1994.
_____. *The Question of Palestine*. London: Vintage, 1992.
_____. *The End of the Peace Process*. London: Granta Publications, 2002.
Saleh, B. 'Socioeconomic Profile of Palestinian Militants from Hamas, Palestinian Islamic Jihad and Al-Aqsa Martyrs' Brigades'. Paper presented at the Graduate Research Forum, Kansas State University, April 4, 2003.
Salem, W., 'Paradox of the UN 1947 Partition Plan' in *Shared Histories* eds., Paul Scham, Walid Salem & Benjamin Pogrund. Walnut Creek, California: Left Coast Press, Inc., 2005, 182-187.
Sanders, D., 'International Relations: Neo-realism and Neo-liberalism' in *New Handbook of Political Science* eds., Robert E. Goodin & Hans-Dieter Klingemann. Oxford: OUP, 1998, 428-445.
Sarsar, Saliba, 'US. – Key to Solving Israeli-Palestinian Conflict' *Jordan Times, Opinion. Jordan.* November, 1, 2006. http://www.jordantimes.com/wed/opinion/opinion4.htm.
Savir, U. *The Process.* New York: Vintage, 1998.
Scham, P., Salem W., & Pogrund B., eds. *Shared Histories*. Walnut Creek, California: Left Coast Press, Inc., 2005.
Schatz, A. 'Invisible Walls', *London Review of Books*, Vol. 28, No. 15. August, 3 2006.
Schmid, A. & A. Jongeman. *Political Terrorism*. Amsterdam: North Holland Pub. Co., 1988.
Schulze, K. E., M. Stokes, & C. Campbell. *Nationalism, Minorities and Diasporas*. London: Tauris, 1996.
Schwart, Michael, 'Digging up the Past, Destroying the Future' *Challenge*, Tel Aviv, November–December 2005. No. 94. Vol. 16. No. 6, 6-8.
Schweitzer, Y. & S. G. Ferber. *Al-Qaeda and the Internationalization of Suicide Terrorism*. Jaffee Center for Strategic Studies, TAU, November 2005.
Schweitzer, Y., 'Female suicide bombers for God', *Telavivnotes, No. 88*. 9 October, 2003. Tel Aviv University, The Jaffee Center for Strategic Studies & The Moshe Dayan Center for Middle Eastern and African Studies, October, 9 2003.
_____, *"Is there a 'Mind' of a Suicide Bomber?."* Jaffee Center for Strategic Studies, TAU. Undated c. 2005?
_____, 'Suicide Terrorism: Historical Background and Risks for the Future', *Wide Angle; thirteen WNET New York*. June, 18 2004. 2005 Educational Broadcasting Corporation.
Scobbie, Iain, *'Unchart(er)ed Waters?: Consequences of the Advisory Opinion on the Legal Consequences of the Construction of a Wall in the Occupied Palestinian Territory for the Responsibility of the UN for Palestine'. The European Journal of International Law*, Vol. 16. No. 5 © *EJIL 2005*, 941-961.
Scott, T., *The Jews a Blessing to the Nations*, 1810. Held in the British Library.
Segev, T., *One Palestine Complete*. London: Little, Brown & Co., 2000.

Sela, A., 'Israeli Historiography of the 1948 War' in *Shared Histories*, eds., Paul Scham, Walid Salem & Benjamin Pogrund. Walnut Creek, California: Left Coast Press, 2005, 204.

Sfeir, J., 'Education in the Holy Land', in *Christians in the Holy Land*, eds., Michael Prior & William Taylor. London: World of Islam Festival Trust, 1994, 75-88.

Shafir, G. & Y. Peled. *Being Israeli.* Cambridge: CUP, 2002.

_____. *Land, Labor and the Origins of the Israeli-Palestinian Conflict, 1882-1914.* Cambridge: CUP, 1989.

_____. 'Institutional and Spontaneous Settlement Drives: Did Gush Emunim Make a Difference?' in *The Impact of Gush Emunim* ed. by David Newman. London: Croom Helm, 1985, 153-171.

Shahak, I., & Mezvinsky N. *Jewish Fundamentalism in Israel*. London: Pluto, 1999.

_____, 'Jerusalem and the Jews'. in *Jerusalem Today,* ed. by Ghada Karmi. Reading, Berks. Garnet, 1996, 119-132.

_____. *Jewish History, Jewish Religion*. London: Pluto, 1997.

Shamir, I. *Flowers of Galilee*. Tempe, Arizona: Dandelion, 2004.

Sharp, G., 'There are Realistic Alternatives' in *Waging Non-violent Struggle*. Boston: Extending Horizons Books, 2003.

Shearer, D., & A. Meyer, 'The Dilemma of Aid Under Occupation' in A*id, Diplomacy and Facts on the Ground* eds., Michael Keating, Anne Le More & Robert Lowe. London: Royal Institute of International Affairs, 2005.

Shehadeh, R., 'The Legislative Stages of the Israeli Military Occupation', in *International Law and the Administration of Occupied Territories,* ed. by Emma Playfair. Oxford: Clarendon, 1992, 151-168.

Sheridan, S., 'Abraham from a Jewish Perspective', in *Abraham's Children: Jews, Christians and Muslims in Conversation,* ed. by Norman Solomon, Richard Harries and Tim Winter. London: T. & T. Clark, 2005.

Shilhav, Yosseph, 'Interpretation and Misinterpretation of Jewish Territorialism' in *The Impact of Gush Emunim* ed. by David Newman. London: Croom Helm, 1985, 111-124.

Shlaim, Avi, *The Iron Wall: Israel and the Arab World.* London: Penguin, 2000.

_____. 'Is Zionism Today the Real Enemy of the Jew?' *International Herald Tribune,* February, 4, 2005.

_____. 'The Lost Steps', *The Nation,* August, 30, 2004, issue, 31-38

_____. 'The United States and the Israeli-Palestinian Conflict' in *Worlds in Collision,* eds., Ken Booth & Timothy Dunne. Basingstoke: Palgrave Macmillan, 2002, 172-183.

Shulman, D. *Dark Hope*. Chicago: University of Chicago, 2007.

Sid-Ahmed, M., 'The Arab-Israeli Conflict and Terrorism' in *Terrorism and National Liberation* ed. by Hans Koechler. Frankfurt: Lang, 1988, 97-112.

Siegman, Henry, 'The Middle East Peace Process Scam', *London Review of Books* Vol. 29, No. 16, dated August, 16, 2007.

_____, 'Gaza: The Lies of War', *London Review of Books,* January, 29, 2009.
Silberstein, L. J., 'Becoming Israeli/Israeli Becomings' in *Deleuze in the Contemporary World* ed., by Ian Buchanan & Adrian Parr. Edinburgh: Edinburgh University Press, 2006, 146-160.
_____. *Jewish Fundamentalism in Comparative Perspective.* New York: New York University Press, 1993.
_____, 'Postzionism: A Critique of Zionist Discourse' in *Palestine-Israel Journal*, Vol. 9, No. 2, Part 1, March 2002, 84-91; Vol. 9, No. 3, Part 2, October 2002, 97-106. ISSN 0793-1385.
_____, 'Postzionism and Postmodern theory: The challenge to Jewish Studies' in *Modern Judaism and Historical Consciousness: Identities – Encounters – Perspectives,* ed., by Andreas Gotzmann & Christian Wiese. Forthcoming.
_____, 'Religious Fundamentalism and Modernity: Theoretical Issues' in *Jewish Fundamentalism in Comparative Perspective,* ed., by Laurence J. Silberstein. New York: New York University Press, 1993, 22.
_____. *The Postzionism Debates.* New York: Routledge, 1999.
Silke, A., 'The Devil You Know: Continuing Problems with Research on Terrorism.' *Terrorism and Political Violence*, winter 2001, Vol. 13, No. 4, 1-14.
Simeon, C. *Horae Homileticae 21 Vols.* London: Holdsworth and Ball, 1832.
Sinclair, A. An Anatomy of Terror. London: Macmillan, 2003.
Sizer, S. *Christian Zionism.* Leicester: Inter-Varsity Press, 2004.
_____, 'The International Christian Embassy, Jerusalem: A Case Study in Political Christian Zionism', in *Speaking the Truth about Zionism and Israel,* ed. by Michael Prior. London: Melisende, 2004, 104-125.
_____. *Zion's Christian Soldiers.* Nottingham: IVP, 2007.
Skinner, J. *I & II Kings.* Edinburgh: T. C. Jack & E. C. Jack, 1926.
Sluka, J. A., ed. *Death Squad: The Anthropology of Terror.* Philadelphia: Univ. Pennsylvania Press, 2000.
Smith, A. D. *Chosen Peoples.* Oxford: OUP, 2003.
Smith, H. *The Jerusalem Bishopric.* London: Bertheim, 1847.
Sohlagheck, D. *International Terrorism.* Canada: Lexington, 1988.
Solomon, N., R. D. Harries, Winter T., eds. *Abraham's Children: Jews, Christians and Muslims in Conversation.* London: T. & T. Clark, 2005.
Solomon, N., 'The Ethics of War: Judaism' in *The Ethics of War* eds., Richard Sourabji & David Rodin. Aldershot, Hants. Ashgate, 2006, 108-137.
Souef, A., 'Under the Gun: a Palestinian Journey', in *The New Intifada,* ed. by Roane Carey. London: Verso, 2001, 45-68.
Sourabji, R., 'Just War From Ancient Origins to the Conquistadors Debate and its Modern Relevance' in *The Ethics of War* eds., Richard Sourabji & David Rodin. Aldershot, Hants. Ashgate, 2006, 13-29.
Sourabji, R., & D. Rodin. *The Ethics of War.* Aldershot, Hants. Ashgate, 2006.
Sprinzak, E., 'Gush Emunim: The Iceberg Model of Political Extremism' in *The Impact of Gush Emunim* ed. by David Newman. London: Croom Helm, 1985, 27-45.

_____. *The Ascendance of Israel's Radical Right.* New York: OUP, 1991.

_____. 'The Politics, Institutions and Culture of Gush Emunim' in *Jewish Fundamentalism in Comparative Perspective* ed., by L. A. Silberstein. New York: Routledge, 1993, 121.

Stern, Jessica, 'Holy Avengers'*, Financial Times Magazine,* June, 12, 2004. Issue no. 59, 14-17.

_____. *Terror in the Name of God: Why Religious Militants Kill.* New York: Harper Collins, 2003.

Sternberg, D. *How to Complete and Survive a Doctoral Dissertation.* New York: St. Martin's Griffin, 1981.

Strauss, A. & J. Corbin. *Basics of Qualitative Research*, Second Edition. London: Sage, 1998.

Studdert-Kennedy, G. A. *The Unutterable Beauty.* London: Hodder & Stoughton, 1927.

Stunt, T. C. M. *From Awakening to Secession.* Edinburgh: T&T Clark Ltd, 2000.

Sugden, J., & A. Bairner, eds. *Sport in Divided Societies.* Oxford: Meyer & Meyer, Sport. UK 2000.

Sugden, J., & J. Wallis, eds. *Football for Peace?* Oxford: Meyer & Meyer, Sport. UK 2007.

Sukarieh, M., 'Life in the Camps', in *The New Intifada,* ed. by Roane Carey. London: Verso, 2001, 287-292.

Svirsky, G., 'The Israeli Peace Movement since the Al-Aqsa Intifada', in *The New Intifada,* ed. by Roane Carey. London: Verso, 2001, 321-332.

Tams, Christian J., 'Light Treatment of a Complex Problem'*, The European Journal of International Law. Vol. 16. No. 5 © EJIL 2005,* 963-978.

Thompson, T. L. Ed. with S. K. Jayyusi. *Jerusalem in Ancient History and Tradition.* London: T&T Clark International, 2003.

Tibawi, A. L. *British Interests in Palestine 1800-1901.* London: OUP, 1961.

Tobias, P. *Liberal Judaism: A Judaism for the Twenty-First Century.* London: Liberal Judaism, 2007.

Tuchman, B. *Bible and Sword.* New York: First Ballantine Trade Edition 1984.

United Nations, *Costs of Conflict: The Changing Face of Bethlehem.* UNSCO and OCHA, December 2004.

Vereté, M. 'The restoration of the Jews in English Protestant Thought, 1790-1840' in *Middle Eastern Studies: January, 1972,* 3-50.

Victor, B. *The Last Crusade.* London: Constable, 2005.

Viorst, M. *What Shall I do With This People?.* New York: The Free Press, 2002.

Wagner, D., 'Marching to Zion: Western Evangelicals and Jerusalem Approaching the Year 2000', in *Jerusalem: What Makes for Peace!* eds., Naim Ateek, Cedar Duaybis & Marla Schrader. London: Melisende, 1997, 73-93.

_____. *Anxious for Armageddon.* Scotdale, PA: Herald Press, 2001.

Walker, P., 'Jesus and Jerusalem: New Testament Perspectives', in *Jerusalem: What Makes for Peace!* eds., Naim Ateek, Cedar Duaybis & Marla Schrader. London: Melisende, 1997, 61-72.

Wallensteen, P. *Understanding Conflict Resolution.* London: Sage, 2002.

Walzer, M. *Just and Unjust Wars.* London: Allen Lane, 1978.

Wardlaw, G. *Political Terrorism.* Second Edition. Cambridge: CUP, 1989.

Warschawski, M. Translated by Peter Drucker, *Toward An Open Tomb.* New York: Monthly Review Press, 2004.

Watson, J. *Listening to Islam: with Thomas Merton, Sayyid Qutb, Kenneth Cragg and Ziauddin Sardar: Praise, Reason and Reflection.* Brighton: Sussex Academic Press, 2005.

Watt, D. C., 'Terrorism', in *The Fontana Dictionary of Modern Thought*, eds., Alan Bullock & Oliver Stallybrass. London: Fontana, 1977, 628.

Weir, A., 'Gaza: A Report from the Front', in *The New Intifada,* ed. by Roane Carey. London: Verso, 2001, 159-164.

Weisburd, D. *Jewish Settler Violence.* Pennsylvania: Pennsylvania State University, 1989.

Wessels, A., 'The Significance of Jerusalem for Muslims', in *Jerusalem: What Makes for Peace!* eds., Naim Ateek, Cedar Duaybis & Marla Schrader. London: Melisende, 1997, 45-60.

White, A. *Iraq: Searching for Hope.* London: Continuum, 2005.

Whitfield, G. V. *Amity in the Middle East.* Brighton: The Alpha Press, 2006.

_____. *The Roots of Terrorism in Israel and Palestine.* Lexington, Ky: Emeth Press, 2007.

Wilkinson, P. *Terrorism and the Liberal State.* London: Macmillan, 1977.

_____, 'Trends in International Terrorism–the American Response' in *Terrorism and International Order,* eds., Lawrence Freedman, Christopher Hill, Adam Roberts, & R. J. Vincent. London: Routledge, 1986, 37-55.

Williams, C. *Terrorism Explained.* Sidney, Australia. New Holland Publishers, Pty. Ltd., 2002.

Windsor, P., 'Middle East Terrorism', in *Terrorism and International Order*, eds., Lawrence Freedman, Christopher Hill, Adam Roberts & R. J. Vincent. London: Routledge, 1986, 26-36.

Wistrich, R., & D. Ohana, eds. *The Shaping of Israeli Identity: Myth, Memory and Trauma.* London: Frank Cass & Company, 2005.

Woodward, B. *The War Within.* London: Simon & Schuster, 2008.

Wright, G. E. *The Challenge of Israel's Faith.* London: SCM Press Ltd., 1946.

Wybrew, H., 'Churches of the Holy Land. Obligations and Expectations: a View from Outside', in *Christians in the Holy Land*, eds., Michael Prior & William Taylor. London: World of Islam Festival Trust, 1994, 217-224.

Yahya, A., in *Shared Histories,* eds., Paul Scham, Walid Salem & Benjamin Pogrund. Walnut Creek, California: Left Coast Press, 2005.

Yuval-Davis, N., 'Conclusion: Some Thoughts on Post-Zionism and the Construction of the Zionist Project' in *The Challenge of Post-Zionism* ed. by Ephraim Nimni. London: Zed Books, 2003, 182-196.

Zaru, J., 'Justice and Peace', in *Christians in the Holy Land*, eds., Michael Prior & William Taylor. London: World of Islam Festival Trust, 1994, 65-74.

_____, 'Pathways to Christian Unity II', in *Jerusalem: What Makes for Peace!* eds., Naim Ateek, Cedar Duaybis & Marla Schrader. London: Melisende, 1997, 28-30.

_____, 'Theologising, Truth and Peacemaking in the Palestinian Experience', in *Speaking the Truth about Zionism and Israel,* ed. by Michael Prior. London: Melisende, 2004, 165-189.

Zertal, I., & A. Eldar. *Lords of the Land.* New York: Nations Books, 2007.

Zoughbi, Z., 'Local Community and Tourism', in *Jerusalem: What Makes for Peace!* eds., Naim Ateek, Cedar Duaybis & Marla Schrader. London: Melisende, 1997, 111-113.

Index

A
Abrahamic Covenant 14–25, 32, 53, 85, 88, 124–31
Abu Ghraib 149
Africa 31, 36, 45–46, 137
Agudat Yisrael 46
Ahmedinejad, President Mahmoud 21, 144
Ai 36
Albright, Madeleine 74
Alexander, Rt. Rev. Professor Michael Solomon 98, 104–10
Aliyah 64, 80
Allon, Yigal 44, 59
Amalekites 144
Amanah, Amana 64
Amery, Leopold 34–35, 39
Ancient Israel 21, 134
Annapolis 37, 67, 74, 139, 161
Apocalyptic 15, 89
Arab Peace Initiative 164
Aran, Gideon 41–42, 53, 60, 65, 67–70, 76–81
Argentine 30, 51
Armstrong, K. 130, 134
Ashkenazi 46, 48, 54, 69, 77, 84
Ateek, Rev. Naim 142, 158
Australia 31, 137
Avnery, U. 34, 39, 81, 140, 153, 157, 159, 163, 166

B
B'tselem 75, 82, 146, 155, 158–59
Ba'al Hatzor 61
Babylon 33, 47, 130–31
Baker, James 70
Balfour Declaration 15, 29–37, 47, 55, 83–85, 110–13, 120
Baptist Missionary Society 91
Barak, Prime Minister Ehud 71, 147
Barenboim, David 156, 159, 161
Baring, Rt. Hon. Thomas, MP 98, 117

Bedouin 29–30
Begin, Prime Minister Menachem 44, 59, 63, 66–67
Beit Hanoun 162
Beit Jala 158
Ben-Gurion, David 152
Benvenisti, Professor Eyal 140, 143, 157–58
Berith 32
Bethlehem 34, 39, 79, 82–83, 126, 146, 157, 158
Bicheno, Rev. James 89–91, 111, 114
Bickersteth, Rev. Edward 102
Bilezki, Professor Anat 143–44
Block of the Faithful 55
Bnai Akiva 48
Bogue, Rev. David 91, 95
Brighton, University of 12, 17
British Council 12
British Mandate 30
Broyde, Michael 73, 82
Bruderlein, Claude 148, 159
Buber, Martin 50–52, 56, 78–79
Bunsen, Chevalier 105
Burder, George 93
Bush, George 70
Bush, George W. 140, 154, 161, 163

C
Camp David 24, 67, 147
Campbell, Patrick 104
Canaan 16, 29, 35–36, 50, 62, 77, 87, 121, 123, 126–27, 133
Carey, William 91, 115
Carmel, Alex 106–107
Carter, President Jimmy 67, 81, 142, 158, 162
Carus, William 96, 98, 116–17
Cavanaugh, Kathleen 34
Celtic 33
Checkpoints 22, 75, 138, 143, 145, 150
Christ Church, Jerusalem 104, 108–109, 118–19
Clements, Professor Ronald 105, 119, 124, 132–34
Clinton, President Bill 147, 158
Co-existence 21, 31, 57, 135
Colonialism 27, 36, 45, 137, 143, 158
Committee for Jewish Affairs 92
Covenant 13–16, 23–25, 32–33, 47, 49–53, 62, 69–70, 76–77, 84–90, 121–34
Crusades 27
Cyrus 47
Czar Alexander I of Russia 98

D
d'Alema, Massimo 140

Dalton, George 101
Davies, Professor W. D. 30, 32, 36, 38–39, 73, 75, 82, 123–24, 132
Debellatio 37, 39, 73, 75
Dershowitz, Professor Alan 22–25, 142, 151, 158–59, 164–67
Dialectic 41
Diaspora 29, 48, 73, 80–81, 84, 113, 123
Disease 13, 22, 136, 145
Dispensation 16
Dreyfus Affair 45
Dugard, Professor John 142–43, 158
Duke of Kent, HRH 94–98, 111

E
Egypt 24, 29–30, 45, 53–55, 61, 63, 67, 77, 87, 105, 121–22, 126–27, 133, 137, 145, 153
Ein Yabrud 61
El-Sarraj, Dr Eyal 162, 166
Eldar, Akiva 57, 62, 79–81, 139–40, 147, 154–59
Elon Moreh 44, 61–63, 73
English Premier League Football Clubs 12
Eretz 24, 32, 46, 55–56, 61, 71, 75, 109, 121, 125, 140, 163
Euphrates 24, 32, 54, 77, 87, 121, 133
European Union 136, 147, 151
Evangelical 15, 33–34, 53, 63, 76, 83–95, 103, 105, 107, 109–11, 114
Exile 33, 43, 47, 89, 130–31
Exodus 29, 39, 55, 90, 126, 128, 132–33
Extermination 36, 121–22, 125, 127–28, 149
Ezekiel 49–50, 78, 98, 117
Ezra 131

F
Faber, George Stanley 98, 117
Farran, J. 103
Fatah 13, 34, 136–37, 154, 161
Feige, Professor Michael 48–49, 71, 78, 81
Finch, Sir Henry MP 88
Finkelstein I 128, 134
Finlayson, Geoffrey 105, 118–19
Finn, James 109
Firman 108
Fisch, Professor Harold 43, 49–51, 77–78
Fisk, Robert 72, 82
Flora London Marathon 12
Football for Peace 12
Fourth Geneva Convention 58, 62, 138, 140–41, 157
Frankl, Viktor, 23
Free Gaza Movement 162
French Revolution 89
Frey, C. J. 91–117

Friedman, David 27–28, 38, 72, 81–82
Fuller, Rev. Andrew 16, 51, 94, 111
Fundamentalism 33, 51, 54, 65, 71, 76–81, 87

G
Gahelet 54, 60
Galen 15, 17
Galway, University of 34
Gaza 14, 16, 23, 37, 45, 67–68, 74–75, 136–37, 145, 150, 152–55
Gazit 57, 66, 71, 74, 79, 81– 82
Genesis 23–39, 77–79, 87–90, 12–22, 126, 128, 132–34
Genocide 28
Germany 29–30, 38– 47, 86, 105, 146, 152
Gershon Shafir 45
Gerstmann, Dr. Albert 106
Ghada 37, 86, 138
Gidney, W. T. 95, 97, 100, 116–18
Gobat, Rt. Rev. Bishop Samuel 109–10
Goldberg, Rabbi David 87–88, 113–14, 120
Goldstein, Dr. Baruch 16, 72
Guantanamo Bay 149
Guardian 134, 162–67
Gush Etzion 46, 57, 60

H
Ha'aretz 35, 37, 159, 163, 166–67
Hafrada 142
Hague Regulations (1907) 58, 141
Haim Be'er 71
Halakhah, Halacha 42–43, 53–54, 57
Halper, Professor J. 56, 74, 79, 82, 145, 157–58, 162, 166
haluka 84–85
Hamas 13, 22–23, 31, 34, 70, 136–38, 144, 149–54, 159, 161–62, 164–65, 166–167
Haniyeh, Prime Minister Ismail 164
Hannukah 63
Haredim 48, 54
Hareven, Shulamit 71, 81
Hasidim 84
Hass, Amira 166
Hebron 44, 52, 57–59, 72, 77, 126, 129, 143
Herzl, Theodore 21, 36, 45–46, 48, 55, 112
Hess 51
Higher Criticism, School of 38, 86, 89, 103
Hill, Christopher 88, 114
Histradut 46, 144
Hitler 28, 30, 34
Hitnachalut 61
Hizbollah 22, 28, 31, 144, 149
Hodder, Edwin 102, 109, 118–20, 132

Holocaust 13, 21, 23, 30
Horne, The Rt. Rev. George 96, 111
Husseini-Haj Amin al 30, 34

I
Ideological 11, 13, 15–16, 33, 36–37, 42–43, 44, 46, 51, 53–54, 61–69, 71, 76, 78, 83, 87, 112–13, 124, 127–48
Impasse 14–15, 21, 31, 37, 80, 88, 104, 108, 136–37, 149, 152, 163
Indigenous 11, 16, 24, 29–30, 36, 45–46, 50, 56, 74, 137
Inquisition 28
International Crisis Group 161, 166
Iraq 24, 30, 54, 121–22, 127, 149, 161
Isaiah 49, 78, 135
Israel Defence Force (IDF) 42, 55, 75–76
Israel Supreme Court 44, 141, 151

J
Jabotinsky, Vladimir 21, 72
Jacob 49–50, 62, 90–91, 95, 125–26
James, Fleming 70, 89–90, 105, 109, 114, 134
Jericho 36, 127
Jerram, Rev. Charles 90, 114
Jerusalem 16, 21, 39, 42, 47–53, 57, 62, 64, 67, 71, 74, 80, 83, 85, 99–164
Jewish Labour Movement 45
Jewish National Fund 46
Johnson, President Lyndon 58
Jordan 30, 36, 71, 145
Joshua, Book of 16, 29, 35–36, 39, 62, 80, 125–33
Josipovici, Gabriel 30, 38
Jowett, Rev. William 99
Judea 42, 48, 53, 60, 67–68, 128

K
Kadum 62
Kahn, Mustaq 136, 157, 159
Karmi, Ghada 37, 154–55
Keating, Michael 136, 138, 145–46, 152, 157–59
Kedumim 62
Kfar Etzion 44, 57
Kibbutzim 45–46, 58, 63
Kimmerling, Professor Baruch 38–39, 43, 73, 77, 82
King Arthur 33
King David 16, 124, 128–29
Kiryat Arba 44, 57, 59, 72, 77
Kissinger, Henry 63
Kook, Rabbi Abraham 42–79, 112
Kook, Rabbi Zvi Yehuda. 48, 52, 54, 56–57, 60, 64, 69
Koran 34
Kretzmer, Professor D. 140, 151, 157, 159

L

Land of Israel Movement 53, 60–61
Lebanon 24, 28, 30–31, 100, 127, 139, 145, 164
Leo Baeck College 32, 38
Levinger, Rabbi Moshe 57, 58–59, 62, 64, 68
Lewis, Don 90, 100
Likud Party 66, 72
Lloyd George, David 34, 112
Logotherapy 23
London Jews Society (IJS) 79, 85, 88, 93, 113, 115
London Missionary Society 91, 98, 113, 115
London Society for the Promotion of Christianity Amongst the Jews (LSPCAJ) 113–120
Lovett, Richard 91–92, 115
Lustick, Professor Ian 43, 53–54, 59–60, 65, 71, 77, 79–82

M

Malory 33
Matrix of Control 11, 56, 74–75, 138, 150
Mattiyahu Droble's Settlement Plan 66
McCarthy, R. 166–67
McCaul, Professor Alexander 105
McGowan, Dr. Edward 106, 109
McTernan, Oliver 73, 82
Mercy 21, 31, 58, 101, 127, 130
Merkaz HaRav 48, 52, 64
Meron, Theodore 58
Messiah 14–15, 27, 43–47, 53–113
Messiah's Donkey 45, 47, 60–61, 113
Messianism 44, 56, 65, 72, 114
Meyer, Anuschka 140, 146, 157–58
Mezvinsky, Norton 47
Military 22, 30, 36, 41, 43, 51, 53, 56, 58, 60–89, 107, 128, 138–67
Milner, Lord 35
Mishnah 15
Mizrahi 46, 54
Monarchy 129
Montefiore, Si Moses 85, 106
Morrison, David 46–47, 77
Mosaic Law 70
Moses 15–16, 29, 36, 41, 47, 51, 85, 106, 123–30
Mossad 151
Mount Moriah 125, 128
Muhammad the Prophet 130
Muslim 21, 28, 110, 134, 164

N

Nablus (Shechem) 52, 62, 126
Nahal 58
Nakbah 31

National Religious Party 54, 66
Nationalism 45, 48, 54, 61, 63, 65, 72–73, 85
Naudi, Cleardo 99
Nazi 29–30, 123
Nehemiah 131
Netanya 74
Netanyahu, Prime Minister Binyamin 71–72
Neumann, Professor Michael 33, 39, 132
New Zealand 137
Newman, David 66–67, 79, 80–81
Nicolayson, John 99–118
Nile 24, 32, 61
Nishool 142
North America 31, 36
Numbers, Book of 35, 39, 126, 132–33

O
Obama, President Barack 163, 166–67
Occupation 16, 24, 28–33, 42, 45, 53, 58–60, 72, 113, 127–28, 131, 136–49, 153–64
Occupied Territories 57–58, 62, 67, 72, 74, 140, 142–43, 155, 163
Occupying Power 72, 136, 138, 140–41, 143, 163
OCHA 143
Olmert, Prime Minister Ehud 157, 163–64, 166
Operation Defensive Shield 74
Oral Law 15, 126, 133
Origen, Adamantius 15, 17
Orthodox 33, 42, 46–48, 52, 54–57, 64, 70–71, 106–107, 110, 123
Oslo Accords 67, 71–72, 152
Ottoman Empire 21, 100, 107, 137

P
Palestine Place 95, 97, 100, 109
Palmerston, Lord, 102–103, 105–107
Park Hotel, Hebron 58
Partition 30, 32, 112, 150, 163, 166
Patriarchs 41, 124–25, 127, 129
Peled, Y. 77
Peres, President Shimon 44, 62, 156, 164
Perushim 84
Piterberg, Gabriel 39, 45–46, 77, 137, 143, 155, 157–59
Pogroms 28–29, 45, 85, 149
Politicide 31, 37–39, 73, 75, 77, 82
Pollard, Arthur 96, 116
Porat, Hanan 43, 49, 77–78
Power 21, 29, 36, 42, 44, 46, 60, 71–72, 75, 89, 111, 124, 128, 136, 138–48, 151, 154–56,   163–65
Pragai, Michael 88, 112, 114, 120
Promised Land 14, 34, 56, 60–61, 76, 89, 120, 123, 137
Prussia 104–105, 109

Q
Quran 34

R
Rabbis for Human Rights (RHR) 75, 82, 146, 155, 158, 165–67
Rabin, Primister Yitzhak 62–63, 67, 71–72, 133, 147
Rachel 62, 126
Rachman, Emmanuel 73, 82
Red Cross, International Committee 72
Refugees 24–25, 31, 35, 60
Reinhart, Tanya 32
Reiss, Albert J. 63–64
Richardson, Professor A. 130, 134
Road Map, 2003 147, 161
Roberts, N. 159
Rose, Hugh 79, 108
Rowley, Gwyn 70, 81
Rubinstein, Danny 35, 62
Rubinstein, William 34–35
Russia 29, 35, 46, 59, 98, 101, 147–48, 151

S
Saa'd, Philip 28
Sabeel 142, 148, 158–59
Sadat, President Anwar 67
Samaria 42, 48, 53, 60, 62, 67–68
Scott, Thomas 89–90, 96
Scranton, William 62
Sebastia 61–63
Second Temple 131
Security 21–23, 27, 29, 31, 36–37, 62–63, 66–69, 72–76, 128, 135–36, 139–65
Security Wall 74, 136, 139–40, 161
Segregation 131
Semitism 12, 27, 34, 45
Sephardi 45–46, 54, 70, 84
Settlements 24, 28, 41–42, 45, 51, 55, 57, 59–78, 113, 136, 138–61
Settlers 22–23, 41–46, 59, 61–75, 122–23, 137–39, 146, 150–51
Shafir, Gershon 45–46, 77
Shaftesbury, Earl of 85, 90, 96, 101–106, 109–11, 114, 117–20
Shahak, Israel 47, 77
Shakespeare, William 166
Shamir, Prime Minisdter Yitzhak 59, 70, 72
Sharon, Ariel 44, 62, 66–67, 69–71, 73–75, 139–40, 146, 153–54
Shearer, David 140, 146, 157–58
Sheridan, S. 133
Shlaim, Avi 37, 39
Shoah 21, 23, 29–31, 37, 50, 123, 149, 152
Shulman, Professor David 74, 82
Siegman, Professor Henry 142, 156, 158–59, 165–67

Silberstein 79–80
Simeon, Rev. Charles 84, 95–96, 98, 100, 102, 111, 116–17, 120
Six Day War of 1967 44, 52, 55–56, 59, 78
Solomon, Rabbi Normal 105, 109, 128–30, 133
Sprinzak, Professor Ehud 52, 54–57, 79
Steadman, Rev. William 97
Stunt, Timothy 89, 114
Survival 29–36, 68, 97, 126, 150
Sykes, Mark 34
Syria 28, 30–31, 61, 100, 103, 145

T
Taba 24, 147
Talmud 15, 29, 84, 122, 126, 133
Terrorism 13–14, 16, 21–32, 41, 68, 73–76, 84, 113, 135, 138, 142, 152, 156, 164
Theological 15, 38, 42, 48, 50, 75, 87, 100, 111, 113, 134
Times, The 103
Torah 15, 29, 38, 41, 46, 49–50, 53–60, 69, 84, 87, 122–23, 126–27, 131, 133
Tschoudy, Melchoir 99–100
Tuchman, Barbara 103, 112, 118, 120
Tutu, Archbishop Desmond 162, 166

U
Uganda 30, 46, 50–51
Ultra Orthodox 52, 54
UN Security Council 151
United Nations 30, 37, 43, 59–60, 62, 70, 112, 140, 143, 147, 150–51, 162, 164–66
Universal Declaration of Human Rights 37, 151
USA 11, 22, 24–25, 123, 148, 154, 162, 165–66

V
Vance, Professor Norman 15, 33, 38
Versailles Treaty 138
Viorst, Milton 38, 42, 48, 56–57, 59, 72, 76–82

W
Wadi El-Arish 61
Wailing Wall 57
Way, Lewis 21, 24, 37, 43, 52–53, 60–61, 63, 65–66, 71, 88, 97–98, 100, 105, 107–108, 122, 125, 127, 137–38, 148, 150
Weisburd, David 63–64, 67–68, 80–81
Weisglass, D. 154
Weizmann, Chaim 112
Wilberforce, William MP 94–96, 102, 111, 120
Woolf, Rev. Joseph 99–100
World Sports Peace Project 12
World Vision 148, 159
World Zionist Council 21

Y

Yamit 45, 67
Yaron Perry 88
Yedioth Ahronot 163, 166
Yehudah Etzion 61
Yesha Council 68
Yishuv 47
Yisrael Galili 62
Yom Kippur War, 1973 14, 29, 42, 44, 53, 55, 59–60, 71
Young, William Tanner 37, 57, 94, 103–104, 108–109

Z

Zechariah 47, 77, 80, 90, 120
Zertal, Professor I 57, 62, 79–81, 139–40, 147, 155–57
Zion 49–50, 78–79, 81, 86, 105, 119, 128, 130–31
Zionism 17, 23, 39, 42–43, 45, 47–51, 55–56, 57, 59–61, 65, 72, 77, 84–86, 114, 117, 121, 136, 157–59

About the Author

Geoffrey Whitfield is no stranger to war, violence and terror. He was made familiar with them from an early age when, at the age of five, he was evacuated from his parents in London, three days before the outbreak of war in 1939. In a short time, the city was emptied of children, who were dispersed all over the country and beyond. Having been away for two months he was one of a very few who were returned, after which he endured the nightly Blitz by German bombers in the first year of the war. At the end of the war, at the age of eleven, he went to his mother's home in Ireland where IRA sympathisers in the village would frighten him with stories of how they would destroy London. At the age of 18, he was to enter the army to do National Service for two years in the Kings Dragoon Guards during the time of the war in Korea.

From 1953, after his return to civilian life and then college education, he became involved in issues of industrial strife, social and political unrest in the UK and international injustice overseas. Conflict prevention and resolution have therefore been part of his personal and professional life over the decades. Towards the end of his professional career, and after his formal retirement, he became particularly engaged in Israel and Palestine, where he had close friends in both communities. His work across the divide was officially recognised and led to his being made a Member of the Order of the British Empire in 2004 by Her Majesty Queen Elizabeth.

This book is the third he has written on Israel and Palestine. The first, *Amity in the Middle East,* was the product of the sports project he set up in 2000 for youngsters in Israel and Palestine and which now functions on an ever-increasing scale in Israel. His next book, *The Roots of Terrorism in Israel and Palestine: The Uses and Abuses of the Abrahamic Covenant* was published in 2007. The present book arose out of his personal experience with Arabs and Jews in Israel and Palestine, combined with his research at UK universities.

His professional career has covered a number of disciplines but he always describes himself as, "an ordinary, non-conformist Baptist minister." With his wife Jean, they live in Lewes in East Sussex, England, and have four sets of families, three in different parts of the UK, and one on the island of Kona, Hawai'i.

About the Author

Geoffrey Whitfield was made a Member of the Order of the British Empire in 2004 by Her Majesty Queen Elizabeth for his reconciling work among Arabs and Israelis.

---

*Photographs of Her Majesty Queen Elizabeth II are used by permission.